DATE			

FORM 125 M

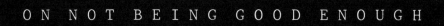

ON NOT BEING GOOD ENOUGH

ON NOT BEING GOOD ENOUGH
writings of a working critic

ROGER SALE

New York   Oxford
OXFORD UNIVERSITY PRESS
1979

Library of Congress Cataloging in Publication Data

Sale, Roger.
    On not being good enough.
    1. American fiction—20th century—Book
reviews.   2.   English fiction—20th century—
Book reviews.   3.   Criticism—Book reviews.
I.   Title.
PS379.S2   813'.5'409   78-25560
ISBN 0-19-502559-8

Printed in the United States of America

Acknowledgment is given to the following for permission to reprint the essays and reviews that first appeared in their pages:

The American Scholar for "Unknown Novels." Copyright © 1973 by Roger Sale.

Denver Quarterly for "Novelists, Readers, Critics." Copyright © 1974 by Roger Sale.

The Hudson Review for "René Wellek," "Hugh Kenner," "Marvin Mudrick," "Jane Jacobs," "Lionel Trilling," "Huxley and Bennett, Bedford and Drabble." These essays were originally published in *The Hudson Review* under the following titles: "René Wellek's History," "The Art of Hugh Kenner," "The Great Reviewer," "Thinking About Cities," "Lionel Trilling," and "Huxley and Bennett, Bedford and Drabble." Copyright © 1966, 1969, 1970, 1971, 1973, 1975 by Roger Sale.

The New York Review of Books for "Hawkes, Malamud, Richler, Oates," "Mailer and Lessing," "Toynbee, Ellul, Safdie, Negroponte," "Williams, Weesner, Drabble," "Alfred Kazin," "Mumford and Fuller," "Dashiell Hammett," "Robert Stone," "Bradley and Maclean." Copyright © 1971, 1972, 1974, 1975, 1976 by Nyrev, Inc. Reprinted with permission from *The New York Review of Books*.

The New York Times Book Review for "Leslie Fiedler," "Irving Howe," "Philip Roth," "Kurt Vonnegut, Jr." These essays were originally published in *The New York Times Book Review* under the following titles: "The Collected Essays of Leslie Fiedler," "Irving Howe, The Critical Point," "Philip Roth, Reading Myself and Others," and "Slapstick, or Lonesome No More." Copyright © 1971, 1974, 1975, 1976 by The New York Times Company. Reprinted by permission.

Ploughshares for "The Golden Age of the American Novel." Copyright © 1978 by Roger Sale.

I would like, in addition, to express special thanks to Frederick Morgan of *The Hudson Review* and Robert Silvers of *The New York Review of Books* for their many acts of support and kindness over the years.

For
Bill Pritchard

Contents

Introduction   ix

FICTION

Unknown Novels (1973)   3

Mailer and Lessing (1971)   21

Hawkes, Malamud, Richler, Oates (1971)   30

Williams, Weesner, Drabble (1972)   42

Novelists, Readers, Critics (1974)   53

Robert Stone (1975)   66

Dashiell Hammett (1975)   73

Philip Roth (1975)   80

Bradley and Maclean (1976)   84

Huxley and Bennett, Bedford and Drabble (1975)   93

Kurt Vonnegut, Jr. (1976)   105

The Golden Age of the American Novel (1978)   110

CRITICS

René Wellek (1966)   129
Hugh Kenner (1969)   136
Leslie Fiedler (1971)   144
Lionel Trilling (1973)   148
Alfred Kazin (1974)   157
Irving Howe (1974)   163
Marvin Mudrick (1971)   166

CITIES

Jane Jacobs (1970)   177
Toynbee, Ellul, Safdie, Negroponte (1971)   188
Mumford and Fuller (1974)   202

INTRODUCTION

Some years ago I gave a speech to the California Association of Teachers of English that I called "On Not Being Good Enough." Its subject was teaching, especially teaching in the early 1970s; I wanted to say I thought I was a good teacher, just as many in the audience were, but also that I was not sure if any of us were good enough to do what I thought we had to try to learn to do. Limitations of space, and the desire to give this collection at least a modest shapeliness, have prevented me from reprinting the speech here, but I decided I did want to commandeer its title to use here. The circumstances under which many of the following pieces were written, and perhaps the circumstances under which the objects of their concern were written too, lead me to say, very often, "Good, yes, yet not good enough."

Most of what appear here as essays were originally reviews, of current fiction, criticism, and a few non-literary books, mostly about cities. The not-good-enough-ness of reviewing is well known to anyone who has tried it and to most who spend much time reading reviews. Marvin Mudrick says a reviewer is always catching something on the wing. An editor sends out a book or a group of books and wants 2500 words by September 15, a date two weeks to three months hence. I live far from the publishing marts and spend most of my life thinking about other things than current books, so I am usually content to accept whatever comes, especially since the two editors for whom I have most frequently reviewed, Frederick Morgan and Robert Silvers, have interesting tastes and good eyes for finding books they think I will enjoy reading. Still, the circumstances under which the work must be done are no one's idea of the best.

In my first years as a reviewer I felt not good enough most often when reading a book I really liked; I kept worrying that I liked it too much, or even that I shouldn't like it at all. It is no fun reviewing bad books, but it is usually not difficult to trust one's taste with bad books, and their quality is usually easily enough revealed with a few quotations. But in the first batch of novels I was ever sent to review was a first novel, *Catch-22,* and with me and that book it was as with Yossarian and the priest, love at first sight. It was funny, and I laughed, it was moving, and I felt like crying. I read some jokes to my friends, and they did not laugh; I read some early reviews which praised the book, but never for being funny or moving. Could I possibly trust myself; could I afford to say what I thought? Had everyone else known these jokes from their cradles? Well, everyone knows *Catch-22* by now, but a year or so later I had the same kind of experience with Jack Ludwig's *Confusions,* a book that never gained an audience, and some time after that came *Herzog,* which I did not think simply funny and moving but a masterpiece, and the circumstances of reviewing are precisely those where one does not welcome the opportunity to proclaim masterpieces, since many reviewers who have done so have turned out to be anything from pleasantly mistaken to ludicrously wrong.

Over the years I came to see there is little one can do about one's taste. If it isn't good enough, it isn't, and if I was wrong then about *Catch-22, Confusions,* and *Herzog,* I would be now. Of course I get the jokes more readily now than then, but I still enjoy them, and *Herzog* still seems to me a masterpiece, a book that I will leave the task of inveighing against to others. But at the same time as I was coming to accept my own taste, even if it may not be good enough, I discovered another and more enduring cause for anxiousness. Reviews were invented to inform a public about new books, and most specialized reviewing is still done by people with a secure sense of their audience. But general audiences of periodicals with fairly large circulations are, for me at least, amorphous. One may presume readers but one knows nothing definite about them and hears very little from them; I describe the circumstances more fully later on, in "Novelists, Readers, Critics." I am, in addition to being a reviewer, a teacher, and teachers come to learn that what *their* audience wants is not love but attention, and I am quite sure that, gradually over the years, I have come to address my reviews to the authors of the books I was reviewing, speaking not as an instructor but simply as one who says, in effect, "You have written this, and here is what I can say in response to you." One doesn't say this directly, of course, or even feel it directly, but if a reviewer cannot always praise, a reviewer can and must always attend. My own relative isolation, and the relative isolation of most authors, has, I am sure, encouraged me in this.

Yet the conditions of reviewing make this way of addressing oneself risky. I have written books myself, and know it is hard for an author to feel that any review says it right, does the book justice, especially if the review must be brief. A disproportion is inevitably felt. A book may have taken years to write, and a review must be written rather quickly; a book is always long enough to make a brief review seem puny. It may help an author little to realize the reviewer is trying hard, is being as temperate and generous as possible. I persist in believing that reviews are the best way to write about current books—the time for longer essays or books is later, even much later—but that belief doesn't keep me from feeling that my best reviews aren't good enough.

Yet there is another perspective available here. The reviewer's conditions, however special or crimped they sometimes seem, are the world's conditions as well, after all. A real reviewer is a critic, if only as a way of not being an adjunct to the publishing and advertising businesses; to put it another way, a reviewer is a serious reader, and serious readers must admit to being often disappointed, especially when a good book fails to be all it promises to be. It is relatively easy to face a writer like Kurt Vonnegut, Jr., or some other purveyor of the fashionable; with them the task is simply to say why the results seem so distasteful. But with a Robert Stone or a Margaret Drabble the task is harder, not just because their works are more serious but because they are willing to take real risks, and often the risks will not seem to have yielded all that was hoped for. R. P. Blackmur's way of putting it is: "Failure is the expense of greatness." The failures of the best writers of one's own time seem to me the best places to look to see what that time is all about, and so with their work I seek to let them haunt me because the better I can do this the better I can understand everything else; where they are not good enough is where I can best learn about my own failures.

As it has turned out, there are two pressure points where this greatness and this possibility for failure can be most clearly felt, at least by me. With critics, it is their ability to withstand the invitations and onslaughts of the official academic requirements which so often seek to deny or vitiate the critic's need for maintaining clear-eyed independence without falling into self-absorption or nastiness. With novelists the pressure point is the conduct of whatever it is that passes for narrative, of sustaining materials, of exploring them, from the beginning right through to the end, if possible. These, it has turned out, are for me the ways I discovered the greatness, the failures, of those contemporaries I most admire, so that the attempt to state limitations is the heart of the praise, often the most sacred part of the whole enterprise.

If I put the matter this way, I hope I can then add, easily and without obscurity, that for me the search for the ways in which I and others are not good enough has been my means of expressing my gratitude for the body of literature created in the twenty years I have been reviewing books. At the outset of these years no one could find replacements among novelists then writing for Hemingway and Faulkner, and both poetry and criticism seemed arid, dominated by the excessively restrained mandates of the New Criticism. Since then it is as though spring has come again, and the Nile has flooded its banks, so that one can praise this season of two decades for the fecundity of its production, the plenitude of its snakes, the splendor of its mud; really, I meant that. And there have been Cleopatras, too. Criticism, which has *not* been rich, has Irving Howe and Hugh Kenner and Marvin Mudrick; Jane Jacobs has done what few writers of fact or fiction have been able to do, make us realize the understandable splendors of our great cities; the novel, the American novel especially, seems in its heyday not good enough, often not even trying to be, but electric, wayward, almost wearyingly able: Pynchon, Bellow, Malamud, Stone, Weesner, Welch, Woiwode, Howard, Mailer, Updike, Roth, blessed even in its guests, Nabokov and

Singer, its aging saints, Morris, Savage, Buechner. Moment-to-moment in these essays it must seem I am always a little too deliberate, too measuring, too quick to say when a writer has been not good enough. Such I am, perhaps, or such a reviewer must be. If so, however, it is as a way of feeling enabled and grateful that it has been a period anyone might be happy to have been part of, alive in, caring about.

FICTION

UNKNOWN NOVELS

No novel is unknown to everyone; the author, the editor, the agent, some friends of each, *they* know. But hordes of novels are published every year in this country, and most are never heard of or from. If the author is at all serious about the book, it must be very disheartening to struggle to get it right, get it finished, get it into print, only to have it spottily noticed, and then disappear. Maybe a third of the novels of a given year are hopelessly bad, maybe as many as half are cynically produced hackwork confections never meant to be taken seriously, and maybe as many as thirty to fifty of those remaining are seriously reviewed and read in a year; that still leaves as many as a hundred authors, each of whom has a novel, a not worthless piece of work, and each of whom ends up discovering that author, agent, editor, and friends are guardians of a well-kept secret.

Such writers must occasionally look around, or up, and feel envious and bitter. They stand, as it were, at the base of a pyramid, and all the other novelists are somewhere, probably above them. At the top of this pyramid, at what I will call level 1, are those very few American novelists who are always and instantly news; if we do not fuss much about identifying the precise or total membership, we can say that at level 1 right now are Bellow, Roth, Nabokov, Updike, Mailer. Level 2 at its upper reaches blends easily into level 1, and consists of novelists who are guaranteed serious reviews in many places, who win prizes, who have admirers convinced that they are among the very best:

3

Pynchon, Malamud, Morris, Welty, Barthelme, Ellison, Heller, Gass, Vonnegut, Salinger, Oates, Hawkes, Styron, Capote—again, we do not so much need to agree on the names as to recognize the category. Then, at its lower reaches, 2 blends into 3, what might be thought of as the novel reader's level: serious writers who have little difficulty getting work published but whose audience tends to be restricted to literary people. Here one has to begin to give first names: Hortense Calisher, Reynolds Price, Frederick Buechner, Evan Connell, Stanley Elkin, Bruce Jay Friedman, R. V. Cassil, Thomas Rogers, George P. Elliott, Edward Hoagland, Terry Southern, Alison Lurie, James Purdy, Herbert Gold—this list could be greatly extended, of course, which at least can tell us that not everyone is doomed to end up unknown, although many will be only dimly or partially seen. Writers on level 3 often move up the pyramid and even more often move down; with *Augustus,* John Williams may have appeared on level 3, but sometime recently, Vance Bourjailly, perhaps Calder Willingham, or Peter Matthiessen, disappeared from it.

At level 4 we find, first, compartments of people who write things like detective stories, science fiction, spy thrillers, Westerns, Gothic novels; lots of writers in these categories are quite well known, like Chester Himes, Ross Macdonald, John D. Mac-Donald, Robert A. Heinlein, Ray Bradbury, yet they stay at or near level 4 because the world tends to decide that only freaks can take them seriously. But a good deal more of level 4 is just books; one goes to any public library and finds them lining the shelves: *A Tree Grows in Brooklyn, The Caine Mutiny, Battle Cry,* the works of Robert Nathan, Hamilton Basso, Paul Gallico. There may be some excellent books at level 4—I have heard it said, for instance, that Charles Jackson's *The Lost Weekend* is a fine book—but it is very rare that a writer at level 4 is ever accorded the serious attention that other novelists receive. I am quite sure, for instance, that both Raymond Chandler and James M. Cain have offered serious literary people far more pleasure than their contemporary and fellow Californian, John Steinbeck—yet Steinbeck won the prizes, and the recognition.

Then, more alongside than in the pyramid itself, we find James Baldwin, Mary McCarthy, Gore Vidal, Susan Sontag,

Katherine Anne Porter, James Dickey, Robert Creeley—writers better known for their essays, stories, or poems, but who have written at least one novel, and who are in the enviable position of being widely reviewed and advertised even though they are not primarily novelists at all.

The writers at all these levels have had a chance; the machinery of publishing and reviewing and academic criticism has worked well enough in their cases so that they are known by many people who do not know them personally. Of course few writers feel that they have been adequately recognized, or valued, or financially rewarded, and most feel that the novel is never taken seriously enough in this country. Publishers are often alleged to be chintzy, the marketplace is easily compared to a brothel, and the journals of opinion, especially those located in New York, are constantly accused of logrolling. But all writers above level 5 must admit, if only in moments of rare candor, that inadequate praise and critical drubbings are preferable to being unknown; most would admit that good luck played a considerable part in giving them whatever eminence they have enjoyed.

I am not going to stop to ponder these strokes of good luck, these instances of back scratching and greed and blindness; they exist, and they must gall many writers who have never benefited from them. I want, rather, to write about a few books and writers who are, for all intents and purposes, unknown, and who deserve better. I am not concerned here with neglected masterpieces; there may be one in this country, but I don't know it, and I am sure no good comes from looking for that rare object if, in the process, other books, not masterpieces, are casually tossed aside that never received the decent attention and criticism they deserve. There are hundreds of possible candidates, and of course I know only a handful; it would be nice to think that others will respond with their own lists and comments. There is no need to agree precisely on our evaluations since we all know when dealing with minor novelists that the reader's temperament plays a large role in determining that evaluation. I have tried here, however, to avoid books for which I can identify my temperamental affinity, and I have not pretended to be fully rounded in my judgments, since there is no point in carefully listing the shortcomings of novels that very few people know. Mostly I have tried to indicate what sort of book it is that I am discussing, and the kinds of pleasure that one can find there.

All of the books that I am considering are American, and were written within the last generation; none falls into a special generic category like the detective story or the children's book; all are level 5 books, as far as I can determine. I am not so much interested, then, in the underrated or the wrongly classified, as in the unknown. To indicate the distinction I am trying to make, let me describe a yardstick I found myself using. Gina Berriault and Edward Lewis Wallant are both good and not well-known novelists, but each, I discovered, had been borrowed more than twenty times from my local library in the last five years, and that makes them, by my rough calculation, level 3 writers, although of course both could sink to level 5 very easily. On the other hand, the novels of Thomas Savage have been borrowed from the same library about once every other year. Such reckonings are crude and may be quite inaccurate, but often, in making my choices, I had only these guidelines to follow. Finally, let me add that I have tended to ignore more recent writers who have as yet written only one or two books; they may well be doomed to oblivion, especially if they write no more, but it is a little too early to tell.

A note, to show the kind of thing these level 5 novels are up against. As I begin, four books plague me, because I can't honestly claim to know them although they have been in the recesses of my consciousness since I began work on this project. The first is Cynthia Ozick's *Trust*, a huge book that I noted on the shelves because I had read some of her stories and essays. I simply didn't get down to it until too late, and so read barely a hundred pages, and they didn't deeply excite me, so I regretfully laid it aside; I hope someone who knows it is a wonderful novel will rebuke me. Second and third, H. F. M. Prescott's *Man on a Donkey*, and Edith Simon's *The Golden Hand*. People I admire have lavishly recommended both books, and I started both more than once, but never wanted to go on. Both are very long, and I simply felt defeated at the prospect of reading three hundred pages to see if I wanted to finish them; I conclude that there is a kind of long minor novel one is willing to give every chance, and another kind one isn't. Fourth, Margaret Boylan's *The Marble Orchard*, which I read years ago and rather liked, but which I simply could not get hold of to reread. It is about a blind girl who suddenly discovers she can see but tells no one she can; I remember it mostly for details, especially, for some reason, a passage about the way the girl's parents speak of things only by brand names—not coffee, but "the Beech Nut," not car wax, but "the Johnson's." Since many books are memorable only for such details, I can only say I'm sorry that, around here, *The Marble Orchard* is not just unknown, but unknowable.

I begin with two regional novels of my own region, the Pacific Northwest. Presumably every state has its authors, but in the postwar years the only regions nationally acknowledged are Jewish New York and the South. In the Northwest the only novels that have gained real recognition are H. L. Davis's *Honey in the Horn* and Ken Kesey's vastly overrated *One Flew Over the Cuckoo's Nest* and *Sometimes a Great Notion*. But, being a young region, it tends to have lots of writers and few really good ones; there is no novel, however ordinary or flaky, from which someone who knows and loves the area cannot learn something, but there are only two that I am sure someone from elsewhere could like.

Jack Thomas Leahy's *Shadow on the Water* (Knopf, 1960, out of print), in its best moments achieves a wonderful harmony of a Huck Finn story of a lad coming to learn of the corruption and ineffectuality of his elders with a background of the last territory ahead there will ever be, an Indian village on the Washington coast, a town so far from anywhere that Seattle is a long trip away. This is Leahy's only novel, and that is rather a pity since its major fault results from an awareness of technique discovered in creative writing classes, which is precisely the sort of defect one easily grows beyond. The novel demands the technique, a naïve storytelling equally suited to the boy's consciousness and to the stories he hears from his grandfather about the Indians; both the boy and the Indians are ground under and stupefied by the heartlessness or the indifference of the older whites. The trouble arises whenever we become aware that behind the innocent narrator is a knowing author, when we know far more than the narrator or the Indians do about what is happening to them, as in a sequence in which the boy and his Indian friend are picked up by a homosexual in Seattle and we know, but the boys don't, what is happening to them. But the advent of the new white exploiters, first a team of anthropologists, then developers who turn the Indians into a sideshow, is wonderfully done. At the end, when the boy's Indian friend is crushed under a horse he has been made to ride because "Indians ride horses" (even though the coastal tribes had never seen them), we find Leahy and his narrator at one:

> I turned then, and looked toward the mountains, the peaceful mountains, and I wondered how they could remain so beautiful. I knew, then, suddenly, what Grandfather had tried to tell me. I knew that where there was beauty, there was now ugliness; that where there had been joy there was now despair; that where there had been the truth of the heart, there was now only the emptiness of the soul. And, knowing that, I walked away from the beach.

One notes the effortful posing, the first novel shining through, but when one comes on that moment one wants to swallow it whole, so telling has been the rendering of the beauty that was and the ugliness that is. Since Leahy, writing in the late fifties, had no Third World or environmental fashions to buttress him, had to invent for himself a method that would bring the boy and the Indians into a single focus, he sometimes stumbled. By the same token, since the fashions weren't there, he could bring real freshness to his details and sense of place. *Shadow on the Water* is a fine little book, one that needs no regionalist, no fashionable perspective. It means its language to be of the heart, and that is what leads to its sentimentalities, but its language really is of the heart, too, which is another matter entirely.

Allis McKay grew up in what was becoming the apple country along the Columbia River, and she grew up convinced both that it was a possessing landscape and that it had possessed her mother more than it could her, so that when she sees the cliffs, the orchards, and the river, she sees her mother in the landscape. She left it when she grew up and moved to Chicago, but came back to start asking the older people how it had been. The result is two novels, *They Came to a River* (Binsford & Mort,

1941, in print, but hard to find outside the Northwest) and *Two Women at Pine Creek* (Macmillan, 1966, out of print). Both are good; it doesn't matter which you start with, but the first is better. It is a very long novel that works entirely with rhythms and anecdotes—no rich human creations, no fine writing, no driving plot, but a real shape. The anecdotes that are best all bespeak a telling innocence—a lad climbing arduously out of the valley to see Halley's comet, only to discover that he can't locate it even from the highest rim; a woman reading Greek myths that she can barely understand to her children so they will at least have heard the names; a man who finally admits to himself after years of accumulating evidence that his brother is cheating him of all he loves, and who then kills him, dumbly. But the cumulative effect is of experience gained and held; the path from innocence to wisdom is taken not so much through experience as through the rhythms established by repeated loyalties to neighbors and to harvests. Which is why the book must be long; it must abjure not only melodrama and big scenes, but plot as well, in order to gain its shape, the arc of a generation. Where a writer like Ken Kesey is pitifully nostalgic, McKay is winningly direct, and thereby tough, claiming not some mythic America but only these lives, this place, as her subject. But all this, which is the source of her strength, is also what keeps her from being any better. Allis McKay can trust her experience, but her trust is passive, so she never grasps, never transforms; never needing a method beyond her trust, she never attains one. But what she worked to get right she got right, and it rings true and clear and bright.

Moving out of the Northwest only slightly, we come to Thomas Savage of Montana, who is perhaps the most striking instance among my authors of the uses and disasters that are liable to accompany the unknown. Savage, now nearing sixty, is the author of seven novels, and if he hasn't one great book to show for his career, he has one that is very good indeed, and a number of others that are interesting. It is not easy to locate copies of his books, so if you do, buy or borrow them; even when he is not at his best, he is not dull. Savage has two great virtues, or rather, two versions of the same virtue operating on different scales. On the one hand, he is superb at destinies, at creating a sense that this life had to end up as it did; he is in no sense a determinist, but he does convey a fine sense of fatality, so that even in his lesser books he keeps the fatal end in view without being particularly portentous or foreshadowing. On the other hand, Savage is excellent at conveying the fixity, the unyieldingness of environments, the obduracy of the people and things in one's landscape, so that, given this person inside that environment, the result is destined. The first quality cannot be demonstrated without lengthy illustration, but the second yields itself to quotation:

> Once the three were inside the store (the teen-aged girls suppressed their giggles, the eyes of the boys were scornful, watchful) the tall dark wife began to handle and inspect a spongy head of lettuce from a crate on the counter. Under the very eyes of the painted peppery owner she tossed back the head of lettuce and held up another. She shrugged and dropped the second, plunk. She would have no lettuce.
> "All gone by," she said, loud enough for all to hear.
> There was a crackling silence, for she had flouted the owner, who considered the lettuce good enough to offer. Anyway, around there they didn't think much of people who always had to have lettuce. Before the development the owner never got lettuce in at all. Why, before the development there was a *lot* of stuff she never bothered with. This Pepperidge Farm bread, and garlic. They were always after garlic.

This is all there is to the store, but the relation of the owner to the tall dark wife, of old-timers used to cans, and newcomers from the development who want fresh lettuce and garlic, is all there, in a hundred words, and the economy of the writing assures us that this antagonism is irrevocable. Now, into that same development put a young wife, not the one in this scene, but one, rather, who shares the attitudes of the store owner. No lettuce, garlic, or Pepperidge Farm bread for her, but nothing else either; nothing she wants to do. Give to her, then, a husband whose virtue is kindness and all of whose other qualities are irritations, and you have the atmosphere of a life about to reach a totally unfulfilling climax. The husband catches the wife sleeping with another man, and he is fascinated, ignorant of causes, feeling only that it must be his fate to be a cuckold:

Inevitably, she tried to smile. Her face, her nose especially, had the sharpness of someone very old. "Sheldon! He doesn't even love me!" And now behind that mad, vacant smile he saw the terror. "What will I do? What will become of me?"

"Become of you?" He looked into her face and shook his head in a kind of innocent bewilderment. He spoke quietly, honestly. "I don't know."

Then she began to weep.

He leaves, and we hear no more of the wife, nor need we, because, as far as Savage can see, her destiny is complete. Start with almost any set of details, and you can see in their fixity the way people will strain against them, but they must yield to their destinies, and, at his best, Savage's stories of these people are truly mysterious.

The passages above come from *Trust in Chariots* (Random House, 1961, out of print), one of the better books. The best one, the one fully successful novel, is *The Power of the Dog* (Little, Brown, 1968, out of print), a Western about two ranching brothers that does not falter once in its tremendous evocation of details and their power to articulate whole lives. The store described in the first passage quoted is in a Boston suburb, something Savage found out about relatively well along in life, which may make his sense of its details clear, but the urban landscapes of *Trust in Chariots* don't have the same haunting power as the Montana range in *The Power of the Dog*. He had tried in his first two novels, *The Pass* (Doubleday, 1944, out of print) and *Lona Hanson* (Simon & Schuster, 1948, out of print), to do Montana, as it were, but except for a wonderful rodeo sequence at the beginning of *Lona Hanson*, the landscape just isn't there yet, and so the destinies seem forced. But in *The Power of the Dog* we have five major characters, and for each there are tellingly characteristic objects and habits of life, so that when they clash in some grand climaxes, the objects all become supercharged with a marvelous sense of inevitability.*

* I would be more detailed about *The Power of the Dog* were it not the focus of an essay in *Colorado Quarterly* [1973] by Jack Brenner, who also reports that at a meeting of the country's experts on Western American literature no one had ever heard of Savage.

Why women become alcoholics, why men madly put their trust in chariots or in horses, why some people cannot break out of self-created cages, why some lives become so possessed that they lose all ability to derive pleasure from the little things that make others content—these are the stories Thomas Savage knows. He is much better with men than with women, which is why *Lona Hanson* and *Daddy's Girl* (Little, Brown, 1970, out of print) are not so good as the two novels mentioned above. *Daddy's Girl* has lots of good details and vignettes, but it haggles and insists on Daddy's Girl's fate rather than evolving it, and manages to show, mostly, that there is a considerable difference between showing why masculine men fail and showing what makes a major woman's destiny. We will, later on, run into the question of what happens to a writer of talent when his or her work is consistently neglected or ignored; for now let it be said that Savage is a good writer, with a real body of work, one fine novel, and firsthand things to tell us about.

A note here. Although his work spans three decades, Savage's novels are very much of the fifties, and so remind one of a number of other novelists of the period who enjoyed or suffered similar fates. In the early fifties Oakley Hall earned some fame for *Corpus of Joe Bailey* (Viking, 1953, out of print). Hall is always a bit crude, and his highest estimate of human motives is no more than the wish to be good, but, like Savage, he can be very clear about destinies, and can be even better than Savage at knowing the stories to tell that play them out. In addition, there are sequences in Hall's work—driving a bulldozer in *So Many Doors*, the Berkeley scenes of *Joe Bailey*, bafflements about the relation of parent to child in *Mardios Beach*—that are memorable beyond the booming postwar California that is the milieu of these books. Hall, on the other hand, was seriously reviewed twenty years ago, and that cannot be said for the remarkable work of Davis Grubb and Richard Bissell. Grubb wrote *The Night of the Hunter* (Harpers, 1953, out of print), which was then made into a wonderful movie by James Agee and Charles Laughton, although that never seems to have made the novel at all well known. Grubb can be both pretentious and wearyingly sentimental, but he can also be haunting and exciting; I know no one who has not been frightened by parts of *The Night of the Hunter*. The major

reason is Grubb's wonderful sense of the dreariness of the West
Virginia landscape; in at least the first half of this book and in
briefer sections of *The Voices of Glory* and *Shadow of My
Brother*, Grubb invents a place, and a way of living to fit it, that
is all his own, and unique. Bissell is lighter fare, also much less
uneven, also best in his novels of the early fifties, also with a marvelous sense of place. *Stretch on the River (1950)*, *High Water*
(1954), and *7½ Cents* (1953), all Little, Brown, all out of print,
are wonderfully durable books, funny, sweet, touching. The
scene is the Mississippi, on the river, in a small town in Iowa;
Bissell, never sure whether or not to take himself seriously,
writes with a breezy freshness that bespeaks simple firsthand experience and offers no sense of Sinclair Lewis, Sherwood Ander-
son, or Mark Twain. But *7½ Cents* was turned into *The Pajama
Game*, which may have made Bissell rich and which may have
contributed to his becoming an Easterner. Once out of his habitat, he dwindled rather quickly and rather badly. But the early
novels are fine reading indeed.

Next, two novels that were totally unknown to me until fairly
recently, and whose excellence has shamed me into realizing that
there may be other good novels that I have never looked at
because they are about historical figures. Henrietta Buckmaster's
And Walk in Love (Random House, 1956, out of print) and
Gladys Schmitt's *Rembrandt* (Random House, 1961, out of print)
were published and advertised, I am quite sure, as the stuff of
Literary Guild best sellers. They may even have been read as
such, although it is hard to see how, for neither partakes for even
a page of the métier of Irving Stone, Frank Yerby, and Samuel
Shellabarger. It may well be that an almost sure formula for remaining unknown is to write a serious historical novel; who will
believe it isn't *Désirée* or *Dinner at Antoine's?* So far as I know,
only Mary Renault is consistently read as a serious historical
novelist.

    And Walk in Love is based on the life of Saint Paul, and
surely no one is more apt to be repellent to novel readers than
he. Novels demand flexibility and generosity; Paul is insistent
and dogmatic. He is reputed to have given Christianity not only

its fame but a fatally wrong direction, and he certainly provides a wonderful target for anyone who wants to hate Christianity, or, perhaps, any religion. Yet Henrietta Buckmaster makes all that, even if true, mostly irrelevant, and she does it not by hedging the issue but by being extremely diligent and chaste. There is none of the history-in-the-making heart-thumping of *Ben-Hur* or *The Silver Chalice*, and nothing either of that phony wisdom that finds the real heroes to be Barabbas or Judas or Pilate. One neither learns nor cares if Buckmaster is herself a Christian. What she has done is to brood, to take Acts and Paul's letters and let them evoke her hero, so that nothing in this quite long novel is not mentioned or easily allowed for in the New Testament itself. In her source the characters, as is well known, tend to lie pretty flat on the page, and Buckmaster, without altering a detail, broods, presses a little here, fills in a landscape there, and the story comes to quiet, shimmering life. Perhaps her greatest success comes early in the novel, when she gives herself one invention—that Saul knew and loved Stephen the martyr—and then shows Saul persecuting the Nazarenes out of torment and the need to believe in some absolute truth. He is, thus, quite ready for the vision on the road to Damascus when it comes. It does not turn his life around, only clarifies it, sets it on its true path, the one he had long been seeking. No one believes in either visions or conversions who does not want so to believe, that is Buckmaster's assurance, and it gives her strength, her sense of the kind of love this forbidding man could feel, the kind of trouble he would have with those who wanted to keep Christianity a Jewish sect, and the very different troubles he would have with those Gentiles who just wanted to be converted to something. There's not a cinemascopic moment in the novel, although the fact that the title is taken from Ephesians does not keep it from being an unfortunate one; there is none of the ordinary historical novelist's fatal need to explain the unexplainable with decoration in details. The world that Paul moves in is there, clear enough at all events, because he himself is clear. The writing is undistinguished, but it is always diligent and serviceable, a rather plain rhetoric that is sufficiently like Paul's own that when he speaks words we all recognize as his we can read without embarrassment. Her Paul really does say that faith, hope, and love abide, these three, and she makes us feel that he might well have said just that, when he does, in the situation that she provides. The characters are sculpted, and so rather stiff, but that stiffness is Henrietta Buckmaster's dignity. She needs it, and justifies it.

There's nothing particularly chaste or dignified about *Rembrandt,* which is a huge and lavish book. Gladys Schmitt really does imagine that she was there, familiar with the streets and houses of Amsterdam and Leyden, with the commerce and politics of being a painter, an apprentice, a master of apprentices. We have seasons and weather here, richly described rooms and faces. What makes *Rembrandt* so much brighter and thingier than *And Walk in Love* is precisely its fidelity to its source. As Buckmaster has brooded on biblical texts, Schmitt has on paintings and etchings. The book is best on Rembrandt at work, Rembrandt taking the people around him and making them Saint Peter and Aristotle and Danaë, Rembrandt's rapacity in being able throughout a long career to do just that, to see everything as the subject of his works. He emerges as a great bear, insolent, warm, sensual, often naïve, convinced of his greatness, never capable of or interested in removing that greatness from the world he moved in. It is a book to read with a book of reproductions open at all times right alongside.

Perhaps the most remarkable fact about *Rembrandt* is that it succeeds very well despite one major shortcoming: Gladys Schmitt does not know why Rembrandt is one of the greatest of painters. Having rightly insisted on the rootedness of his provinciality, having seen how much she could learn about his world just by looking closely at his work, she can't reverse the process and imagine how and why the result is as magnificent as it is. Fortunately, what she cannot do she does not try to do; fortunately too, Rembrandt's absorption in his life is so enormous and so fully rendered that we do not miss what we most long for except at rare, if crucial, moments. For it does not slight Rembrandt to make him so rooted in his world. Wherever the mystery of his genius resides, it is in the way his almost complete self-assurance released him into seeing others with a rich sense of their uniqueness even while he was being careless in his relations with them, even while struggling to find a life that could make him truly indifferent to the pettiness of so much that surrounded him. So he is tied to his world, passive even, yet remote, alone. The figure Schmitt creates is almost totally convincing—until one asks why Rembrandt is not Hals, or Brueghel, but one of the very greatest. Still, *Rembrandt* is 650 big pages long, and never anything but episodic, yet totally engrossing to read and vivid and bright in the memory.

These two books are the only ones of their authors I have yet been able to read. Henrietta Buckmaster has written a number of other novels, one on Shakespeare, one on a secretary general of the United Nations, that I have been unable to locate. Gladys Schmitt has written a whole host of books. Her first novel, *The Gates of Aulis* (1942), according to *Twentieth Century Authors*, was widely and seriously reviewed, although not always favorably. But after that she took to writing historical fiction, and as a result seems simply to have dropped from any sustained consideration. It is a pity that we seem quite able to read the historical novels of Scott, Tolstoy, Mann, Isaac Bashevis Singer, perhaps a few others, yet remain convinced that the fact that most historical novels are trashy makes it an inferior type; most novels of any type are trashy, after all. It was good to see Gore Vidal speaking out on this subject in a recent issue of the *New York Review of Books.* Judging by *Rembrandt,* I would not advise anyone to try Gladys Schmitt's work as bedtime reading; her intention and talent are far too serious for that.

Last, I want to mention some books that fall into a category that may be at least as capable as historical fiction of begetting oblivion, namely, the early novels of writers who turn out to write only one or two. We have, well up in the upper reaches of my pyramid, Joseph Heller and Ralph Ellison, which is to say we have *Catch-22* and *Invisible Man*, with little prospect of more from either writer. It is possible, thus, to become and to stay famous as the result of just one book, but it is rare and unlikely. Since first novels tend to have more heat than light, more suggestion than achievement, one wants more. Yet there can be good or bad reasons why one novel is all we get: failure to find a publisher, failure to be able to write more than one good autobiographical novel, desire to do something else. And so the first novel tends to get lost and never found again. I think of Floyd Salas, author of *Tattoo the Wicked Cross* (Grove, 1967, out of print), a seared and searing book about a boy in a reform school. Salas is so completely inside his experience that what in many other novels is treated as sensational lore is here only the setting for the boy's experience. The moment the doors are locked behind him, the boy has nothing but his tenaciously held street codes of honor to remind him of who he was and is, but those codes are precisely what doom him when he confronts the brutalities of the reformatory. First the outside world fades, then the officials prove ineffectual, then the other boys are divided into the strong and the weak, so the hero, with his code of never squealing, is left alone to face a group of brutal and much stronger boys; the result is an awful homosexual rape, about which Salas will let us know only the hero's hurt and humiliation. He has trusted the truth of his experience to give him the truth of his novel, and it has not failed him. Salas has, so far as I know, written nothing after *The Wicked Cross;* perhaps he has nothing else to write, but this book should not have been allowed to disappear.

Even stranger is the case of Rudolph Von Abele and *The Party* (Houghton Mifflin, 1963, out of print). This was not his first novel, but *The Vigil of Emmeline Gore,* published the year before *The Party,* is totally unobtainable, and the two represent the sum of Von Abele's fictional output. But almost twenty years before these novels he wrote a biography of Alexander Stephens and some years after the novels a book on Hawthorne; at one time or another I know I've seen poems of his in magazines. How, from this, to imagine *The Party,* a novel that can quickly be described as being about Hermann Göring and by Henry James? It is a wonderful tour de force, and if it doesn't reread so well as it reads, that is in part due simply to one's amazement the first time that such a book could exist. It takes 400 pages to describe the events of one evening with, obviously, great slowness and concentration. The matter is the experience of an army colonel who, late in the war, is beginning to learn of the horrors of the camps, who is only meagerly able to understand his own meager life, and who is invited to a party at the Marshal's chateau in Austria. It is one of those books that are marred by their authors' decisions to "do something," in this case name everyone except the hero by role: the Pastor, the Superintendent, the Businessman, et cetera. But the gallery is vivid, and the slow stupefaction of the coming defeat of the Reich brings out the interesting worst in everyone, except for the Marshal, huge, splendidly selfish, and cruel, who decides to be nice to the hero because the hero has been reticent and detached toward him. Halfway through the book is a chamois hunt by moonlight in the mountains, in which Von Abele brilliantly catches the crisscrossings of the suddenly revealed temperaments of people who are strangers to each other. And the night goes on—like most real parties, unlike most fictional ones, the late, anticlimactic moments are important, quietly, carefully described, as the officer realizes he has been implicated in the Marshal's baiting of him, caught in his own refuge of silence to hide his fear, to offer a mask of moral superiority. At the end:

> Nothing would interpose to make commitment easier; know what he might, he could foresee himself already, sitting in the greasy armchair in his rented, cluttered room, revolving endlessly the difficulties of rebellion, which he also saw would be compounded now that he had come to know and, for a time, almost to love the Marshal. Perhaps the war would end somehow, and by ending would relieve him of the anguish of decision, and also of the anguish of the knowledge that he seemed, especially after this adventure, perfectly, Platonically incapable of making a decision. If he had been in the habit of praying, he would have prayed for the end of the war.

There have been lots of novels that have tried in one way or another to rework the central proposition of Kafka's *The Trial,* and the more self-consciously they have done this, like *1984* or *Player Piano,* the less well they have worked. Von Abele seems nowhere near so interesting a man as George Orwell, and may be no more talented than Kurt Vonnegut, but *The Party* repays one for its slowness, compensates for its lugubriousness, by the density with which it evokes a real relationship between the Big Man and the Little Man, shows how a single night can clarify if not alter the course of a whole lifetime, and in so doing poses all the implicit moral and political issues in a truly imagined world.

I have closed with Salas and Von Abele because it is the most convenient way to bring me down a little closer to the present. Earlier I disqualified recent books from the present discussion because it seemed to me that subsequent work by a number of writers might begin to earn them the wide audience that their first novels did not seem to gain. But what if these first, or second, novels are, for whatever reason, all there is to be? They will almost certainly vanish, in five or ten years be as assuredly unknown to any reading public as Allis McKay or Thomas Savage is now. I think, mostly, of Theodore Weesner's *The Car Thief*, published in 1972, which seems to me the best American novel I have read since, say, *Herzog*. It wasn't, by the usual standards, ignored, but neither was it widely acclaimed, and since it is a very slow and painful book to read, it just may not make its way in the world. Its subject is not very much different from Floyd Salas's, except that most of the action takes place outside the reformatory, but it is much better than Salas's simply because, whatever his actual personal relationship to the young car thief, Weesner is triumphant and not just compellingly honest with his story; Salas tends to blurt out his pain, and Weesner knows when to blurt out, when to back off, and the cumulative effect of his apparently simple sentences is sometimes staggering. If Weesner goes on writing, I trust he will be recognized, but if not, someone ought to make sure to buy a hundred remaindered copies of *The Car Thief* to give away as presents. I think, too, of a novel by James Guetti, called *Action*, which, much more than Weesner's novel, is in danger of disappearing without ever having been seen, and if it does, it would be hard to blame Guetti for shutting up or turning to hackwork. *Action* is the best novel I know about gambling, and indeed is so much better than most that the others cease to count. Furthermore, it has a grand opening sequence that is, by itself, a first-rate short story, and, to boot, a wonderful indicator for any wary reader of what is in store.

One could go on. All the time that I have been reading, rereading, and writing, I have been plagued with the sense that there are, first, other writers who for some reason I've misplaced in my memory, and, second, hundreds of other books that I'll never read that may be, for all I or perhaps anyone knows, as good as any of those I've mentioned, or the next Roth or

Updike.* There is, for some, great joy in writing, in imagining a fiction, a full story, and it may well be that the joy of the writing is enough and what happens to it after it is in print doesn't really matter. But while this may well be true for a novel or two for many writers, the evidence is quite strong that continued neglect demands its payments. Many give up, and quite a few who go on get worse, as my early-fifties novelists can show. What makes any person, or any person's talent, continue to develop and grow is of course a mystery, but I know of no instance where it can be said that a writer has thrived because he or she has remained unknown. Perhaps the one way neglect seems to hurt most novelists is with the prose, line by line. Most first and second novels, no matter how strongly conceived, are underwritten or overwritten, often considerably. In the absence of an audience, especially an intelligent critical audience, these defects tend to go uncorrected, perhaps because they are never properly recognized. My guess is that lonely writers hug their conceptions to themselves, nurture their stories and characters with wounded pride, but rather ignore the moment-to-moment quality of their writing. Almost all the writers that I have discussed read better than short quotations can reveal. Of course premature adulation and fame can hurt, too; this, I am convinced, has proved to be the case with Roth and perhaps with Updike too, but those are the rare fates, after all. Much commoner are those we can discern only as questions: What happened to Richard Dohrman? Why did Clara Winston not go on, or, why did Richard Gehmann settle for writing for *TV Guide?* Did Dexter Masters ever write anything after *The Accident?* To ask such questions is to begin to think that it isn't very much worthwhile once more to go out and measure the size of the ego or the achievement of Norman Mailer.

For, of course, it is not just the writers that suffer from being unknown, but the rest of us as well. The novelists themselves,

---

*To wit, Janet Lewis, gifted with an almost scary neat and tidy prose, author of two fine novels, *The Wife of Martin Guerre*, short, tricky, nasty, haunting; *The Ghost of Monsieur Scarron*, long, violent, evocative. Both are set in seventeenth-century France. Also, Maureen Howard's *Bridgeport Bus*, a very sad and funny novel about a smart, dowdy single woman who discovers admirable ways to accept life as she busily tells us how it ought to be better than it is. I've passed these books among friends—until someone forgot to return them—and have never had a disappointed reader.

after all, may be living on quite happily in oblivion, but anyone who has known the experience of a book that remains memorable knows also that one cannot have too many such experiences. Of course there are lots of things to read besides novels, and lots to do besides read. But the very fact that there are so many good unknown novelists, that at any moment of the day hundreds of novels are being conceived and written and rewritten, shows that it is still our form, our major literary way of saying who we are, and why. One only wishes life were somehow different enough so that the books we should read, the books that could be memorable, could always be announced to us. It is part of our great abundance that we have so much, written in our lifetimes and within a single genre, that is worth knowing. It is the curse of that same abundance that we may never begin to know the extent of our riches.

MAILER & LESSING

When Norman Mailer's "The Prisoner of Sex" appeared in *Harper's* [Mar. 1971], it served to shove his *Of a Fire on the Moon* into the background, and even his admirers did not seem unhappy. Mailer admits he wrote it because he needed money, and his way of giving value for money was to write a book almost 500 pages long; moreover, it is about the flight of Apollo 11, about which no one has cared for some time. So it was good of Mailer to appear again quickly, and writing about women as well.

In favor of such a position it can be said that the first and third sections of *Of a Fire on the Moon,* the Mailer sections (he calls himself Aquarius), are quite bad, and the long middle section, on the moon flight itself, has some boring stretches. Mailer is, say, at a dull news conference in Houston, or he is hot and tired the night before the liftoff at Cape Kennedy. For years he has been assuming he can bludgeon his feelings even at his worst moments and end up with news, but it doesn't work this time:

Aldrin gave a disconcerted smile. "I hope I don't have a tender foot walking around the moon." It was so bad a joke that one had to assume it was full of reference for him, perhaps some natural male anxiety at the thought of evil moon rays passing into one's private parts.

Who could say the ride of the Indian with whisky in his veins was not some conflagration of messages derived from the silences of the moon? Now tonight were the ghosts of old Indians awakening in the prairies and the swamps?

Give Mailer a "one had to assume" or a "who could say" and, of course, he can launch into Mailerese, but the effort here seems forced and most of the launchings abort quickly. Mailer has on his hands a "hovering of machinery" and it costs almost "twenty-five billion dollars," so he must make something of it. The machinery, thus, "is preparing to go through the funnel of an historical event whose significance might yet be next to death itself." Which is silly, and Mailer seems to know it, so he backs off, changes the subject.

Most of the book is like that. Mailer will be content for a while to report straightforwardly, but then, as if he feels he were being paid to be Norman Mailer, he lurches off: Is the trip to the moon a fulfillment or a defiling of God's will? Is the American Wasp God's answer or His Curse? Does this or that malfunction in a computer or a hatch portend the long-feared moment when the machines strike back, asserting their own will? He is committed to trying to see the very big in the very little, to make all events potentially symbolic, because his whole success as a reporter has been based on his ability to do just that. But here, where he really has very little to say about what is happening, we are left, often quite embarrassed, with a technique that suddenly makes Mailer seem a driveler and a show.

In one place, though, everything seems to go right, and it is perhaps significant that it comes when Mailer is talking about questions of scale, but is not trying to make the big out of the little. The subject is the pictures taken of the dark side of the moon:

> . . . and indeed nothing for hundreds of miles before the eyes but swellings and distensions of the terrain like a skin

beneath which furies must have wrung themselves, a bewildering endlessly worked-over expanse almost without rays, a stretch of bumpy knobby pock-marked upthrown churnings equal to the view from a low boat—without horizon one could never sight a level, a direction was hopeless, a windtwisted choppy sea had been frozen on the instant to stone. So one had no sense of scale. . . .

Mailer is free now to speculate almost at will, but interestingly, he turns to the history of art:

Aquarius had been devoted to painting for close to thirty years; an amateur of the mysteries of form, it took him close to thirty years to comprehend why Cézanne was the father of modern art and godfather to photographs of the far side of the moon.

He proceeds to earn it all, both the leap to Cézanne and the assertion about him:

Before Cézanne, did a painter work a canvas properly? Then one could cut out a square inch of canvas, show it to an unfamiliar eye, and the response would be that it was a piece of lace, or a square of velvet, for the canvas had been painted to look exactly like lace or velvet.

Cézanne, however, had looked to destroy the surface. A tablecloth in any one of his still lifes, taken inch by square inch, resembled the snowfields of mountains; his apples could be the paint-stained walls of a barn, or the clay roundings of a rock; the trunks of his trees were stems, or pillars, or hairs beneath a microscope. His skies, patch by patch, could be taken for a sea as easily as a light-blue throw cloth; the skin which ran from a man's eyes to the corner of his mouth was like the sun-beaten terrain of his hills. . . . Something in that vision spoke like the voice of the century to come, something in his work turned other painters out of their own directions and into a search for the logic of the abstract.

Mailer like this, free, wanton, thoughtful, makes all the rest worth it.

Still, what Cézanne is telling him, Mailer seems not really to have learned. To take a small thing, a flower in the crannied wall, and to render it as though it might be a mud pool in a desert or a distant galaxy alone in space is to instruct and dizzy the imagination with the possibilities of a universe of visible forms torn loose from scale and context. No one who looked at the moon while Aldrin and Armstrong were on it could fail to be staggered with such or similar possibilities. But when you take that same flower and you feel endlessly obliged to say what therefore God and man is, you probably have the surest prescription for inflated rhetoric.

Two years ago Mailer was looking at Apollo 11 and trying over and over to decide whether it was the herald of sunrise or of night, whether the century was ending or beginning. Apollo 11 had to be that flower in the crannied wall—but it wasn't. Cézanne teaches a humility that Mailer, nineteenth-century romantic that he is, simply cannot learn because neither his vision nor his ambition will let him. He knows he has very little to say here—at one point he longs for a great heavy-weight championship fight to write about because that would "sear the brain with excess of perception" while "in NASA-land the only thing open was the technology." So technology it is, right scale or wrong scale, because Mailer has forced himself to say there is little to say and then to write a very long book trying to make that little interesting, even grand.

Not that the technology is badly done. Mailer once studied engineering, he says, and one remembers that the best parts of *Why Are We in Vietnam?* concerned big guns and helicopters. The descriptions of the relation of physics to engineering at various points on the trip are fine. But he will not be content with such straightforward reporting because it is his secret pride that he can fathom technology and Wasp America and show he is not simply literary and New York. About Wasp America, though, he has nothing new to say here—the vision of the spectators the night before the launching is similar and inferior to the vision of the soldiers who challenged the marchers on the Pentagon in

Armies of the Night—and about science and technology he is only like other intelligent amateurs.

Which is to deny Mailer his ambition, at least for now. We must still prize him only for his occasional stunning and exhilarating passages, of which he has quite a few more elsewhere than in this book. The short essay on American fiction in *Cannibals and Christians*, the meditations on women's peace groups in *Armies of the Night*, the passages on Lawrence and the Jews in "The Prisoner of Sex"—one can feel about these as one does about the great things in Ruskin, and the comparison holds in a number of ways.

Both Mailer and Ruskin are great and incorrigibly egotistical writers obsessed with the urge to tell us who we are and where the world is headed; both seem to have to write much too much in order to write anything good at all, and we can treasure both not for their books, but for those passages that turn, stop, explode, only to turn and explode again, and again. Giddy with contemplating their grandeur or the world's doom, the brain of each seared with excess of perception, surely it is only in eras when we *want* others to tell us who we are and where we are going that such writers appear, become famous in ways mere literary types never are, feel needed, indeed, because they are.

If the metaphor for Mailer is Ruskin, mad stylists making the world the arena for their seriousness about themselves, the metaphor for Doris Lessing may be George Eliot, finger on the pulse of Everything. Unlike Ruskin and Mailer, George Eliot and Doris Lessing write real and whole books, and at least once, in *The Four-Gated City*, Mrs. Lessing has written a book as good as many of those of her predecessor. Like George Eliot, Doris Lessing is often thought of as ponderous, clumsy, a thinker rather than a real novelist; which is all nonsense. The style of both writers is fully answerable to their vision of our lot; neither "writes stories" and yet both can do what only the great storytellers can do, sustain intelligent interest over hundreds of pages;

both manage to convey the most urgent concerns of their eras by the way they write about the domestic lives of a relatively few people.

The last section of *The Four-Gated City* is Doris Lessing's vision of the ghastly future before us. At some time in the 1970s the totalitarian, bureaucratic technology collapses in an accident and the land mass occupied by the Western world becomes mostly uninhabitable. The enormous demands made by the society on the individual, for conformity, for efficiency, for cheerfulness, have led to an increase in the number of people who "hear things," have extrasensory perceptions, who come to learn to live in "their world" as they are forced out of "ours"; they are our messengers from the life of the future.

Such visions are very common in science fiction, and, considered strictly as a vision, Mrs. Lessing's is not as good as one it closely resembles, Arthur C. Clarke's *Childhood's End.* But where Clarke is weakest Doris Lessing is a mastodon of strength. His is all vision while hers is the full outgrowth of 600 pages of densely imagined lives; he had an idea, and she has a great novel. Her vision of the future is mostly "what happens next" to Martha Quest and to Mark and Lynda and Francis Coldridge, and her sense of history and of the inner workings of the mind are the consequences of, and not the antecedents to, her curiosity about her characters.

Briefing for a Descent into Hell is shorter, more programmatic, more simply satirical. The assault on the society's treatment of the "mentally ill" is much more directly mounted. A man is picked up on the London Embankment and taken to a hospital. He is taking an extraordinary mental journey in the Atlantic, and two doctors, named X and Y, try to "control" this journey with drugs. X wants to try shock treatment and seems a monster, while Y, kindly, but narrow, wants to work with some brand-new drugs; both agree the man's journey is simply hallucination. Both receive venomous treatment from their author, as her names for them show. The idea, thus, behind *Briefing for a Descent into Hell* is easy, too easy; suffice it to say it resembles the flashy insistence of R. D. Laing that the insane are the only truly sane. But there is a difference between an idea and a vision which embodies that idea, and even in this novel, where Doris Lessing is too close to carping for comfort, there is much that is convincing.

The journeying patient is washed up on the shore of an island, discovers an abandoned city, becomes crazed by the moon as he watches some lurid blood sacrifices, finds himself surrounded by hordes of dog-rats and then by monkeys. The two groups of animals fight horribly, then the man is removed by a Crystal disc come from the sky for which he has been hoping and waiting all along. Above the earth he looks down on the awful encrustation that is mankind as it asserts its ego and will to pollute and destroy, but then he soars once again:

> But man-wise, microbe-wise, I am before the Crash and in a cool, sweet loving air that rings with harmony, is harmony, Is, yes, and here am I, voyager, Odysseus bound for home at last, the Seeker in home waters, spiteful Neptune outwitted and Jupiter's daughter my friend and guide.

Throughout this long vision the writing is firm and absorbed, controlled in a way that makes us know here what home is, know that the voyager is at the end of his vision but also before it, before the Crash and the pollution.

There follows a long scene, the briefing of the title, which unquestionably does not work. The vision is now in the third person, the voyager is present only implicitly, Minerva and Mercury and others in the solar system are planning a descent into the hell that is earth. The use of the celestial gods, which seems right when the voyager is made Odysseus, is jarring here, especially when the principals are called Merk Ury and Minne Erva and there is a Descent Team and a Permanent Staff. I can only say that it seems all wrong, thin in argument, nagging in tone. What becomes clear, though, is that the patient is going to descend to earth, his vision over, his drugged sleep ended, his self recovering in the eyes of the doctors, but lost in his own. But he cannot remember where he has been, or where the doctors are trying to take him from, though he knows he longs to return.

A series of letters then tells us that the patient's name is Charles Watkins. He is a professor at Cambridge and he has never quite maintained normal relations in life, and to others he has seemed something of a brute; what we call life has never quite touched him or seemed important to him. Doctory Y has him write down something he remembers and he tells a moving story of joining a group of partisan guerrillas in Yugoslavia during the Second World War which ends when a girl with whom he is in love is fatally impaled by a doe protecting her new fawn. But we also learn that Watkins never was in Yugoslavia, that he had a long and fearfully grinding experience during the war which ended with a three month recovery in Cornwall spent with a man who *was* in Yugoslavia and to whom the experiences Watkins describes may or may not have happened.

Watkins's long vision at the beginning and his story about Yugoslavia are things that are his, events in his mind, not because he is Watkins so much as because those who descend into the hell of earth have such experiences. The effect of the drugs on Watkins is that of Wordsworth's prison house: the drugs are simply one of the world's ways of giving the soul her earthly freight which lies heavy as frost, and deep almost as life. The suggestion is clear that something like this happens to all of us. Watkins wants terribly to be able to remember the vision he has lost, but he also wants to do as he is told, to return to "normal life." Against his better judgment and that of an adolescent girl who becomes his only friend after he awakens, Watkins submits to shock treatment in the wan hope it will make him remember. But it doesn't, he is instead "cured" and he goes home to his wife and children.

Although Mrs. Lessing has stiffened her ideas and is using her characters in a much more clinical way than in *The Four-Gated City*, she manages nonetheless to make Watkins's story compelling. He is also an "other," one briefed for his life on earth, so he is a case. But his author's understanding of *him* is never clinical, he escapes her more mindless satirical moments, he experiences almost nothing offered by ordinary human life, yet his instance is touching and beautiful. We do not feel in reading about him that only the insane are truly sane, but rather that these terrible and wonderful events have happened to him. If he is defeated at the end, Doris Lessing is not, and we need not be.

But to say that is perhaps to deflect too soon or too easily from what she, and Norman Mailer too, are trying to see and tell us.

Both have become increasingly and insistently visionary in their recent books; both feel it is not preposterous to invoke the moon as a potentially magical and mystical power; both seem certain that if we persist in seeing the moon only as the methods of modern science have taught us to see celestial bodies then we are doomed. In "The Prisoner of Sex" Mailer speaks of the Devil as having "wished to cut man off from his primitive instincts and thereby leave us marooned in a plastic maze which could shatter the balance of nature before the warnings were read." Here is part of Charles Watkins's vision, in a similar vein:

> Some sort of divorce there has been somewhere along the path of this race of man between the "I" and the "We," some sort of terrible falling away, and I (who am not I, but part of a whole composed of other human beings as they are of me) hovering here as if between the wings of a great white bird, feel as if I am spinning back into a vortex of terror, like a birth in reverse, and it is towards a catastrophe, yes, that was when the microbes, the little broth that is humanity, was knocked senseless, hit for six, knocked out of their true understanding, so that ever since most have said I, I, I, I, I, I, I, and cannot, save for a few, say, We.

Not since the Victorians have so many very good writers been so completely in earnest as they feel themselves become watchmen of the night.

The reasons are so familiar as to need very little rehearsal. In any era where power becomes centralized at a rate faster than anyone's ability to comprehend, when official voices seem to insist that average citizens deny the evidence of their senses, when it seems in very truth that true wit is near allied to madness, then there must be a terrible blurring of scale and proportion. At such times the temptation is great to see what God and man are by looking at the flower in the crannied wall—any flower, any God, any definition of man just so long as it gets rid of the blurring and seems to yield proportion.

Thus: R. D. Laing, Charles Reich, Jacques Ellul, so many of Norman Mailer's bad moments, so many similar bad moments for all of us. On the day I write the newspaper reports two events, more or less as a matter of course: the FBI issues instructions to its agents to infiltrate radical groups simply to increase the paranoia of their members; James Michener has interviewed students at Kent State and says that one quarter of them told him their parents believed the students who were killed got what they deserved and their own children deserved the same. What *is* one to say, what evasion or explanation can satisfy even for a moment?

Doris Lessing seems to say that trying to learn to live with the polluted flowers in our crannied walls works to defeat what is precious in us. We would be better off, perhaps, breaking down and away from the terrifying evidence, psychically shivering, rejecting, because human beings can take only so much. And she takes us there, showing us that those who do this are not simply defeated, indeed, they seem at times to expand their consciousnesses and possibilities by so doing. At the end of *The Four-Gated City* there is no good or understanding human gesture of which Martha Quest seems incapable, and near the end of *Briefing for a Descent into Hell* Charles Watkins achieves his finest moment of human contact, just before submitting to recovery and defeat. She is no Laing, no touter of the void, to use Herzog's phrase, as though it were so much real estate. The preciousness, the terror, the rejecting, the achieving I speak of are in her work densely realized and vivid. Personally I do not see her scale or vision as being triumphantly right, yet no other writer in recent years, not Mailer or Bellow, has upset me as she has done.

HAWKES, MALAMUD, RICHLER, OATES

John Hawkes's *The Blood Oranges* fails because it is the work of a contemptible imagination. Hawkes has always seemed to me more an unadmitted voyeur of horror than its calm delineator, but in this new novel the pretense that what is being described is horrifying is dropped, and we have only the nightmare vision of a narrator unable to see how awful he is. He is a "sex-singer," a middle-aged expert in love who is frequently delighted to tell us in what good shape he is, how he looks in his trunks, how skilled he is in bed. He and his wife want and capture other people, in this case another couple, and they insist the world should learn to have its sex with the same impersonal, erotic ennui that is their staple emotion. Their insistence that they are flexible and free is belied by the rigid emptiness of their daily round: sit on the beach, climb a hill to see a peasant or a goat, screw expertly.

There is cruelty here that, because unadmitted, is not even palliated by the relish of sadism. The two men see a peasant girl in a barn and the narrator says: "Perfect, let's hunt her down." They do, and force her to strip so they can take pictures of her, and the other man is delighted by things like the hairs on her chin because he is making a collection of photographs of peasants: "That's perfect. Now let's just shove her over against the beam." Great fun.

And when the friend decides later on that he doesn't much like the idea of the two couples making a sexual foursome, we get lectured: "Need I insist that the only enemy of the mature marriage is monogamy? That anything less than sexual multiplicity (Body upon body, voice on voice) is naïve?" When the other man wants to keep his wife to himself, when the other woman collapses after the death of her husband and the departure of her children, they are to shape up, and to *this* standard: "It is simply not in my character, my receptive spirit, to suffer sexual possessiveness, the shock of aesthetic greed, the bile that greases most matrimonial bonds, the rage and fear that shrivels your ordinary man at the first hint of the obvious multiplicity of love." This deeply *un*receptive narcissism has so little aesthetic greed, furthermore, or even mere desire to write well, that we find, on almost every page, something like "The sun was setting, sinking to its predestined death," or "And already the seeds of dawn were planted in the night's thigh."

Hawkes has many admirers, which means some will note that I have completely missed the fact that it is all a put-on; some others will suspect I am guilty of all those sins that Hawkes's narrator so cleverly exposes in your ordinary man. So be. But when horror becomes a pastime it should announce itself or at least know itself; when reticence and shyness become the great human vices, then their opposites should be clearly and ably defended; when the man who does not want his wife sleeping around makes her wear a rusty and viciously designed chastity belt, then narrator and author should not imagine it is chastity's fault; when life is insistently joyless it should not be called good, or even particularly tolerable; when people stop mattering to a novelist, the writing will suffer and the writer should stop.

Bernard Malamud's case is altogether more interesting. He is a much better novelist than Hawkes to begin with, and he is still struggling to write good novels. Something goes seriously wrong with his latest, *The Tenants*, but we know, as we try to identify what and why, that Malamud has been there before us, calculating his difficulties, daring his possibilities, perhaps deciding that his way was the only way, despite its unsatisfactoriness.

He begins with a situation which seems, though obviously contrived, ideal for his morose and witty genius. Long ago Harry Lesser wrote a good first novel that no one read, then a bad second novel that was popular. For years he has been engaged in writing a third novel, one worthy of his talents and the years of his labor. As *The Tenants* opens he is having a terrible time seeing how it should end. He has decided he cannot move until he finishes the book, even though he is the only person still living in a condemned building whose owner is barred by the rent control laws from evicting him. One day Lesser discovers a young black with a typewriter in the abandoned apartment next to his. He is called Willie Spearmint and he is working slowly, painfully, and passionately on his very black and rather clumsy autobiographical novel.

The relation between Lesser and Willie that begins to evolve is filled with mistrust and inherited prejudice, but also with mutual respect for each other's privacy and intense dedication to writing. The early scenes between the two work well because Malamud can accept them both as types without ever becoming gossipy or journalistic. Here they are in the middle of a party in Lesser's apartment where everyone is smoking hashish:

What's your book about, Lesser?

Love, I guess.

Willie titters, rowing calmly, steadily, his muscles flashing as the water ripples.

It's about this guy who writes because he has never really told the truth and he's dying to. What's yours about, Willie?

Me.

How's it coming?

On four feet, man, in a gallop. How's yours?

On one. Clop.

I'm gon win the fuckn Noble Prize. They gon gimme a million bucks of cash.

After me, Willie. I've worked since the ice age and to-morrow is another day. . . . What's more I'm writing my best book. I want all the good people on both shores waving their little paper flags, all those grays and blacks, to admit Harry Lesser is King David with his six-string harp, except the notes are words and psalms fiction.

That's Malamud, sure of what he is about: clear, relaxed, gloomy, witty.

But there is trouble ahead. Malamud's intuition tells him the relation between the two will fail even though both seem to want it to succeed, in so far as either cares about anything other than his writing. It will fail because Lesser is a Jew and Willie is a black, because those facts will come to mean everything to Willie and because Lesser can do nothing to prevent becoming a vic-tim. There may be something self-pitying about Malamud's intu-ition, but there is truth enough, too. Malamud knows that Lesser will be a victim not just because Willie is an angry black but also because Lesser's novel is about "Love, I guess." Had he been writing a long short story here, I think Malamud could have sim-ply followed his intuition and created a kind of fable that would make his asserted truths about the fate of Willie and Lesser seem the necessary facts.

Instead, he decided to write a novel, and in novels simple intuitions and assertions are not enough. The end of the book may have been clear to him, but the way to get to the end was not. Malamud offers us Willie's white chick, with whom Lesser falls in love, and some of Willie's black friends, who see no reason to treat Lesser with anything but contempt; he then lets these minor characters provide the impetus and motive for the final clash between the tenants. Lesser takes over the girl, in whom Willie is increasingly less interested, then Lesser tells Willie he has done so. Willie and his friends smash Lesser's apartment and destroy his novel, the two meet with ax and razor and kill each other.

What might have been simple and powerful turns out to be blurry. After Lesser and the girl fall in love, she keeps insisting to him that she must be the one to tell Willie, if anyone does, so when Lesser does instead we have to think that all might have gone differently had the girl been able to handle it her way. Worse still, the girl is uninteresting and Lesser's falling in love with her is foggy. We are not led to believe he wants her because she is Willie's, yet we have no other explanation for a celibate man in desperate need of finishing his book suddenly becoming entangled like this, dreamily and dangerously. We can't even say he does it to run from his novel. So all that is potentially most interesting about both Lesser and Willie becomes dissipated and then lost in novelistic workings up of plot which needn't have been there in the first place and which probably would not have been there had Malamud seen he had a situation better suited for a much shorter story.

Inevitably, *The Tenants* will be compared with *Mr. Sammler's Planet* because both are by Jewish writers of distinction and eminence, and both explore the consequences of discovering that New York is no longer Malamud's or Bellow's, Lesser's or Sammler's, and perhaps is not even habitable by them. Both novels lose their central urgency in a tangle of minor characters; Malamud's should have been a short fable, Bellow's a monologue. Neither writer has seen a way to bring a black man into a novel and still have it be a novel, though the blacks themselves in each case are rather impressively handled. Both seem to have reached at least a momentary impasse with the racial problem, yet knowing that each sees that problem as his world and frontier makes one hope they do not retreat now, but instead try to see how a full story would go that has Jews and blacks as its central figures. The other well-known frontiers, involving women and the young, are not for these writers anyway, and this one is every bit as important.

The two remaining novels under review are by much younger writers than Malamud and John Hawkes. They are also much longer and more ambitious and easier to recommend to someone interested in reading a good book. Both are full of faults, but both are so energetic, so filled with their authors' expanding sense of novelistic powers, that the faults seem as much a badge of exuberance as a sign of limitation. Neither Mordecai Richler nor Joyce Carol Oates seems in danger of becoming first-rate soon, but they are good to read, to praise, to hope for.

Richler's *St. Urbain's Horseman* begins with a fine title and accompanying dust jacket designed by Alice and Martin Provensen. It is one of those current extravagant performances, with a raconteur for a narrator, Canadian (this time) and Jewish jokes and pain, lore about stages of life and recent history. If you don't like the manner you can't like the book:

> Back in Montreal Jake made straight for the bar in Central Station, ordered a double whisky, and paid for it with American money.
> "Montreal is the Paris of North America," the waiter said. "I trust you will enjoy your stay, sir."
> Jake stared at his change. "What's this," he asked, "Monopoly money?"
> "It's Canadian."
> Jake laughed, pleased.
> "Canada's no joke. We're the world's leading producer of uranium. Walter Pidgeon was born in this country."

or:

> In the afternoons they studied for their bar mitzvahs at the Young Israel synagogue and at night they locked the door to Arty's room, dropped their trousers to their ankles, and studied themselves for bush growth. Pathetic miserable little hairs, wouldn't they ever proliferate? Duddy Kravitz taught them how to encourage hair growth by shaving, a

sometimes stinging process. "One slip of the razor, you schmock, and you'll grow up a hairdresser. Like Gordie Shapiro." Duddy also told them how Japanese girls were able to diddle themselves in hammocks. Of course Duddy was the bushiest, with the longest, most menacingly veined, thickest cock of all. He won so regularly when they masturbated against the clock, first to come picks up all the quarters, that before long they would not compete unless he accepted a sixty-second handicap.

Well, that is the most familiar tone now in fashion; you can quote it easily, like it or not like it equally easily, feel superior to it at whim or peril.

The question is not, Is it art? but, Can you make a novel out of it? To which the theoretical answer is a forceful yes while the answer in practice is usually a qualified no. Malamud's self-pity shrinks to nothing beside the self-regard of Richler's narrator. There is nothing he will not try to package with humor and anguish: the fifties, Jews on Germans, assimilation, modern London, Toronto, the sexual and hygienic trials of the middle-aged rich, the sexual revenges of the downtrodden, the tendency of lives to approach tabloid journalism. Richler's aim is almost encyclopedic, and he knows full well he has left himself wide open to the charge that he offers nothing new:

> Years and years ago, he recalled, another Jake, ponderously searching for a better way than St. Urbain's, had started out on his intellectual trek immensely heartened to discover, through the books that shaped him, that he wasn't a freak. There were others who thought and felt as he did. Now the same liberated bunch dissatisfied, even bored him. The novels he devoured so hopefully, conned by overexcited reviews, were sometimes diverting, but told him nothing he had not already known. On the contrary, they only served to reaffirm, albeit on occasion with style, his own feelings. In a word, they were self-regarding. . . .
>
> To read of meanness in others, promiscuity well observed or greed understood, to discover his own inadequacies shared no longer licensed him, any more than all the deaths that had come before could begin to make his own endurable.

A nice point.

For any novelist, the way out of the box that Richler so cleverly constructs around himself here is not to go on trying to convince others that they are not freaks, which is the usual praise of his kind of book. It is to test his style and his anecdotes and his autobiography by means of a real story. Richler senses this, and he tries to keep his narrator from being only another instance of charming and arrested adolescence. At the beginning of the novel Jake Hersh, a wealthy television director in London, is going on trial for participation in some wild sexual shenanigans. As we go along we gradually learn what the shenanigans allegedly were; near the end we come pretty close to knowing Jake's complicity in them. And that is all carefully connected with Jake's boredom with the present, his fear of death, his search for his tawdry but heroic lost cousin, the first St. Urbain's horseman, and with his co-defendant, a really funny and grubby pervert from the East End.

But "connected with" is all we can say here. Richler wrote, before this, three rather ordinary raconteur novels, and he saw he needed a story. But the one he comes up with, neat and "connecting" though it be, is a raconteur's story, shaggy and timed, incapable of testing anything. And the test of *that* is the narrative voice. If the story were really a story, the voice would alter as it encounters the changes the plot forces it to recognize; consult *Catch-22*, that very good novel, on this point. As yet Richler sees the need for testing with his story more than he knows how to do it. He simply is too attracted by his own gaudy attractiveness, and the only limits he allows for are those he defines for himself, not those discovered in a fiction. The voice in *Catch-22* changes each time it retells its story, which means we do not end up where we began; the voice in *St. Urbain's Horseman* is by comparison static, completing itself, encountering nothing anew. I like Richler's voice, but wish it would give itself sterner tasks to do.

Joyce Carol Oates's strengths are Mordecai Richler's weaknesses, and vice versa. She is humorless where he is witty, filled with a pressing tale where he is chatty, deeply concerned with her characters where he is content with the masturbatory feats of Duddy Kravitz. *Wonderland* is a great anguished slab of a book, filled with real grotesqueness rather than with the cardboard wildness that Richler calls the grotesque. The novel opens with a December day in the life of an adolescent boy in a very small town in western New York. Something is wrong: the father is morose, out of work, his gas station is for sale and that greatly embarrasses the boy and his older sister; the sister and the mother quarrel at the kitchen table before school; the boy himself is sick to his stomach during a Christmas assembly. Step-by-step Miss Oates puts her pieces together beautifully until the father appears in the store where the boy works, yanks him out, and drives him home, and slowly the boy begins to realize that the father has killed everyone else in the family, and means to kill him. He runs, is wounded, ends in a hospital, the only one in his family left alive.

It is the best thing in all four novels, profuse and precise in detail, yet driven by a strong sense that something is still to happen. When this kind of climax comes so early in a very long novel one is left wondering if anything like this can be sustained, and how. The answer the rest of the novel offers is never convincing; it lurches and drives, often with considerable intensity, but as a whole it is obscure. It should be that this is a novel about a boy and man whose family is destroyed in a mass murder, but Miss Oates cuts that off by having the boy flee so completely in body and mind that he, and the novel, cannot register his past, and a book that cannot register its past is a book whose form must end up being created arbitrarily.

But the novel's second long sequence is almost as good as the first. The boy goes to Lockport as the adopted son of a huge, corrupt, immensely persuasive provincial doctor, a figure at least as grotesque as the boy's father. The family lives at meal times, when the doctor asks his children to give recitations, and they, and he, respond to the pressure he thereby builds up by eating and eating, each successful performance celebrated and defeated by more food. They are all very fat, and hungry all the time. The doctor's wife finally tries to escape and asks the boy's help. They flee to Buffalo, and in a particularly wild scene they eat two full

Chinese meals and endless snacks, thereby rendering themselves liable to be hunted down by the doctor. Which they are.

If it all sounds grand and mad, it is. Miss Oates builds scenes and sequences of scenes very well; she has a fine sense of the way one powerful and grotesque person can transform everyone into himself, and this makes for some splendid writing. But then, as we watch the boy go through college and then medical school, it slowly becomes clear that Miss Oates means for us to take her wild and mad collection of people and know it is America. When in doubt, call it social commentary, and we realize that for all their many differences she and Mordecai Richler have much in common.

The effect of her book is of course much different from Richler's: with *St. Urbain's Horseman* you learn early on that the plot is mostly a hoax and so you can relax with the commentary; with *Wonderland* you are led to believe from the great opening bursts that something fine is going to happen, then you become increasingly depressed as Miss Oates dwindles her story into a metaphor for Modern Times that Richler could spin better in ten pages than she can in three hundred. She ought to be better than he is because she respects rather than regards herself, but she ends up worse. The idea that the boy keeps on trying to flee his past as he becomes a man is for many pages only an excuse to ignore earlier parts of the work. Gradually the story turns into a fable of loneliness and success, the inhumanity of great doctors, etc.—we might as well be reading one of the later novels of John Dos Passos.

Miss Oates's talent is for unfolding horrors and mysteries in big scenes, which means that as we read we must be quite passive, letting her strip away each layer of apparently placid domestic detail. When she has no mystery to offer, when the horrors become banalities, we can realize this only after the fact, after the promised big guns have not gone off, and it may well be that Miss Oates is as powerless as we are in this matter. She seems to have to write herself into her big scenes before she can really know how they're going to go, if they're going to be good, and if the guns are going to go off.

This is particularly telling at the very end of *Wonderland*. The boy, by now a doctor approaching middle age, becomes obsessed by the flower child waywardness of his second daughter. She writes him loving and hating and tantalizing letters from all over the continent and he finally tracks her down in a grungy Toronto street. She is there with her man, and there is a constant threat that the doctor will kill them both—and so become like his own father?—but the scene lurches hither and yon, the shootings don't happen—because he is not like his father? because the times they are a-changing? Who knows? Father and daughter end up on a boat, where he is reduced to wailing: "All of you . . . everyone . . . all my life, everyone . . . . Always you are going away from me and you don't come back to explain." The doctor and his author, it would seem, are equally baffled. As the final clarity of a huge and ambitious novel, it is pathetically inadequate.

The truth, I think, is that Joyce Carol Oates is as yet only a writer of short stories just as Mordecai Richler is only a raconteur of gossip and anecdote. They don't see well enough how life goes to sustain a whole novel, and each has let his great talents and energies obscure this fact. Both tend to lapse into thinking that their interesting and strange angles on life are really its central truths, and then to let that lapsing serve as a vision of our common contemporary lot. Since there is nothing they can't write about, they tend to drift, to write about everything. Richler gives us a long account of a softball game on Hampstead Heath played by wealthy and middle-aged Jews in show business in London. We are told their life stories, how they do at bat, in the field, in the market, in bed with this wife or that mistress. It's all supposed to matter, but it doesn't.

Joyce Carol Oates goes on for pages about her doctor and a woman named Reva, whom he has seen somewhere but can't place, with whom he becomes obsessed, apparently for years, though it's quite clear to her and to us that she isn't worth it. He even leaves home to track her down to a shack in northern Wisconsin; she seems willing to go away with him, but it turns out his love for her is merely suicidal, and he leaves.

In Richler's case, the softball game is only another excuse for display; in Miss Oates's, Reva is only an invitation to write some big scenes that resolutely won't come off and so turn into metaphors for the doctor's need to run from life. In each case—and both authors have many more—one suspects the writer realized that a dead end had been reached, but to have deleted the episodes would have been to ask more strictly than either was willing to do what really belonged.

Yes, oh dear yes, the novel tells a story, says E. M. Forster despondently in *Aspects of the Novel.* He assumed the modern novel should try to liberate itself from storytelling somehow, but it turned out that modern novelists at their best were only finding new stories to tell and new ways to tell them. It's not that we can't get rid of story in fiction, but that to try to do so is to evade the central truth that to say what happens next is to say what you mean. Of course good novels do superb things in addition to telling their tales, just as inferior novels will have inferior stories that are nonetheless in their way often more fully completed than those of better novels.

John Hawkes's story is as fully rendered as any of the four novels here being considered. If you accept its terms all else follows, and it is only the terms that are intolerable. But with Malamud, Richler, and Oates the question of story is more interesting and indicative of why their current novels do not succeed as well as they should have. Malamud's trouble, his fuzziness about how to get from his premise to its conclusion, seems more a miscalculation than anything else, of a kind that plagues even the best of writers. He seems mostly to have overestimated his material, or to have imagined he was more interested in it than he really was. But he is an experienced and wise enough writer to accept this. If *The Tenants* does not finally work, then tomorrow, as Lesser says, is another day.

With Mordecai Richler and Joyce Carol Oates, however, one feels that all is neither already lost, as with Hawkes, nor pretty generally known, as with Malamud. They have rich talents and badly need to use them more rigorously, to accept their strengths as being by now given and assured, to acknowledge their weaknesses as defects of their virtues and so as something that must be lived with, looked into, slowly overcome if possible. There is great potential waste as well as considerable potential achievement in both of them. They need now to put themselves in the position of Malamud's Lesser, paralyzed and refusing to finish until he sees how his story should go right through to the end and how that ending says his sense of life. So long as his novel is about something as vague as "Love, I guess," he shouldn't finish, and so he can't.

That is the current lesson of this particular master. One of his epigraphs is from a Bessie Smith song: "I got to make it, I got to find the end." Richler and Miss Oates have, in one sense, made it already; they still have got to find the end that will make the beginning and everything in between clearer and truly revealing.

WILLIAMS, WEESNER, DRABBLE

By all rights, John A. Williams's *Captain Blackman* should have been much worse than it is. Its method is documentary, its aim is consciousness raising, not the loftiest of fictional ways and goals. Williams has, apparently, gone over every inch of ground where, at any time in American history, black soldiers have fought. As he did so, he tried to imagine not only the men he knew had been there but also a binding single figure, a soldier named Abraham Blackman, who fought in all the battles, from Lexington to New Orleans to Petersburg to Fort Sill in the Indian wars, to San Juan Hill, to France, Spain, Italy, Korea, and Vietnam. As the novel opens Blackman is wounded in Vietnam trying to shield some of his company from slaughter, and the rest is his dreams and hallucinations of his role in all the earlier battles.

As a novel the book doesn't even begin to count. Blackman himself may not be superhuman, but he is strictly a fantasy figure: huge, strong, brave, serious, always right, always able to speak the deeper ironies. His women, most of whom are named Mimosa Rogers, are always strong, sexy, eager, and tough-minded. The episodes, though many and varied, always carry the same message: whites are always willing to use blacks in battle, always afraid of the power blacks might have if properly rewarded for their service, always willing to find ways to ignore, degrade, or simply kill black soldiers who become a problem. So Williams has given himself practically no fictional room to move in. The coins have to keep falling exactly as Williams calls them.

But, given this, *Captain Blackman* is not without merit. At the beginning, when Blackman finds himself walking toward Lexington with Peter Salem, he says, "This is 1775 and you're on your way to Lexington because a cat named Paul Revere rode through these parts last night talkin about the British're coming." It looks as if a long read is ahead. But soon Williams takes Blackman's foreknowledge away from him, and it all begins to move more smoothly. It reads less like "You Are There" in jive talk. Williams's travels have given him a clear sense of the history of the army, and why it acted as it did, and he keeps showing the way it is racist, though not always bigoted. Whites assume the rightness of their history and their institutions, yet in moments of crisis, when they declare blacks expendable, they can see the folly and irony of their behavior as well as the blacks can. Though of course they very seldom try to do anything about it.

At the beginning of World War II, for instance, a high-level meeting is called to decide what to do about the race riots that are breaking out at army and navy bases all over the country. A Southerner says: "Now, god-dammit, you just cain't take northern nigras and station em in the South," and someone answers: "But we did because you wanted the bases there to give your economy a boost." The general in charge then wonders where the blacks can be sent, and he is told the Aussies are nervous, and Gruening doesn't want them mixing with Eskimos. "Panama wants us to remove a company of Negroes." "Isn't that something! That damned canal was built by niggers!" Chile and Venezuela say no, there are political reservations in China, and the Belgians in exile say no black troops in the Congo. It is all cartoon work, but Williams is never blind to the comic fact that whites simply don't know what to think or do about black soldiers. That damned canal *was* built by niggers, but of course the Panamanians don't want black troops.

Or, later, in Viareggio, a general discovers that two hundred black troops have deserted and taken up a position in the swamps. The general is stuck:

> Take these people, kick them in their asses all their lives, then put them in an incomplete unit, with all kinds of shitheads for officers; court-martial a bunch of their own Negro officers and send them out to fight. What the hell for? Of course, Blackman's right. But what am I to do, let all of what's wrong come to rest on *my* shoulders, ruin *my* life? Am I supposed to be the guy who says, You're right? Quit, don't fight, desert into the swamps of Tombolo and Migliarino? I can't change history.

So he orders his men to go in and kill the deserters, but he also, doing as much as his thin strain of decency will allow, tells Blackman the orders too so he can give warning. Grim, sad, awful.

So if Williams's fictional device is clumsy, and many of his attempts to flesh out history are vulgar, the central vision is one worth reading. It may not matter much that we learn about this or that incident that we've never heard of, but the grim joke that is our racial history does need to be told over and over, and the very sameness of the joke in each of Williams's many episodes is necessarily part of the telling, the irony, the joke. We may like to think that by now we've moved beyond such simple versions of the story, but that is exactly what people said in response to Richard Wright's *Native Son,* and they were wrong, and that was more than thirty years ago. *Captain Blackman,* like *Native Son,* is not a novel, but it is hard to wish that either had never been written.

Theodore Weesner's *The Car Thief* is an almost unbearably grim and painful book. After a hundred pages I wanted very much not to go on, to escape to the much simpler world of *Captain Blackman*, yet every word is haunting, forcing one on. The novel is set in small city America, an automobile factory town in Michigan. It is a scummy November morning, after a flash snowstorm, and Alex Housman is driving around the city and countryside in a car he has just stolen, his fourteenth. He parks outside a school where he might see a girl he has picked up a few times who wears a coat he stole and gave her. He peers into the tavern run by his mother's husband, where his brother lives, but he has seen none of these people for years. He flicks the dial on the car radio, trying to find music he can float away on. He goes back to the city, to his own school, but can't stand the idea of afternoon classes, so he goes to a movie. He goes home, sleeps a while, and is awakened by the girl, who calls to say she has told her parents of Alex's thefts and they have called the police. His father comes home from the second shift at the Chevrolet factory and for once he is not drunk. The two have a desultory conversation, then go to bed. The next day Alex is arrested and sent to a detention home.

It is not easy to say or show why the prose in these early pages is so awful and wonderful. It seems naturalistic, but compared with the simple pile-it-up naturalism of, say, James T. Farrell, it is sharp, pointed, locking us into each moment, suspending us from all other possible moments, giving us a sense that something is going to happen soon:

> He had a nickel in his fingers now but he had no desire to play the pinball machine, no more than he wanted to be there. Still, he worked the nickel flatways into the slot, pushed the handle in, held it as the balls fell, pulled the handle out. The machine lighted and clicked itself back to zero, alive under his hands. But he stood mute. His mind's voice was telling him, trying to tell him, that he did not want to play it. Nor did he want the packaged pie he had bought, or the Pepsi-Cola. He saw everything going this way, the way of this morning, driving here, driving there, doing things he did not want to do.

All the actions seem arbitrary, pointed nowhere, each one suspending us from the past by giving us so little connection to what has preceded, each one thus locking us into its own charged, sullen, pointless atmosphere.

What we have is something like the prose of short stories, where events can be described but not explained, where we get our slice of life and have our brief clarifying vision. Weesner takes this prose, but keeps insisting that clarity is not yet, perhaps not ever, and we must pay attention to that very fact. Alex Housman is almost totally without any sense of himself, and because Weesner is interested in showing us what that means, he must move very slowly, so we can discover the disappointment and frustration of its tedium. We are given material for a dozen sociological or psychological explanations for Alex—grimy factory town; a child of a brief wartime marriage; an unknown mother and an alcoholic, willing, failed father; Alex's only companion, his brother, taken from him some years earlier. But such explanations are, in a sense, short story explanations, neat and tidy, and Weesner scorns them and forces us to do so too.

In the detention home Alex does almost nothing for two months, and slowly he begins to remember things that have happened to him, living in foster homes, learning about his father, playing in a muddy river with his brother, clinging to the edges of his very few pleasures. But we cannot say whether he ended up a car thief because he wanted something to do, because he sought some revenge, or because he wanted to be caught and for someone thus to pay him attention. Best to say that when the car was stolen something was defined, yet that definition turns to nothing in the detention home. Thus, when he is released and sent home and back to school, Alex is free, given a chance, yet nothing has happened. He tries to do better in school and even partly succeeds, but it makes no sense or difference to him. He goes out for the basketball team and does very well for a while, but quits when he realizes he is being given little chance because he is a jailbird. He then can act out his sense of being excluded only by becoming more voyeuristic. He takes a paper route and peeps in early morning windows. He seeks a girl he has always dreamed of, but when she responds he cannot accept her kindness.

Page by page, as Weesner patiently builds, we realize we are coming better to understand Alex, or at least better able to accept and even to predict some of his apparently aimless and desperate actions. The truth of novels, after all, is that lives do have shapes, even this one.

One afternoon the girl he is following catches him watching her, and "he had the thought that something was wrong." Voyeurism has become intolerable; if he insists he is nothing he will become nothing. He goes to a blue movie but must leave quickly:

> . . . he saw himself, alas, as a mean and worthless son of a bitch, invulnerable, and cruel, and saying to himself, *I don't give a shit, I don't give a shit, they can go fuck a duck*, believing he desired not the detention home but the fierce world of the penitentiary. He had known, leaving the theater, that he was going after a car.

As he does, Weesner at last shows us why he stole the first car, and each detail is clear and defining; even that "alas," which is so strange, seems just right.

This comes after 250 pages and, regardless of what comes after, is enough to make *The Car Thief* the best American novel I've read in some time. Despite the grimness, despite Weesner's refusal to resort to even a moment of wit or humor, I felt something close to exhilaration approaching this moment in the book. As a form the novel has always tended to repudiate tragedy and to embrace pathos in the rendering of ordinary lives, and Weesner, claiming only that Alex's life demands patience and clarification, justifies that repudiation.

What happens after this is not bad, but it is nowhere near so good. Alex does take the car, but he isn't caught or sent to the penitentiary, because, and I think rightly, Weesner feels that would be too simplifying, and would yield the book up to Alex's sense of his worthlessness when the whole point is that Weesner values Alex where Alex himself cannot. He also feels, and rightly, that just getting to the moment where he takes the car is a kind of triumph for Alex, a demonstration that no old solution will work and that new ones simply must be found. But this leaves Weesner with the pattern of a *Bildungsroman*—Alex leaves school, and after a summer of slow dying, joins the army, leaving home for a new life. This of course is much too easy, and Weesner knows it, so he resorts, oddly and arbitrarily, to the suicide of Alex's father as a means of somehow paying for the failures of the past and opening the doors to the future. But the father's steady drinking is not the despair of suicide but of slow dying, so the event is uncalled for.

The repudiation of tragedy has always left the novel plagued with the problem of climactic actions. Countless novels like *The Car Thief* resort to gratuitous violence near the end to resolve issues that have become intractable for their authors. The wrongness in this case is only a sign that Weesner has been unable to see his story through on its own terms, but this does not injure the excellence of the first three-quarters of the book.

Margaret Drabble's *The Needle's Eye* raises all the same issues as *The Car Thief,* but in a very different way. The fact that parts of Weesner's novel appeared in *The New Yorker, Esquire,* and the *Atlantic* means that it is not doomed to obscurity by any means, but by comparison Margaret Drabble already has a following. She is a writer that many already find they prefer to her elders and presumed betters, Iris Murdoch and Doris Lessing. Like Weesner, she writes about people not in themselves very interesting but for the care she pays them. One knows, especially after having read a number of her books, that this care is not the result of self-identification but of a deep curiosity and absorption in the facts of daily life.

The Needle's Eye is her richest book to date. As a narrator Theodore Weesner is endlessly patient and slow; Margaret Drabble is by comparison expansive, brilliant, meditative, obtrusive, so that *The Car Thief* is Alex Housman's book and *The Needle's Eye* is Miss Drabble's. There are characters here, and a story, but they exist not so much in themselves as to allow their author another chance to say what she sees. The thing to do with her is to quote:

> The week before she had been waiting in the queue to buy some stamps, and a girl in front of her had been trying to

post a parcel. She was a nice girl, a timid girl, and she said very politely, as she stuck the stamps on, "Do you think it will get there by the end of the week?" "Don't ask me," the post-office lady replied, crossly. "Oh, I'm sorry," said the girl, immediately apologetic, sorry to have annoyed her: whereupon the post-office lady glowered ferociously through the grill (which took on the aspect, suddenly, of a restraining cage) and said, "Look here, you're asking me for a cast-iron guarantee, aren't you, a cast-iron guarantee about whether that parcel of yours will get there by the end of the week. Well, I'm not going to give you one, it's not my job. I don't give cast-iron guarantees to no one." The girl looked shattered by this attack, as well she might: but a sense of pride and justice compelled her to assert, as she moved away, "I wasn't asking for a guarantee, I only asked."

Had Doris Lessing written that incident it would have been a portent of an impending breakdown in English society, or at least in the bureaucracy. Had Iris Murdoch written it she would have gone on with a long story showing how the post-office lady came to be so awful. But for Margaret Drabble it is simply there, at most a sign that the woman doing the remembering, the heroine, knows her neighborhood. If the writing doesn't justify the telling, little in the context can.

Here is another passage, this time meditative. Miss Drabble's meditations are usually quite long, so one has to break in, and some of the accumulated force is lost. A man is thinking about the results of having been raised by his mother:

Perhaps, after all, his childhood had been in sum more nearly what she had intended than what she had achieved? She had fought herself, valiantly, she had courageously denied the truth of the bleakness which was what she truly had to offer. If she had not aspired she would have sunk or died. Oh Christ, it was exhausting, this living on the will, this denial of nature, this unnatural distortion: but if one's nature were harsh, what could one do but deny it, and repudiate it in the hope that something better might thereby be? It was for him that she had hoped, and so on, through

the generations. And to what end, to what end, to what
right end of life, to what gracious form of living, to what
possible joy? . . . He thought once more of John Stuart
Mill and the despair that had seized him: to conceive the
right end, and then to despair, that was a fate he had feared
often enough for himself, and his petty tinkerings and his
niggling readjustments and his dreary slow calculations.

These quotations may not be the best things in the book, but
they are characteristic, so if they attract or repel, so will the
book. *The Needle's Eye* is not all fragments, but mostly occasions
for Miss Drabble. The characters, except for the heroine, are
worthless, the dialogue is aimless, the big scenes are few.

But there are cumulative effects nonetheless. The vignette
with the post-office lady, for instance, is only one of what seems
almost a series. The novel opens with a marvelous scene in a liquor
store, it too has a line of customers, and there are bits scattered
throughout about gardeners and servants and helpful and helpless lawyers and a hateful governess and a defeated baby sitter.
But we are not asked to think about the decline of servants and
service in a welfare state, but only to see or to remember that of
course these things are the stuff of our lives. So too characters
here think hard about their children, fret over their memories of
their parents, worry about money and its presence and absence,
and they do so directly, passionately yet unevenly, the way one
does in life, the way that never happens in novels that force
themselves more strictly to attend to story and scene. The violence here will not be that of a climactic suicide, but of a remem-
bered bad marriage. The big scene, so called, is a walk to the
beach where the major concern is how to keep the children from
whining.

The effect is to make one greatly interested while reading,
but not altogether certain if or how it all adds up after one has
finished. What keeps it interesting is the intensity of Miss
Drabble's absorption, her sense that life has meaning that cannot
be rendered in narrative and that is far too tremblingly ordinary
to be subjected to experimental prose. In the average person's
thoughts over a ten-minute span a great deal happens. To render

the span as a stream of consciousness is to insist that the actual motion of the thoughts is crucial, and we all know that is a little bit clinical and therefore fake. To put the same span into a strong narrative is to insist that the thoughts be important and lead to important events, and that too can lead to falsities.

To take the span, and to reassemble the images, memories, and odd thoughts so that the merely associative is thrown away and the importance, say, of a disturbing memory is heightened, is to do some injustice to the ten minutes themselves, perhaps, but it may begin to do great justice to the life being lived. Margaret Drabble takes away the unit of ten minutes, transforms the disturbing memory into a vignette or a meditation, showing that this is how to clarify the facts and quality of our lives. Her intelligence and sensibility are so traditionally novelistic that it is easy to overlook the originality of her method.

But to make it all add up is hard. Rose Vassilou, a wealthy heiress who hates her money, marries for love. The first pathetic fact is that by the time she marries the struggle against her parents has been so great that she no longer loves the man she marries. The second pathetic fact is that he is not a fortune hunter but a man baffled in his clumsy efforts to love her. The third is that even after she divorces him and achieves the plain domestic squalor she has so avidly sought she cannot rid herself of her passion for renunciation and so wears herself away by foolishly agreeing to take back her husband. But to put the matter this way is to give the book a shape that Miss Drabble insists on not giving it. The first two facts I've mentioned have long since happened by the time the novel opens and are discovered only in meditation, and the third takes place in an epilogue.

The wind bloweth where it listeth, she says more than once in *The Needle's Eye;* passions and meanings come and go and a good life is one that knows this and fusses little. As a sense of life it has great validity but it also tends to make what happens, the individual scenes and events, unimportant. It is one's sense of this, I think, that creates the suspicion near the end of the novel and afterward that maybe Miss Drabble just hasn't looked hard enough at her subjects and situations, that even their failure to resolve could be more clearly seen.

The big scene on the beach, for instance, is wonderfully and enticingly low-keyed. The ex-husband has spirited off the children and has even threatened to take them out of the country. Rose and her lawyer friend scurry around getting injunctions, then rush up to her parents' East Anglia estate, where the ex-husband and the kids were last heard from. Indeed they are there, but it turns out that no kidnapping was ever seriously intended, and so the excitement dwindles down to the afternoon excursion to the sea. But Miss Drabble knows this won't quite do. To leave the matter there is not just to say that the wind bloweth where it listeth but to evade the issue of what will become of her characters. So she adds an epilogue, and that leaves her announcing some important events in a nonchalant tone that is annoying.

Unlike the ending of *The Car Thief*, this one does mar one's sense of the whole book because it leads one to think that in some ultimate way Miss Drabble hasn't cared enough and so has exploited her characters but not fully attended to them. I'm not sure how serious a defect this is, and I suspect I stress it precisely because *The Needle's Eye* is so good page-by-page and because it is the work of someone who seems on the brink of being a major writer. Margaret Drabble has come a long way from *A Summer Bird-cage*, even from *Jerusalem the Golden*. She is much freer, much more conscious of what she can do, than before, and this leads to a wonderful freshness of tone and detail. However flawed, *The Needle's Eye* is that rare thing, a book one wishes were longer than it is.

The novel remains the bright book of life, both in its ability to celebrate our lot with pathos and in its insistence that we all do have lives, lives that shape into strange and bitter forms, perhaps, but shape nonetheless. It thus remains able to be its own critic, expose its own flaws. The closed-circuit work of John A. Williams, however clever or even moving, remains closed-circuit work and to that extent without life. The intense care of Theodore Weesner for Alex Housman shows us the book is flawed when that care becomes blurred. The superb intelligence and curiosity of Margaret Drabble create regret, even as they make us grateful, that she has not stuck longer with or looked more deeply into her fiction. The novel insists that we plunge into life, also that we understand and literally come to terms with it. Williams has not plunged; Weesner and Miss Drabble have. For all their shortcomings they also have gone toward giving us the final assurance that a writer can know the pain and squalor of life and yet gain, in their presence and despite them, an individual, an action, that yields up a pathetic triumph.

NOVELISTS, READERS, CRITICS

Nostalgia is always easy. There was a time when . . . a time when a novel could count on reviews—even the Brontë sisters from an obscure Yorkshire parsonage got reviewed. A time when a publisher knew the novels the firm was publishing, and what audience each might expect to reach. A time when young people read novels that were not handed to them by their elders in a classroom. A time when people read new novels the way people now seem to go to new movies. A time when there were some good popular novelists—Marquand, say, or Conrad Richter. A time when some things seemed to matter that seem to matter no longer.

I restrict myself to novels because I do in fact read new novels, and don't in fact read a great deal of new poetry and see no new plays. At some point in the past, if one heard such a statement being made in public, one could safely conclude the speaker was a barbarian. Novels, but not poems, not plays? How? Why? What sort of reader or critic is *that?* You can't read literature, but just a certain kind? Why, it's as though someone read "I listen to symphonies but never hear operas or string quartets." Nonetheless, it's true, and true because, among other reasons, the audience for one genre is seldom in fact the audience for another; if I spoke about novelists and their audiences and then implied that what I'd said held true for all current literature, you wouldn't believe me, you'd spot ignorances and falsities everywhere. And the situation is worse than that, really. If I pretended to you that I know about current fiction in the way I might pretend that I know about Jane Austen or Dickens, you'd catch me out quickly. Let me just name some novels published in the last year or so that I have *not* read: *The Sunlight Dialogues, Fire Sermon, Transparent Things, Necessary Objects, Breakfast of Champions, The World of Apples.* In most years I will read a goodly selection of those novels published during the one quarterly period I am responsible for doing a fiction chronicle; my chances, thus, of reading the right novels, seldom get better than one in four.

Yet not only do I continue to stand here, pretending to discourse about new novels and their audiences, but feel reasonably sure it's not totally fraudulent; I miss a lot of books, because of failures in time, energy, and access, yet I guess I read more novels than almost anyone I know or hear about. So we come to an unpleasant, nostalgia-making, but not uninteresting fact: whatever the audience for fiction is, it is not and cannot be an audience of experts, as that term is usually employed; it is a diffuse audience, probably without centers except centers of gossip and commerce. The ramifications of this truth make up most of what I want to talk about this afternoon. The point is not that an audience for novels does not exist, and I am not one who believes that the point is that the audience is hopelessly vulgar or stupid—which was the point for Wordsworth and Henry James and most people down to approximately Gore Vidal—but rather, the audience for fiction cannot be identified. If this is even close to being true, we are all thrown back either on being theoretical in some socially scientific way, or else on our own experience. I am not a social scientist, and believe that no theory of audience constructed by socially scientific methods could help us much. But I have had some experience, and I want next to tell you a story.

In fall 1971 I wrote a review of some novels for the *New York Review;* I'd done some other pieces for them on what they, perhaps, took to be more important things, like cities and

America, but I had asked for novels and so was sent some. I think by now, if anyone remembers my review at all, it will be for the first sentence. I'd called the thing "How Novels Fail" (a title they changed), and, coming off that, the first sentence read "John Hawkes's *The Blood Oranges* fails because it is the work of a con- temptible imagination." I then went on about Hawkes's novel, and work by Malamud, Richler, and Oates, finding no real success in the bunch. I think I got more mail on that than on anything I'd written to that time. Since I'd been writing sentences like the one about Hawkes for ten years, I conclude that the mail was at least as much due to a lead review in the *New York Review* as to me. I was asked what business I had presuming to be stupid in print about America's finest novelist; I was also asked by a British publisher to write a general book on the English novel. You never can tell. The most interesting letter, however, was a long one from the late Hiram Haydn, editor of *The American Scholar*, and he wanted to know if I'd do something for him on current lit- erary reputations, especially inflated ones; he had in mind mostly, I gathered, not Hawkes, but Nabokov and Updike. Well, writing such essays takes a lot of work, especially since you have to read all the works by people you don't much like, so I de- clined, with a counter-proposal: an essay about novels and novel- ists that may be said to have suffered because of these and other inflated reputations. I knew Haydn himself was a novelist few people knew; I knew he had worked hard to get little or unknown novelists started while an editor at Bobbs Merrill, Random House, and Atheneum, so I thought he might be interested, as indeed he was. He told me to go ahead, and then sent me a lengthy list of possible candidates, and added four novels written in the fifties by someone I'd never heard of, and the fifties were the days when I really knew what was happening, if I ever did. So, an ideal sponsor. I dithered with the thing for a long time, trying to find genuinely unknown writers; soliciting help from friends who always seemed to have the name of a Danish or Bul- garian or Argentine writer, but never one of an American; read- ing Haydn's suggestions; rereading quite a few things I could find that no one knew. That part was great fun, but I sensed the writ- ing itself would be no fun, and it wasn't, because it's hard enough writing reviews of new books, harder still to write assessments of older unknown books without simply becoming a reviewer, telling the story of each. But I finally finished last spring, and Haydn, lovely man, both liked the piece and had lots of good suggestions and corrections. I read the galleys in early fall, though, and felt stupid: who could care, really, about Jack Leahy, Allis McKay, Thomas Savage, Henrietta Buckmaster, Gladys Schmitt, Rudolph Von Abele, Floyd Salas; above all, who could care that I happened to like and remember them? I don't think I've ever felt less eager to see something of mine in print, especially something I'd worked hard and long on.

So it came out in *The American Scholar* last fall [1973], just three weeks after Haydn died, another fact that made me turn away from the piece, since I felt in some ways it was as much his as mine. Yet the response was tremendous, at least in my experience; much greater than the review of Hawkes or anything else had elicited. I'm sure offensive linemen on the Denver Broncos receive more letters in a week than I did on this, but we hardly live in the same public worlds. Furthermore, though I'd never written in *The American Scholar*, and read it only seldom, I knew that it is no large-scale, mass media magazine; this time I felt something other than myself or the publication was responsible. I got, as I'd hoped but not expected, letters from four of the writers themselves, and all were gratified in gratifying ways; I got, too, as I would have expected had I thought about it, a number of letters from people in publishing houses, a couple pleased that I'd noted an author of theirs, more than that annoyed that I'd not noticed some writer of theirs. But the most interesting point about the rest was they were from people who lived far from the groves of any literary academe, and from people who obviously had never heard of me, from people who read novels. They congratulated me for mentioning someone they admired, they chastised me for not knowing someone they liked, they offered me lists, they offered me paranoid theories about how writers get known or ignored, and one, indeed, turned out to be the author of a weekly book review in the Salem, Oregon, *Capitol-Times* that is as fine a regular commentary on novels as I know. A woman in Adamant, Vermont, a man in Santa Clara, an engineering professor in Joplin, Missouri—one could even feel pride in the geographical diversity.

I need to speculate about what this experience should tell me, but first, a digression of sorts on what I take to be my own audience as a reviewer. Most of the reviews I've done over the years are quarterly reports for the *Hudson Review*, a respected, small circulation magazine, much the best of its kind, I think, year in, year out. Yet after ten years of doing fiction reviews for the *Hudson*, I don't really know what their audience is. It is all a sort of labor of love and silence. Lists come in from the office of twenty or thirty titles and authors, and they come fortnightly for three months—maybe a total of 150 novels to choose from, and no way to choose. I plead with the people in New York to keep their ears open just for gossip, but they don't hear much more than I, and little of it is about the most precious of items, a good first novel by an unknown. Then, after I get and read maybe 30 books and choose a dozen or so to write about, all I can do is move, and much too quickly, from one to the other, so the review has and can have little shape. Who wants to read it, thus? But novels should be reviewed—the young need encouragement, the faltering need to be reminded, developing older novelists need special applause, inflated reputations need prodding, if not puncturing. Yet who reads the review? The people in the office, yes, and some friends, yes—though even they are reduced to a comment or two on the few novels on the list they've read—and, for all I actually know, that may be all. For instance, Floyd Salas, one of my unknown novelists, had never gotten my review of his first book, and a great admirer of his had never seen it.

I conclude from this that my audience as a reviewer resembles that of a novelist: it is there, but cannot be identified. Of course it is much smaller than that for all but the least-known novelists, but it is there, and I can presume its existence until I'm asked to name it, name one person in it.

Now one thing that most of the unknown novelists wanted to know, one thing my correspondents in Adamant and Santa Clara wanted to know, was this: how does it happen? Some authors are famous, some known, some unknown—why? What do I know about the publishing process, the reviewing process, the book-selling process, the fame-making process, the gossip among readers process, that can tell me about the kind of audience for fiction such that we end up with a real, unidentifiable audience that feels powerless to affect what books are known and what are not? Again, if I retreat to the past, I know that I can find at least some partial answers to the relation between audience and fame, but I'm not sure I can do this in the present. Many authors, I know, who get published at all, are inclined to blame either publishers or reviewers, they being the obvious targets. But in a world of over 700 hard-cover novels published every year, a publisher cannot buy an audience for a particular novel without allocating an advertising budget in excess of the novel's possible profit. And if an occasional review helps build a large audience, these are rare indeed; lots of good novelists get quite good reviews and remain generally unread. Indeed, one of my unknowns, Thomas Savage, wrote me that he had a fine publisher, that he had been quite gratified by reviews—yet I doubt if he has ever written a novel that sold more than 2000 copies, and the Seattle Public Library, serving a population of over a million, has one copy of two of his nine novels. To say this is not to claim that publishers and reviewers, or booksellers, or librarians, are unimportant in establishing the reception of a particular novel; it is to say only that one can find little evidence to support demonology or conspiracy theories.

Which leaves us with the reading audience itself: what does it do? does it really exist? does it ever show good taste, or even care that some novels are much better than others? If you talk to people, they all feel passive, the results of processes initiated elsewhere—but that's the way publishers and reviewers and the rest say they feel, too. One thing we can say for sure: too many novels are published for the good of any one novel. I won't say there are too many in any absolute sense; I have enjoyed seeing work of mine in print, and between covers, and since that pleasure can be felt regardless of whether anyone reads the work, I wouldn't say that a book with zero reception shouldn't have been printed, if someone wants to foot the bill. But with 700 novels a year being published, far, far more than anyone can read, the numbers themselves make it hard for any one book to get known. The public must turn to the names it knows, however it knows them, for good or bad reasons. But even among known names there are far too many for most novel readers to do more than sample and hope; good comparisons, thus, are hard to come by, and real means of exercising taste aren't available except when we're dealing with well-known writers. Alfred Knopf said many times that when a good novel fails to reach an audience, the reason was not poor taste of the public, really; the trouble was just that the book was not good enough. In a rough way he is assuredly right. There has been one novel, Theodore Weesner's *The Car Thief*, that I've read in the last five years that I could whole-heartedly recommend to anyone willing to read a serious novel. Since it appeared in paperback last fall, when I could recommend it without fear of losing my own copy, I have pushed it at lots of readers, none of whom has been disappointed, many of whom have been greatly moved. *The Car Thief* is not *à la mode;* it will be years, if ever, before it is the staple of classrooms that now accept some new confection by Barth or Vonnegut. So be. One can't organize the world as one likes. But *The Car Thief* now has a real, sizable, and growing audience, because it is good enough. To say this isn't to claim that the reading public, or I, have great taste, that we can't prefer confection to the real thing. It is only to say that our collective taste is good enough.

Let us take stock of where that leaves us: there is a real but unidentifiable audience for novels; there are too many novels published for the good of any one novel; if there is skullduggery, stupidity, and greed involved in the creation of this audience, there isn't so much that we can stop there and content ourselves with deploring the existence of such things in the world; the audiences for novelist and critic may be alike in their silent presence. I would now like to try to move out to some hints, facts, and guesses about the kind of novel that will be written under these conditions.

On the face of it, it would look as though the kind of influence an audience can exert on a writer were less than ever before. It is almost axiomatic that one can respond better to a known than to an unknown audience; one great stimulus to nostalgia is to hearken back to a world, the community of the mead-hall, of the theatre, of a small public of people both literate, leisured, and able to afford printed books—in such worlds a writer knew where he or she was, got immediate responses, could shape and reshape material in the secure knowledge that the audience was there that might recognize care, nuance, patience, in the writer. Dickens had a mass audience compared with Milton's or Pope's, yet he could take the sales of each issue as an index of where the preceding number had left his audience, and he then could calculate what he did or didn't want to do in response. The audience for the novels of Henry James or Conrad or Virginia Woolf was much diminished compared with Dickens's, but it was there, and from the beginning of their careers, in ways that later, less secure, and lonely writers would have to envy. Perhaps the last secure audience we know of (if we except the very famous, who at least know they have an audience and know something of what it thinks) was the audience for experimental fiction during a period that conforms pretty closely to the mature years of the best-known novelistic experimenter, James Joyce. I'm using experimental fiction in a restricted sense, to mean the kind of thing we meant by the term in the years when most of us were growing up: Joyce, Henry Miller, William Burroughs, Anaïs Nin, Lawrence Durrell, etc. This seems to have been a cosmopolitan, international audience which, however much it saw itself as small and struggling, which, however small and struggling it actually was, existed so the word got around, the latest work was quickly known and studied and commented upon. That kind of audience has pretty well disappeared for all but a few writers, most of whom are either New York and Jewish or white and Southern—and even at that some pretty good Jewish and Southern writers exist in relative obscurity. It may well be that the only ongoing community audiences left are among the minority groups; seeing it strictly from the outside, it looks as though literary blacks know each other's work pretty quickly and pretty well, and the same seems to be true among Chicanos and Indians. But by and large, that kind of audience has gone.

That does not mean, however, that its absence cannot exert as much of a force in its way as the other earlier audiences exerted in theirs. The most obvious result of a loss of a known or identifiable audience is a loss of restraint, and this can work for good and ill, has indeed done so, I would say. Since the novel may have modes but can have no real fixity of form, a lack of restraint has no clear effect on the form the book takes; that has always pretty much been left up to the individual writer. But lack of restraint is also a tone, and in a great deal of current fiction it takes the form of assertiveness, of extravagant performance, of a rich inventiveness that seems to follow more the inclination, inspiration, or even whim of the novelist than anything else. I have the sense about a great many novels I read that I am reading something that in essentials, in fundamental inspiration, is very close to first draft. The experimental novelist of a generation ago was an intellectual, a theorist, among like-minded readers, and their novels cohered to a theory of language, a theory of character, a theory of plot or plotlessness—its last traces are easily found in the French *nouvelle vague*. The current novelist is more improvised, more reliant on the words that come into the head than the words that are dictated by an idea of art or life; he or she is all, triumphantly celebrating his or her own imagination, ability to invent, freedom to do anything, unrestrained. I don't mean formlessness at all, though the form that operates in, say, *Catch-22, Invisible Man, Gravity's Rainbow, V., Why Are We in Vietnam?, Herzog* and the other longer Bellows, *Hermaphrodeity, Little Big Man, Portnoy's Complaint, Giles Goat Boy*—the list goes on and on—the form that operates in these books is almost always only a form that knows where the end is, how the plot will turn out, and that leaves the way taken to get there pretty wide open, free to be invented moment-to-moment.

I call this kind of novel imperial, the work of writers whose imaginations are powerful, inventive, conquering. Novels tend to be performed, gaudy passages are preferred to sustained characterization; plots are now in fashion, but they tend to be careless and extravagant, signs that our author has brought it all off. Shyness has disappeared, as has privacy; what used to be considered intimate details are now shown off, paraded, with the implication that we all are crazily alike in such matters; all males, at least, in fact or fantasy, masturbated like Alex Portnoy, had circle jerks like Duddy Kravitz, respond easily and knowingly to a man who says to a friend as they look at a girl on a beach on page 5 of a recent novel: "I'm going to rape her." I call all this imperial because it is aggressive, unrestrained, I call it that even more because it is possessive of its imagination and experience and casual in its presumption that its readers go right along with the show. The single imagination is unredeemably single and isolated, but it is also everything. Here, say, are the opening sentences of Alan Friedman's *Hermaphrodeity,* a novel, incidentally, that I liked a lot more than most of its contemporary fellows:

> Coarse? Well, maybe I am. One of the magazines called me a "coarse old lady poet." I won't argue the point. Naturally, I get coarser as I grow older, like most of you. I don't mean only my indecent turn of mind, which comes automatically with age. I mean those mannerisms which even lady poets develop and which never get into print. I can rarely eat without getting food all over my mouth. And these days whenever I eat anything I really enjoy, I make a sharp whining involuntary noise under my chewing. And the smell of my feet, which has grown stronger with age—well, would it really shock you if I said I like it?

Well, there we are; it's the current mode, and, as I say, Friedman's version seems to me very entertaining for considerable stretches of his very long novel. But the voice that confronts us is not one to be quarreled with; it not only gets coarser with age, but insists we all do, too. There's no way into such an imagination; it is all lavishly, frontally there, right in front of us, carrying on, inventing, enjoying itself, imperial. By the way, *Hermaphrodeity* is a nice repudiation to conspiracy theories, because it is an *à la mode* novel, written by a Jew, published by Knopf, the receiver of at least a couple of good reviews—yet it didn't seem ever to catch on.

But what I am most interested in here is neither the novel's reception, nor how Friedman came in fact to write it. Rather, its relations, and those of its fellows, with the kind of unknowable audience I have been describing, for I am convinced there is a genuine connection between them. Take away from the novelist any sense of the particular qualities of his or her audience, leave only the general sense that it does in fact exist, and you are taking away from the writer security, the voices that speak back as he or she writes; the situation is precisely the opposite of the one in which the budding creative writer, sitting in a creative writing class, has if the teacher of that course is any kind of presence at all. No good writer will write for an audience in the sense that the words are dictated by that audience, but the student in the class can almost hear the teacher reply while the writing is going

on. And for the contemporary novelist that is no longer there in
any way that can interest, or buttress, or offer counter-speech.
The voice of the imperial novel says there is no restraint, nothing
it cannot do, and does this in part because the restraint of an audience is not there. The novelist is thrown back on the native
ability to invent, carry on, perform, but being powerful, but-
tressed by the great surging strength of the country as a whole,
the inventions are confident, aggressive, I would even call them
bullying if there were any clear sense that there was anyone out
there to bully. All those old myths of the modern period at the
beginning of the century—man is lost, alienated, wandering in
cities, victim of machines rampant with power—all those are by
now not only old hat, but, it turns out, precisely the sources of
power that were once taken to be reasons for powerlessness.
America not only survived the modern age, it thrived on it, became abundant and endless and powerful in it, capable of publishing 700 novels a year in it, capable of losing its particular
shapes even as it asserted its powerful existence. The audience
lost its shape, and if its continued existence, if its great increase
in numbers, gives it a presence, it may be powerful, but it is
silent, not there for the writer as he or she writes. Beyond the
writer lie a few friends, maybe, an agent, an editor, then a void. I
get letters now and again from a novelist who has read some
reviews of mine and who had written, novel enclosed, saying,
"This could be something you'd like." One might think this
merely a pitch, as though I had power I don't have to get a
review placed somewhere, but the tone, as I read it, is more ten-
tative: "Maybe, if you do read it, maybe, if you do like it, I can
get some shape to my audience, and otherwise I have nothing to
go on." Why shouldn't the novelist trust native imagination, invention, intelligence—what else, perhaps, is there to trust? Of
course there are lots of reasons why the current novel in America
is imperial, and I am not trying to say that the nature of the audience creates the nature of the novel. I am only trying to say,
beyond question of cause or extent of cause, that the two continue to have an intimate relation with each other. The novelistic
voice is noisy, clamorous, yet relaxed, self-indulgent: "Coarse?
Well, maybe I am." The audience is there, but where? who? A
woman in Adamant, Vermont, a book review editor in New York,

or Atlanta, a book reviewer in Seattle—their geographical diversity bespeaks amorphousness of shape and taste. Not being a true answering voice, the novelist turns it into something to be performed for, all the work to be done by the novelist, in loud, splashy, gorgeous tones and colors.

Given this as the dominant form, what about the novelists who do not write in that form? Imagine Theodore Weesner with *The Car Thief*, John Williams with *Stoner*, Thomas Savage with *The Power of the Dog*, intent, careful fictions, realistic one once called them, filled with particulars, of this time, of that place. The very intensity of their care procures shape, but such care and such shapes are quiet, loving, respectful of persons, and therefore demanding an answering voice that probably cannot be met these days. The novelist is making an implicitly social gesture—that being the relation created between writer and character, it becomes the essential relation of writer to reader. One enters into these fictions, works with the author, cares enough to be slow with them. But who is this reader? If there is a woman in Adamant, an engineering professor in Joplin, a book reviewer in Salem, they seem like such isolated cases, beleaguered people, novel readers in the old sense, almost obsolete. My sense of such people is that they seem to see themselves as freaks. And the less well known the novelist is, the more tenuous the relation with any audience, no matter how much such an audience is needed to complete the essentially social relation established by the novelist's social creation of time, place, and character. In many cases the result for the writer is bafflement and increasing inarticulateness. Most of the little known and very good novels published in this country in the last generation were written by people who did not go on, and, perhaps more telling, those who do go on often do not get better. They need the cutting edge of a real audience, and they don't get it. Not being imperialists, performers, they work more slowly, less well, go silent. They are the real victims of our situation, the ones whose existence one most regrets.

Their counterparts in the audience suffer, too. The isolated novel reader, having little to go on in making choices about what to read, turns to things that don't work as well as they used to: the local book review page, the public library, word of mouth. I tried for a while myself to help select novels for my university

library. A jobber sends in maybe twenty novels a week for in-
spection, and the library, helpless, asks me for help. With a
novel like Friedman's *Hermaphrodeity* I am in pretty good shape
right there on the first page. I know what to expect and have a
pretty good guess how much I'll like what I expect. But the more
flatly written novel of this time and that place doesn't work in the
same way, and one cannot tell about it in a hurry, and one
doesn't want to be able to tell because the rewards of such books
when they are good are slow rewards. So I don't know what to
pick, and gradually stop making my weekly trip over to the library, even though I deplore the buying that the library does do.
The library and I are both victims, able to spot only the performing imperial novels that don't assume I exist. We don't very often
find the good ones that need the reader's help, the discipline of
the reader's care.

The conclusions one can draw from all this are not necessarily
gloomy or sad, though in particular cases they can almost break
your heart. But rather than try to conclude, let me look at one
last ramification of the argument that the audience is there but
unknowable. Think of us, you and I here today, for a moment. As
I sat writing this, I felt more than once I was in an echo chamber,
because what I was saying about novelists and reviewers and
their audiences seemed true for me, and you, right then. On the
one hand I could attempt a performance, a speech that didn't
need an audience. On the other hand I could hope to make a
relation, a gesture that said: "I need you, even though I know
nothing of who you are." Strange, is it not? I am no imperialist, I
can't come to you with some wonderful, witty, inventive, self-
enclosed and self-sustaining theory of the novel and its contemporary audience. Every time I feel my voice trying to rise to
something even modestly lavish, I check myself, knowing such
lavishness is almost certainly an attempt to cover up some ignorance, some inadequacy. I have read some novels, written about
some novels, but my relation to the world of current fiction is so
tenuous that if I happened to have read different novels from the
ones I've read I might be saying something quite different. We
work in the dark, says James, we do what we can, we give what

we have—what better prescription for using native wit, inventiveness, imagination—and so I have, if only in daring to make up a subject called the contemporary novel, daring to talk when I know almost nothing about my made-up subject. And since I am not Mailer or Pynchon, nor was meant to be, I have to perform without the necessary willfulness to offer you a sense that I can bring this speech to a ringing conclusion.

We ought, perhaps, to be more uncomfortable than we are about all this. I can say for myself that the reason I'm not terribly uncomfortable is the homely fact that if today I am the performer, mostly I am a reader. I don't like most novels I read, but I would not want to be doing something else. I've realized recently that I do believe in it all, believe in talking to you about a subject about which no one can know very much, believe in writing reviews no one may read, believe mostly just in the reading. It is a way of saying who I am, a way of finding out what world I live in. I don't read magazines, don't go to the movies, but if someone says "Here is this novel," I read it more times than not, as an act of profit and delight, as a battered act of faith. Helplessly, but really, I am an audience, and one reason I am helpless is that beyond that I have little to say, saved only by the sense that I have little need to say.

ROBERT STONE

Dog Soldiers is a truly grim book, relentless in a way that makes other books claiming to look at the dark side of American life seem at least slightly deflecting or palliative in their final effect. Robert Stone's publishers say he offers a "vision of our predicament," but if that were true one could turn aside, call it just a vision and Stone a grouse, and that's not the way it works. *Dog Soldiers* does not expose, or show, or put on a performance for readers. It is an absorbed, realistic novel, telling a story, always working to get it told right, much closer to Theodore Weesner's

The Car Thief in this respect than to *Something Happened* or *Gravity's Rainbow,* which are "visions" of life that a reader can finally take or leave. As a result, one presumes, these books can be popular in a way that *Dog Soldiers*, homely and serious as wood, beautiful only in its integrity, will probably never be.

The setting is Vietnam and California, the time is the sixties, but while Stone is hugely informed about the dreck of war and counterculture, he does not use that information to make it cohere, to hold it together in a vision. The facts just come, and usually they then just fall, with something like a thud. Here, early in the novel, the central figure, John Converse, is in a Saigon bar with a couple of Australians:

> Both Jill and Converse had gone to see the invasion of Cambodia, and both had had experiences which had made them cry. But Converse's tears had not been those of outraged human sensibility.
>
> "You're an entertaining fella," Ian said. "But in general I object to your being around."
>
> Secure behind her porcelain smile, the waitress placed bowls of fish and rice before them. A party of American reporters came in, followed by four Filipino rock musicians with pachuco haircuts. The Honda salesmen and their Japanese girlfriends grew merrier as the *sake* flowed.
>
> "I mean," Ian said, "I love this country. It's not the asshole of the world to me. I grew old here, man. Now when I leave, all I'll be able to think back on is bastards like you in places like this."
>
> "Sometimes," Jill said, "you act like you invented the country."
>
> "They're a pack of perves," Ian said. "You're a pack of perves. Why don't you go watch some other place die? They've got corpses by the river-full in Bangla Desh. Why not go there?"
>
> "It's dry," Converse said.

Flat writing, not without pressure, but the pressure is being applied not to make a Vietnam or an Ugly American but to make a scene. Bring Ian into focus quickly, since he won't be around long, let Converse drift and not mind being called a bastard, since he is drifting, and maybe he *is* a bastard.

When the central character is drifting, the tendency is for the author to become a tourist guide and the character a picaro; that never happens in *Dog Soldiers*. Stone seems to have realized, here more than in his first novel *A Hall of Mirrors*, that he wanted to see the lives of his main characters as having shapes, for all that they seem to have none, and to use plot as his major means of articulating those shapes. Page by page John Converse, his wife Marge, and his partner Hicks live dully and painfully, and they assume and hate their circumstances much more than they observe or understand them. Thus, shortly after the passage quoted above, Converse, Ian, and Jill see a bomb ravage the bar, watch the scurrying around and away, feel their efforts to condemn and to pity the victims. But Converse then leaves Saigon, goes to My Lat to meet Hicks and arrange the smuggling of three pounds of heroin back to the States; the incident in Saigon has disappeared. Before this scene he has gotten high with a schemer named Charmian, and before that, at the beginning of the novel, he has sat on a park bench talking briefly with a missionary who is returning to the States following the death of her husband. Before that, we presume, Converse had been to Cambodia, and had cried, but not tears of outraged human sensibility.

The events bear no visible connection with one another and they thus seem to express Converse's inability to understand his life. But Stone will not absolve Converse, let him leave his past behind or his present free of whatever consequences attend his choices, however small or meaningless those choices may seem. We come to see that for all his wandering, he is also what Stone cares about, and so we will not see him become a vehicle for some vision about the American presence in Southeast Asia. So too with the others. When Stone turns to Hicks, with his heroin stash in San Francisco, he works with the same low-level intentness with which he has created Converse, who has called Hicks a psychopath. Converse may be right but even psychopaths must get off boats, go to bars, get drunk, plan their tomorrows. We pick up Marge, and she is popping pills and working in a porn theatre and worrying about her daughter and whether the plan to sell the heroin will work.

It's not daily life in the usual sense we are considering, because these lives have no habits or direction; still, it is only the moment-to-moment experience in which Stone is interested. Even people who have no characters have lives. Stone cannot love his characters, or urge us in any way to admire them, because they are not lovable or admirable. But they count, he keeps insisting, which is why the book is so grim. How much easier it would be to think they don't matter.

Slowly the plot is allowed to take shape. Whatever these three have been, they have never been involved in heroin peddling before, and that becomes decisive in ways they can only fall into recognizing. Some "regulatory agents" who may be federal narcs get onto the trail of Hicks and Marge and force them to flee; they also locate Converse soon after he returns and beat him up pretty badly. Where's the stuff? they ask; Converse, who knows only that Hicks and Marge aren't where he thought they'd be, sees he is in some terrible trouble because what had seemed just a deal like other deals in Vietnam has gone wrong. We know that Hicks and Marge are by this time in Los Angeles, looking for someone they can peddle the dope to, inching themselves closer to doing up on the stuff because life has become dangerous and they can't handle it. Converse, back north, glimpses only bits of this, yet his is the life that comes into fullest possible focus first.

Converse is doing no more than talking to a speed-addled stewardess who might know where his wife or daughter are. They begin to get high, to fall into sex, and then, when she calls him a "funny little fucker," he backs off, suddenly remembering the scene he had witnessed in Cambodia, and why he had cried. He quickly leaves the stewardess, and relives his insights on seeing Cambodians bombed by the South Vietnamese Air Force:

> One insight was that the ordinary physical world through which one shuffled heedless and half-assed towards nonentity was capable of composing itself, at any time and without notice, into a massive instrument of agonizing death. . . . Another was that in the single moment when the breathing world had hurled itself screeching and murderous at his throat, he had recognized the absolute correctness of its move. In those seconds, it seemed absurd that he had ever

been allowed to go his foolish way, pursuing notions and small joys. He was ashamed of the casual arrogance with which he had presumed to scurry about creation.

This may be Converse's ultimate vision, and, as Stone's prose rises to its sternest heights, we see it may well be Stone's too. What's best, though, is Stone's sense of timing, so that the insight forced upon Converse in Cambodia is also forced upon him later because he continued to pursue his foolish way, his small joys, with casual arrogance, so that he now is a hunted heroin peddler.

And why?

People passed him and he avoided their eyes. His desire to live was unendurable. It was impossible, not to be borne.

He was the celebrated living dog, preferred over dead lions.

Around him was the moronic lobby and outside the box-sided street where people hunted each other. Take it or leave it.

I'll take it, he thought. To take it was to begin again from nowhere, the funny little fucker would have to soldier on.

Living dogs lived. It was all they knew.

Converse won't mess with the reasons he has gotten himself trapped into being the possible victim of massive and agonizing death. He doesn't know what he has done, or what can happen next, but he is a living dog, wanting to live, a funny little fucker indeed, able to give himself up to the regulatory agents who entrap him so they can use him to entrap Hicks and Marge.

Stone, as I see it, is a nineteenth-century moralist, as eager as Carlyle or George Eliot to make the precise assessments required to judge the choices made by an individual or a society. John Converse has scurried about creation with casual arrogance, and there is no better judgment to be made. Yet if aimlessness, destruction, and institutional wantonness do not preclude choice and so do not preclude judgment, they make Stone's task far different from that of any writer of a century ago. What if one did see the bombs fall on the Cambodians? How easy then to make judgments, and of anything but oneself. Converse, at that moment, only cries. But here, as he remembers the scene, after having chosen to put the world once again murderously at his throat, he neither shrinks nor sentimentally implicates himself in the bombing. He is not one of Ian's perves, come to Vietnam to see it die, yet he was there, and it was dying, and now he is scurrying through the lobby of a San Francisco hotel because he casually fell into its corruption. So he can only soldier on, a dog, but alive.

It is a tremendous moment, and had Stone seen where then to take his novel, *Dog Soldiers* could have been one of the best American books of his generation. The first half does something with all the myths and clichés about current living that no other novel I know has done: it takes on the grimness of our worst fears about ourselves and gives meaning to the lives it thereby embodies. Such unappetizing characters these are, such figures for satire and horror stories—yet that is not the sense we have of them at all.

Nor is it all downhill from here. This scene is immediately followed by one of great ghastliness, which for most readers will be the worst and most memorable one in the book. Hicks is committed to going all the way with Marge but has no idea of the way; Marge is letting the heroin take command of her life; in Los Angeles they're asked to do up a writer friend of the guy they're trying to sell the stuff to, and Hicks, suddenly, cruelly, in vicious judgment of everything, murders the writer by shooting the heroin into his wrist. It is twenty pages that any writer might envy Stone for, but it only forestalls the inevitable truth that if these living dogs live because it is all they know, and if they are deeply enmeshed in a plot, there must follow some headlong action of the sort that always is in danger of simplifying the whole.

Hicks and Marge head east to the desert hideout of an ex-religious leader; Converse, hauled by the "agents," comes down to find them so his captors can find the stash. Everyone comes together at last, and plot becomes plot in the narrow sense, simple action, and through the long hunt and chase the characters remain static. For action to be decisive, lives must have clarifying turning points, and Stone doesn't want that, though he knows this action must kill Hicks somehow. So the chase is followed at the end with a series of glimpses of Converse and Marge that show them shaken but essentially unchanged. But this very fact makes the climactic big scene merely exciting and well done. The more seriously Stone takes his characters, the more carefully he brings their aimlessness to a decision, the more he eventually either jettisons the aimlessness or falsifies the decisiveness and its importance. I'm not sure how he could better have pondered his materials and his wonderful first half, but the remainder is good writing that seems divorced from a wider purpose than its own existence, and so seems just like writing.

The problem here is an old problem, one that has haunted the realistic novel as it has persisted in these latter days when, though the novel itself is alive and well, the conventions with which the realistic novel began certainly seem dead. The myth had it that the atomization of society destroyed the importance the novel as a form had sought to impart to individual lives. To support the myth, one could point to the way many of the best novels of the past generation have invested importance only in the imagination of the performing novelist; language is set free, the result is comic, visionary, and grotesque by turns. But the realistic novel has persisted, and at its recent best, as in *Dog Soldiers*, it does so not as a literary vestige but as a way of still seeing and knowing the life that goes on. Converse, Marge, and Hicks are not complex figures, but they are not symbolic figures or mouthpieces either. The first half of *Dog Soldiers* takes them as they are, and seriously, without once overrating their importance; the second half falls victim to a plot, as so many older realistic novels do, that does not so much realize these characters' lives as finish off an action in which novelist and characters have become enmeshed.

Yet even in its most headlong and least effective pages, *Dog Soldiers* shows Stone's clear eye for detail and clear-eyed determination to see these lives through to some end without sentimentalizing them. Throughout, thus, his integrity gives us a sense of learning at first hand what most of us have known only as hearsay or freakout. He brings the news, as novelists are supposed to do; he makes one think we have only begun to understand our immediate past.

DASHIELL HAMMETT

In the early fifties, when I first read Dashiell Hammett, he seemed to fit perfectly an image my friends and I had then of a writer who had made being a writer into a romantic occupation. He had lived in "the real world," he had suffered years of obscurity and poverty as he learned to write a clean, honest prose, he had written books that were out of print and hard to find, he had gone to Hollywood and drunk too much and stopped writing, he had chosen to go to jail rather than talk at a communist conspiracy trial, he had some undetailed beautiful relation with Lillian Hellman. Compared with that, Fitzgerald and Hemingway were too gaudy, available for anyone's romancing.

About Hammett's writing, I now see, we held an ambivalent attitude that bespoke an uneasiness we could not recognize. On the one hand we pointed to the battered paperbacks we had struggled to find and said: "There, with Op and Spade and Nick Charles, is the real thing, serious writing about crime and detection." On the other hand we implicitly diminished that achievement by dreaming that in the intervening years Hammett had been struggling to write a great, a "mature" novel that would show the world he was as good as we wanted to claim he was. When pressed, I would admit to preferring Raymond Chandler, even to hankering after new young toughs like John D. MacDonald and John Ross Macdonald. But Hammett was the first, and the years of writing stories for *Black Mask* had to be honored somehow. Our conversations would dwindle into asking which was Hammett's best book, and, since claims could be made for many of them, it was easier to talk that way than to ask if any was very good.

By 1961, when Hammett died, it no longer seemed as important to sustain romantic images of writers, though the battered paperbacks had been carefully packed away with each move, and one could hardly fail to be moved by Hellman's eulogy: "He believed in the salvation of intelligence, and he tried to live it out . . . and never, in all the years, did he play anybody's game but his own. He never lied, he never faked, he never stooped." And her 1965 memoir, which may well be the best thing either of them ever wrote, did much to make Hammett into the heroic figure we had all vaguely created years earlier; it was then published as the introduction to ten Continental Op pieces called *The Big Knockover*, and that volume, plus *The Novels of Dashiell Hammett*, which had been published a year earlier, gave his best work the permanence it deserved.

Both collections were well received, but not given the rather lavish attention that has recently been paid to *The Continental Op*, a new book of seven stories selected and introduced by Steven Marcus. I note, for instance, that local libraries that don't have one or both of the earlier hardcover collections have been quick to acquire this one. And Marcus's introduction takes a much loftier tone than any other I've heard in discussions of Hammett. It's all a shame. The stories are inferior work—Marcus might well have done better by rescuing the few minor tales that have never been reprinted from *Black Mask*—and those who come to Hammett for the first time via this volume will get only snatches that show why anyone should read him. With a writer who is very limited at his best, this kind of exposure is especially unwelcome.

Yet one can see what Marcus has in mind, perverse though it seems to be. He wants to take those stories which have almost no interest either as conventional fiction or as conventional detective fiction and to claim that this is where you find Hammett pure. The Op, he says, "undertakes to deconstruct, decompose, and thus demystify the fictional—and therefore false—reality created by the characters, crooks or not, with whom he is involved." True enough, though that is a fancy way to say something pretty obvious. Then:

> It should be quite evident that there is a reflective and co-ordinate relation between the activities of the Op and the activities of Hammett, the writer. Yet the depth and problematic character of this self-reflexive process begin to be revealed when we observe that the reconstruction or true fiction created and arrived at by the Op at the end of the story is no more plausible—nor is it meant to be—than the stories that have been told to him by all parties, guilty or innocent, in the course of his work. The Op may catch the real thief or collar the actual crook—that is not entirely to the point. What is to the point is that the story, account, or chain of events that the Op winds up with as "reality" is no more plausible and no less ambiguous than the stories that he meets with at the outset and later.

Thus Hammett becomes a candidate for existential sainthood. What makes Marcus's point useless is that in so far as it is true, it is mostly a sign of the mediocrity of the stories. We assume, and the Op assumes, that in each case his job is like that of the classic detective: winnow true from false, fact from fiction. We do not assume that a nameless and faceless figure, operating out of a named but equally faceless San Francisco, will act like Philo Vance or Ellery Queen. Nor does Hammett offer his characters in such a way that anyone can care who did what to whom. But if the Op's account of events isn't plausible, it's meant to be, even if it isn't tidy or illuminating. If it isn't to the point that he catch the real thief, then his whole demeanor as an operative—who seeks no reward for himself, who is never violent wantonly—is a fraud. When it doesn't matter what the Op or anyone else does, and that is certainly true in many pages here if not true of whole stories, it makes for very dull reading.

Take "The Main Death," for example, Hammett's forty-fourth published story, so he was no beginner. The Op is asked by a collector named Gungen to find out who killed his employee, Jeffrey Main, and to recover the $20,000 that was stolen from him and that belongs to Gungen. Mrs. Main's story is that she was awakened by a scuffle, found her husband fighting two masked figures, one of whom shot Main. His empty wallet and a

woman's handkerchief are found on the roof of a nearby apartment. The Op sees Gungen and discovers the handkerchief is
owned by his wife. As he leaves he spots a woman leaving too,
and he has her tailed to the apartment of two local con men,
Coughing Ben Weel and Bunky Dahl. From Mrs. Gungen Op
learns that Main had been her lover and that on the afternoon he
died they had been together and he had been robbed by two
men who fit Weel's and Dahl's description. Op finds them,
shakes them down for the twenty grand, masking himself as a
thief and not as a cop so he can then let them go and keep them
from implicating Mrs. Gungen in her affair with Main. All this
means that Mrs. Main's original story was a lie, so Op confronts
her and learns Main had committed suicide and Mrs. Main had
covered up to gain his insurance.

It just isn't true to say of a story like this, as Marcus does:

> What Hammett has done—unlike most writers of detective
> or crime stories before him or since—is to include as part of
> the contingent and dramatic consciousness of his narrative
> the circumstance that the work of the detective is itself a
> fiction-making activity, a discovery or creation by fabrica-
> tion of something new in the world, or hidden, latent, po-
> tential, or as yet undeveloped within it.

The Op uncovers the fabrications woven by Main, Mrs. Main,
and Mrs. Gungen; he himself does not fabricate, nor is his consciousness contingent or dramatic except as the uncoverer of
"real" truths. He does not, to be sure, chortle or offer lengthy ac-
counts of his methods of deduction, or act as though the world
after the uncovering is significantly different from the way it was
in the beginning. If his account of Main's death isn't plausible, it
at least fits all available facts, as in any detective fiction. The Op
is like the queen in chess, able to move both straight and diago-
nally, as it were, in a world of pawns, bishops, and rooks. But he
is a piece, more truly within his world than are most detectives.

This is precisely what's wrong. When the cast is cardboard,
when the relations among the characters are devoid of interest,
when the Op succeeds by allowing for no human motive except
the most simply conceived greed and lust, when the plot moves
these figures around like wind-up dolls, there is nothing to make

any of it matter. No theory, furthermore, true or false, that Marcus can supply can create an interest by saying "But that's the point" and by going on about contingencies and fiction-making detectives. Hammett was not a hero to himself, but he took himself seriously, and Marcus's way of making him pretentious only has the effect of making him trivial.

Perhaps most of Hammett's admirers would not, however, take a line like Marcus's; when he is praised, it is almost always for his writing. In these stories it is drearily literary. The most frequent event here, outside of conversation, is gunfighting, and Hammett could never do anything with guns except pile up elegant variations: "From behind the roadster, a pistol snapped at me, three times"; "An orange streak from the car ahead cut off my wonderment"; "A flash from somewhere near the roadster's heels"; "The girl's pistol barked at the empty touring car"; "Darkness—streaked with orange and blue—filled with noise"; "A gun thundered"; "Gunpowder burned at my face"; "Two points of light near the floor gave out fire and thunder"; "Twin flames struck at me again." Get the Op in a room with a couple of toughs, put him in a car chasing another, and these stiff, self-conscious phrases pile up ludicrously.

Or take a single passage:

> The Kid jumped close.
> He knew knives. None of your clumsy downward strokes with the blade sticking out the bottom of his fist.
> Thumb and crooked forefinger guided blade. He struck upward. Under Billie's shoulder. Once. Deep.
> Billie pitched forward, smashing the woman to the floor under him. He rolled off her and was dead on his back among the furniture stuffing. Dead, he seemed larger than ever, seemed to fill the room.
> The Whosis Kid wiped his knife clean on a piece of carpet, snapped it shut, and dropped it back in his pocket. He did this with his left hand. His right was close to his hip. He did not look at the knife. His eyes were on Maurois.

Perelman, or just ripe for Perelman? In "The Simple Art of Murder," Raymond Chandler says, "Hammett's style at its worst was almost as formalized as a page of *Marius the Epicurean*," and every story in *The Continental Op* shows it: "He looked dead, and he had enough bullet holes in him to make death a good guess"; "Even if I hadn't known Ringgo was looking at me I could have felt his eyes on me."

Nor is it hard to say how such bad writing came to be. Among *Black Mask* readers Hammett was very popular, and he thus learned what made stories sell and kept putting the Op through his predictable paces. He was pretty thoroughly committed, from habit or design, to the idea that human beings were not very interesting, so no character he could invent could hold his interest. Now and again he came up with a good plot which could give his writing some purpose, but since he had to keep writing, good plot or no, there was little for him to attend to most of the time but the prose itself. When that happens, the prose becomes stylized almost immediately, words are pieces in a jigsaw.

Hammett himself must have realized some of this by the late twenties, after he had been writing for seven or eight years. He began to write what the pulps liked to call novelettes; two put together became *Blood Money*, groups of four became *Red Harvest* and *The Dain Curse*. It is still the Op, still cross, double-cross, and triple-cross, but Hammett begins to blow up his writing, to crack wise, to be self-confessedly ornate—not all at once, but you don't find sentences like "The room was black as an honest politician's prospects" or "It was an even mile in the darkness to the head of the stairs we had come up" very often in the stories in the Marcus collection. As can be seen, most such sentences aren't much good, but they allow the Op and Hammett to have a sense of style, rather than force them, as the earlier stories tend to do, into self-defeating stylization. Of course this sense of self as style is not at all what Marcus wants to praise Hammett for, but it was not only what could keep Hammett interested—he stopped writing stories for *Black Mask* in 1930—but what allowed him to do his best work.

To do that he needed someone besides the Op, whose anonymous integrity had worn pretty thin, and he assayed three different characters with three different styles in his last three novels: Sam Spade in *The Maltese Falcon*, Ned Beaumont in *The Glass Key*, and Nick Charles in *The Thin Man*. It is at this point that we can turn to the otherwise deflecting question of which is the best book.

Hammett himself preferred *The Glass Key*, and so, to judge by what he later did with the private eye form, did Chandler; there is much to be said for the preference. *The Maltese Falcon* isn't all that much different from the Op novels, and if Spade is a clearer figure it is mostly because he is more openly selfish and nasty, and there isn't much Hammett can do except let him bark away. *The Thin Man* is silly fun, warmed by the relation of Nick to Nora, warmed as Hammett himself was by his new relation with Lillian Hellman, but otherwise an inconsequential effort to make a casual virtue out of casual plotting. Yet *The Glass Key* is the best because Hammett here tries to make the style of his hero matter; Ned Beaumont's poses are poses, capable of costing something. It is a fumbling book because Hammett wouldn't commit himself enough to what he was doing, wouldn't try to assess how much Beaumont dummies up because of his feeling for a friend, or how much it matters to him that he seem more a gentleman than a thug.

The code always said that one doesn't talk about such things, and the success or failure of *The Glass Key*—and all Hammett, all Chandler, all Ross Macdonald, too—depends on how well the hero's relation to this code is handled. Hold to it completely, act as if there were no prices for so doing, and you have the boring Op; begin to act as if there were prices to be paid and inevitably self-pity begins to creep in: I kept my word, and I took my beating, etc., can lead to some dreary and immoral posing. What Hellman has shown us, however, is that Hammett himself believed in the code, and suffered because he did; the dignity with which he was willing to do so tinged his life with greatness. Better, then, to let the self-pity come in if it must, better to deal with it openly as best one can. Better to say life matters, especially if you really think it does.

Hammett cannot handle all this in *The Glass Key*, but he tries. Beaumont can cry, and attempt suicide after his beating, he can lash out at others because he is unhappy with himself, he can stand paralyzed at the end after he tells his friend Madvig he is going away with the woman Madvig loves and Beaumont does not. The writing in this book is on the edge of all Hammett himself could not write about, but that is not a bad place for his writing to be.

Given this, if Marcus wanted to reprint some currently unavailable Hammett stories he would have been better off, I think, calling his collection "The Early Dashiell Hammett" or some such title. That would give the Op the historical importance he had for Hammett, *Black Mask*, and the hard-boiled story in general. After all, being a Pinkerton agent had given Hammett some material and a way to look at life, but neither plots nor style. The plots he borrowed—not literally, but in the sense that he wasn't going to try to do without them or invent a new kind—and the style had to be invented and evolved even as he had to keep churning out stories in order to live. No need to complain that these stories are crude, primitive, effortful; no need, either, to elevate these very qualities into high art. He did quite a bit in his ten years of writing, and he was a real pioneer. If the best of Chandler and MacDonald and Macdonald is better than his best, if the middling stuff of quite a few writers is better than his middling stuff, there isn't one who doesn't know how much he made them possible.

PHILIP ROTH

Recently I was asked to write an essay about the presumably unhappy consequences for American novelists of there being no tradition of the minor novel in this country. I replied, perhaps hastily, that if there was no such tradition there were nonetheless lots of good minor novelists who seemed to get along very well. But, the editor answered, unquestionably there have been some

victims of pressure to make each new work a "major effort," a
sign of "growth," a willingness not to repeat earlier successes. He
was right, certainly—Anthony Powell is allowed to conceive of
himself in ways that John Updike cannot—though I'm still not
sure what one makes of the fact beyond noting it. But, whoever
has or hasn't suffered from the pressures of excessive and premature expectations, Philip Roth is clearly our most obvious victim.

Roth was still in his twenties when *Goodbye, Columbus*
made him famous in 1959; ten years later, after *Portnoy's Complaint*, he became a national public figure, the most notorious
writer in the country except Mailer. Since then he has searched
restlessly for something new to do, to break out of his apparent
bondage, and the results have not been good. Everyone knows
Roth can write beautifully and that he can be very funny, but the
writing has become self-regarding and the humor has dwindled to
giggles. Of course Roth may well have great productive years
ahead, but at this point he has suffered badly from demands
made on him, by himself and others, to think of himself as a
major talent when what he has to work with is an excellent minor
genius.

Now comes *Reading Myself and Others*, Roth's first work of
nonfiction, a collection of essays and interviews that confirms all
gloomy suspicions. Since *Portnoy's Complaint* Roth has often
been called on to account for his life and career, to justify and
assess his role as an apparently scandalous Jew, to say why he has
written each thing he's done. Inevitably, the result is self-consciousness and self-regard—"The question of moral sovereignty,
as it is examined in *Letting Go, Portnoy's Complaint*, and *The
Breast*"; "Thinking back over my work, it seems that I've
frequently written about what Bruno Bettelheim calls 'behavior
in extreme situations.' " Roth treats himself as an object, an accomplished fact, a figure about to be entombed. He even becomes the central figure in an allegory: "Sheer Playfulness and
Deadly Seriousness are my closest friends; it is with them that I
take those walks in the country at the end of the day." It is all a
shame.

The first half of *Reading Myself and Others* is almost all interviews, embarrassing in their assurance that anything Roth
does is worth his and our closest scrutiny. The second half, too, is

only ostensibly about reading others and mostly a series of attempts to place himself and his work in the context of American Jews and Jewish stereotypes. There is one brilliant essay, "Imagining Jews," which brings these concerns and anxieties into focus and which makes all the others not worth saving. There is another, almost as good, "Looking at Kafka," which places a loving account of Kafka's final year next to a story about Roth's Hebrew teacher, also a Franz Kafka, and a projection of what the Kafka who died in 1924 might have become had he lived, come to America, and ended up living in respectable poverty in Newark. These last two essays can't justify the whole book, but they are awfully good, and show Roth to be a good critic and a good biographer.

The problem remains, though, and what has gone wrong with Roth is not just the result of there being no tradition of the minor novel in America. A number of other circumstances, most of them well beyond Roth's control, seem to have been conspiring to do him in. When *Goodbye, Columbus* appeared, Roth's elders, mostly Jews themselves, were able to hail him as the most recent of what must have seemed an inexhaustible Jewish postwar novelistic talent; he was different from Bellow and Malamud, but in ways that could do everyone credit. In the succeeding ten years or more, however, no one has come along to take Roth's place as the youngest in the pantheon, though of course many young Jewish writers have appeared. As a result, Roth seemed to get more attention, more nagging and somewhat paternal attention—what is he *doing*? what will he *become*?—than is perhaps good for anyone. *Letting Go* and *When She Was Good*, Roth's grindingly realistic and mostly Midwest fictions, seemed not to satisfy, though they seem to me his best work, because in them he really is being the deadly serious and almost holy writer he set out to be, and in them he was not seriously influenced, so far as I can see, by external pressures.

Then came *Portnoy's Complaint*, at the climax of what Roth calls the de-mythologizing sixties, and *Portnoy* did a lot of de-mythologizing. As Roth brilliantly suggests in "Imagining Jews," the novel scandalized and became a best seller because he was imagining a Jew wanting and doing those things that "traditionally" Jews had imagined only the goyim doing; he was even accused of being anti-Semitic. Irving Howe carefully showed the limitations of Roth's work by showing how in important respects it isn't Jewish enough. Howe's is a fine essay, but Roth's is an equally fine reply. The trouble is not that Roth had become a bad boy, but that he had put himself in a position where he didn't know what to do next. No point in repeating *Portnoy's Complaint*, no way to get back to the grim patient realism of his two previous novels. Surely there must be something that can be done with the humor, because *Portnoy's Complaint*, whatever else, is both funny and fun in many places. But what?

Roth was now famous, the subject of gossip columnists as well as of literary critics and Hadassah gatherings; furthermore, Johnson and Nixon seemed to have managed to make America into everyone's subject. Without much in the way of tradition to guide him, without much more that could be made of his native material, with only the uncertain figure of Kafka to act as patron saint, wealthy yet personally retiring, Roth has bobbled, plunged, made one mistake after another.

Everything has become too stylized and too long. Instead of the four-page "The President Addresses the Nation," which is good and reprinted here, we have *Our Gang*, where the same joke is bloated into a book. Instead of the good book about baseball which Roth might have written, we get the truly silly *The Great American Novel*, where instead of baseball we have America turned into pretentious farce; I should have thought one good ten-minute reverie about Ruppert Stadium in Newark would have shamed Roth into never inventing the Rupperts. But take him away from Newark and Chicago and New York and he is adrift in "America," making its mythologies and its audiences his concern. Roth himself disappears, to be replaced by a performer.

But, unlike Mailer, or Pynchon, Roth is not really very happy as a performer, showman, public figure, rhetorician. He is too private a person, too lyrical, perhaps too much, still, a Good Jew, for that. *My Life as a Man* tries to get back, as if in realization of all this, and so, though it is a book mostly swamped in self-justification, there are some passages in it that are moving and lyrical, signs enough that of course Roth can still write. But the rest is all forced, writing projects that seem thought up, abstractions, things that have to be bludgeoned into existence by style. He may one day recover, but as of now everything good he has written is derived from life he had led or known before he became a writer, childhood stuff, growing-up stuff, starting-out-in-life stuff. That material seems to be gone now, and fame and undeserved infamy have taken care of the rest. His present companions, as he says, are Sheer Playfulness and Deadly Seriousness; in such pure form, these can hardly be anyone's best friends; worse still, they become practically enemies when they are one's only friends.

Over the years I have heard many people speak slightingly of Philip Roth's career as a prime instance of New York literary logrolling, and of course such sneers always seem to carry with them an overtone of envy. I hope such people can somehow take a second look, and see how the fame, wealth, and notoriety of Roth have done much to bring him to this pass.

BRADLEY & MACLEAN

"Old man," says a character in Wright Morris's *The Huge Season,* "a book can have Chicago in it, and not be about Chicago. It can have a tennis player in it without being about a tennis player." He then points to a book of Hemingway's:

> "There's a prizefighter in it, old man, but it's not about a prizefighter."
> "Is it about the sun rising?" I said. I knew that was part of the title.
> "Goddam if I know what it's about. . . ."

The province of art is anyplace. Morris did not want sloppy readers saying *The Huge Season* was "about" a tennis player, or that his other books were "about" the West. Mark Harris used this passage as the epigraph to *Bang the Drum Slowly* because he didn't want his readers to make his novel be "about" baseball. Hemingway would have approved.

Still, the claim that novels are not "about" anything has always seemed to me ingenuous, or worse, disingenuous. No reader is interested in everything, and only the very greatest art can withstand the ravages of time, leap the barriers of language and distance, defy the inevitable tendency of readers to be more interested in some things than others. Bill Bradley's *Life on the Run* is "about" playing professional basketball; Norman Maclean's *A River Runs Through It* is "about" fly fishing and working in the Forest Service in Montana. No question but that people who care about these subjects will care more about these admirable books than those who do not. Bradley is thoughtful and engaging about many aspects of basketball that others have written about badly or not at all. Maclean's title story, about fly fishing, seems to me a fine tale. But there's no telling how far or how well these excellences can travel.

Life on the Run is not amusing, or rich in lore and anecdote. Though many pages concern Bradley's New York Knicks teammates, Bradley says little about them an attentive bystander could not have anticipated; the same is true for his account of his own career as a boy from Crystal City, Missouri, who trained himself to be a basketball prodigy, starred at Princeton, and then read history at Oxford as a Rhodes scholar. Even stranger, perhaps, his book is weak in narrative and suspense. Though it uses a few weeks late in the 1973–1974 season as its frame, it rarely mentions whether the Knicks are gaining or falling back on the Celtics. Bradley chooses these weeks, presumably, because it was the end for the old Knicks—Willis Reed and Dave DeBusschere were about to retire—but we don't find out how the season ended. Nor does he say much about the techniques and tactics of this superbly disciplined team.

Which leaves Bradley his subject, the life of an aging professional basketball player, especially life on the road, and it is subject enough.

> As I stand in the cramped shower stall I think about the insulated world we professional basketball players live in. We travel from city to city, sometimes as if we were un-

aware of a larger world beyond our own. Every city we enter is full of crises and problems that never reach us in a hotel room.

Those crises and problems, of course, are what can make those who face them envious of lads who are paid huge sums to play ball. When one feels that envy, one ignores the life of the shower stall, the hotel room, the bus, and the airport:

> The daily worries and pressures of workers concerned about how to pay for food, housing, or medical care never penetrate the glass of our bus window. To do our job, we have to remain healthy and follow orders. In any airline terminal even the sad scene of a soldier's farewell or the joy of a family reunion often by-pass us, making no impression. In the airports that have become our commuter stations we see so many dramatic personal moments that we are calloused. To some, we live romantic lives. To me, every day is a struggle to stay in touch with life's subtleties.

With each sentence here Bradley increases both his scope and his intensity; the phrasing is ordinary but the activity of the mind is not.

Bradley is so insulated that he will speak easily of a friend in this or that city and never once specify the friend's name, age, sex, or the nature of their relationship. All newer players, even those on his own team, are just called rookies, even after they have been in the league a few years. Bradley and Dave DeBusschere roomed for years together and only at the end did one of them ask the other if the friendship could last beyond DeBusschere's retirement, and even at that Bradley is taken aback by the question. Subtleties *are* lost, no question, and Bradley has to ask why he goes on anyway:

> With my dedication to lone practice gone, the team is everything. How the team does affects my feelings about the game and myself; sometimes, I think, too much. I am obsessed with my work of team basketball. In a way, my personality, formed as it was on a steady diet of Calvinist religion, is amenable to the idea of team play. . . . My problem is that my aspirations demand that I create something I cannot control completely.

For years one saw Bradley slide from the baseline toward the top
of the key, saw the screen take form and the pass arrive simultaneously so that Bradley could take his little jump shot and make
up for the fact that he is too short, too slow, and, as his teammates tell him, unable to jump high enough for a Sunday *Times*
to fit between his feet and the floor. One sees him do the same
thing this year, but the ball isn't there and Bradley is left alone
with his obsession: "At times I feel I am an artist in the wrong
medium."

How much of this can interest a reader who doesn't care about
basketball, or who knows little about it, I can't possibly say. Yet
he makes me, a brooding fan, feel I understand more about every
veteran player in the league. There are the old Celtics, Hein-
sohn, Jones, Russell, Sharman, who are coaches now because
their years as players on that team gave them truths their lives
cannot live up to otherwise. There are black players, raised from
playground ball, who slide from starter to reserve to another
team to obscurity because their idea of success involves a different obsession entirely, one too fragile for the endless demands
of team ball. To the casual observer it would seem as though Caz-
zie Russell, who can hit hoops from any angle or distance, is the
artist in the right medium. But he was the forward the Knick's
coach Red Holzman traded, not Bradley, and Holzman was of
course right. Lonely, obsessed, out of touch with life's subtleties,
Bradley is nonetheless in the right medium on the court.

But even those who think sports are only for kids until they
grow up, or that superbly developed athletes are only conspicu-
ous examples of sexuality gone wrong, should not miss, or be denied, Bradley on the subject of growing older. His meditation
begins when he remembers Mickey Mantle describing his current life: "Sometimes after breakfast when the boys get off to
school, I sit by myself and take a scrapbook and just turn the
pages." Bradley is now old enough to understand that:

> When the playing is over, one can sense that one's youth
> has been spent playing a game and now both the game and
> youth are gone, along with the innocence that characterizes
> all games which are at root pure and promote a prolonged
> adolescence in those who play.

The prose is flat, yet "pure," "promote," and "prolonged adolescence" stand in bleak paradoxical relation to each other, beyond the touch of mere alliteration:

> What is left is the other side of the Faustian bargain: To live all one's days never able to recapture the feeling of those few years of intensified youth. . . . The athlete rarely recuperates. He approaches the end of his playing days the way old people approach death. He puts his finances in order. He reminisces easily. He offers advice to the young. But the athlete differs from an old person in that he must continue living. Behind all the years of practice and all the hours of glory waits that inexorable terror of living without the game.

This is a truth too grim for a mere fan. The greater the player, the greater the inexorable terror. The longer the career, the worse its ending.

But here we have almost left basketball behind. No one with any kind of success when young can fail to shiver at the sober accuracy of Bradley's reflections. Bradley may not know it, but people who enjoy their work and work hard burn themselves out, whatever their jobs. Still, in direct proportion to one's caring about Bradley, the Knicks, and professional basketball will one feel the pain of this book, for they are what it is all about. The Knicks played out the string recently against Cleveland, a team maturing as fast as the Knicks are fading. There was Bradley, with nothing to win or lose, obsessed in what have been rumored to be his last games. Behind the screen, out toward the top of the key. Across the middle, setting a screen on the other side. Cleverly defending, taking one step for Bobby Smith's two, keeping between Smith and the ball. Having read *Life on the Run*, I was especially moved by him. Bill Bradley as an author has little art, but he is writing "about" something in this book.

Norman Maclean, twice Bradley's age, retired a few years ago from the University of Chicago, where he had won a number of awards for distinguished teaching. Before now, he was known to me only as the author of two essays in the neo-Aristotelian collec-

tion *Critics and Criticism,* on *Lear* and the Augustan lyric, both
sound, nicely written, and a bit dull. For years, he says at the
beginning, he told his children stories of things that had happened to him, and they finally asked him to write them down.
Which he did, though the result is clearly the work of the current, retired Maclean, not of a father trying to interest young
children in woods and water.

There are three stories in *A River Runs Through It;* two are
long enough to qualify as short novels. The short one is inconsequential, and the long one about being seventeen and in
the Forest Service is flawed by its becoming a variation on the familiar Western tale of a rite of passage. But the 100-page-long
title story, about fly fishing, one might call perfect except that it
makes no pretense to be shapely or artful. At the end, his father
says, "Why don't you make up a story and the people to go with
it? Only then will you understand what happened and why. It is
those we live with and love and should know who elude us."
Maclean, though, does not care about making up a story in which
he will understand what happened; he wants to write about those
he lived with and who eluded him: "Now nearly all those I loved
and did not understand when I was young are dead, but I still
reach out to them." The story is his reaching out.

Mostly to his brother, younger by three years, who did not
move away or become a professor of English. He stayed home,
became a reporter on a newspaper in Helena, Montana, drank
too much, and became a great fly fisherman. At the heart of the
story are the two brothers, Norman and Paul, on the trout
streams of western Montana, loving and eluding each other, fishing. They are the sons of a Scottish Presbyterian minister: "In our
family," is the first line, "there was no clear line between religion
and fly fishing."

As the boys were raised, so we are instructed,

> . . . if you have never picked up a fly rod before, you will
> soon find it factually and theologically true that man by na-
> ture is a damn mess. The four-and-a-half-ounce thing in silk
> wrappings that trembles with the underskin motions of the
> flesh becomes a stick without brains, refusing anything sim-
> ple that is wanted of it. All that a rod has to do is lift the
> line, the leader, and the fly off the water, give them a good

toss over the head, and then shoot them forward so they will land in the water without a splash in the following order: Fly, transparent leader, and then the line—otherwise the fish will see the fly is a fake and be gone.

The first point, then, is that it is simple, though of course the boys did not conclude, as others have, that it was really simple.

But what's remarkable about just a straight cast—just picking up a rod with line on it and tossing the line across the river? Well, until man is redeemed he will always take a fly rod too far back, just as natural man always overswings with an ax or a golf club and loses all his power somewhere in the air; only with a rod it's worse, because the fly often comes so far back it gets caught behind in a bush or rock. . . . Then, since it is natural for man to try to attain power without recovering grace, he whips the line back and forth making it whistle each way, and sometimes even snapping off the fly from the leader, but the power that was going to transport the little fly across the river somehow gets diverted into building a bird's nest of line, leader, and fly that falls out of the air into the water about ten feet in front of the fisherman.

One has to quote such passages, or else the story is reduced to effects, conveying nothing of Maclean's care.

Being a true Presbyterian, Maclean can know about fishing without making us feel outsiders for not knowing, even though most of us are in fact outsiders. Not having recovered grace, haunted by the mysteries of fishing, he would not dream of trying to imply that he has solved the mysteries. A still better fisherman, like his brother Paul, would dream of this even less. So after the rod and the cast came the rivers, and the fish:

One great thing about fly fishing is that after a while nothing exists of the world but thoughts about fly fishing. It is also interesting that thoughts about fishing are often carried on in dialogue where Hope and Fear—or, many times, two Fears—try to outweigh each other.

Thus one fear may be that there is a rock the fish will have to be taken past when hooked, and the line must be pulled so tight if he is taken past the near side he will probably fight free of the hook, especially since the weather has been warm and the fish's mouth will therefore be soft. But the other fear is that if the fish is taken on the far side of the rock the line will get caught under it.

The world narrows, and all one has are the questions one asks, the hopes and fears, and a river running through it all.

> In the arm, shoulder, or brain of a big-fish fisherman is a scale, and the moment the big fish goes into the air the big-fish fisherman, no matter what his blood pressure is, places the scale under the fish and cooly weighs him. He doesn't have hands and arms enough to do all the other things he should be doing at the same time, but he tries to be fairly exact about the weight of the fish so he won't be disappointed when he catches him.

Then, after Maclean weighs this fish at a most satisfying seven or eight pounds, and the fish jumps into the bushes hanging over the water, tying a different knot on every branch he passes, comes disaster:

> The body and spirit suffer no more sudden visitation than that of losing a big fish, since, after all, there must be some slight transition between life and death. But, with a big fish, one moment the world is nuclear and the next it has disappeared. That's all. It has gone. The fish has gone and you are extinct, except for four and a half ounces of stick to which is tied some line and a semitransparent thread of catgut to which is tied a little curved piece of Swedish steel to which is tied a part of a feather from a chicken's neck.

It is an enchanted tale. Paul instructs Maclean a few times, in the sign language of fishers who are also reticent Scots, and once Maclean catches a fish in a hole where his brother cannot because he carries with him special flies, which Paul scorns. There is Maclean's brother-in-law from the West Coast, who fishes with bait, and whom the brothers discover one afternoon, on an island in the river, horribly sunburned, because he and the prostitute with him have made love and fallen asleep in the August sun. There is Paul's drinking, for which there is no explanation other than that to him nothing in life measures up to fly fishing. On the day Maclean learns his brother has been beaten to death in a fight, Maclean and his father talk quietly, mostly about the way all the bones in Paul's casting hand were broken. The story, having a river running through it, generally follows its own path, meandering here and rushing there, but it has to stop at this point.

I have read the story three times now, and each time it seems fuller. Necessarily, I wonder, as I do about Bill Bradley's book, if the very source of the enchantment, its way of being "about" something, must restrict its audience. I have never fished, but I go with a friend who does, to a river only somewhat less wonderful than the big Montana rivers. I have stared at that river, and at others throughout the West, not with the eye of a fisherman, but enchanted nonetheless. I simply don't know what I would make of Maclean's story if I knew no fishers, had never been entranced by trout streams, but I find it hard to believe it would matter as much to me if I knew about none of these things.

There is always something wonderful in reading a book by someone who is absorbed in what he or she does. And that absorption must extend beyond matters of technique and skill. In his Forest Service story Maclean describes a ranger who can pack a whole string of horses and mules so they can walk and climb for days without the packs slipping or the animals becoming hobbled. It must be a rare skill, but then, that is all it is, which is why this story lacks the magic of "A River Runs Through It." Bill Bradley talks well about the skills involved in playing basketball, but it is not that, or that taken by itself, that obsesses him. There is no need to ignore here, for it is not coincidence, the fact that Bradley and Maclean were both raised as Calvinists, and are Calvinists still. They are dedicated, not to work, as those who don't understand these matters like to think, but to the achievement of grace. "To him," Maclean says about his father, "all good things—trout as well as eternal salvation—come by grace and grace comes by art and art does not come easy."

Bradley and Maclean are saints of secular communities, and therefore we must care about the arts they practice in order to enter their worlds with more than passing interest. Patient though both are with readers who do not know these arts, there is no way they can pretend to make their absorption into a magic or an enchantment for everyone. If they could do this, they would be different people, less haunted, obsessed. *Life on the Run* and *A River Runs Through It* should be interesting to the unconverted, and they might seem silly or even wicked to those who scorn conversion. They will be best for those who know, and who, in knowing, need no reminder that mysteries are not meant to be solved.

HUXLEY & BENNETT, BEDFORD & DRABBLE

It's hard to imagine someone wanting to read a full-length biography just for its style or its story; if one could show that Izaak Walton's life of Sanderson were better than his life of Donne it would matter little because people pick up a biography because of its subject, not its author. Even Sybille Bedford's *Aldous Huxley* and Margaret Drabble's *Arnold Bennett* aren't likely to find new readers for their subjects, though they both may well serve an equally valuable purpose and re-create an audience. Bennett and Huxley don't have many loyal fans, people who adore their work, avid readers of their lesser efforts, but thousands have read something of theirs, though often not much and not recently. These biographies can do what most criticism and analysis do not: send one back, to reread and read, to be reminded. Perhaps the major source of the success of each is that they were written out of love and admiration, not because the job happened not to have been done, not to achieve status or promotion for the biographer.

Bedford knew Huxley, and loved him, and she was the choice of his widow, brother, and son to write an official life. For her part, Drabble says, "So I wrote the biography in a partisan spirit, as an act of appreciation." These motives can kill as well as any other, but in these cases they seem to have sustained and guided the biographer over the years of dogged laboring. Bedford and Drabble, themselves authors of novels of intelligent love, love their subjects intelligently, and it makes all the difference in the world. Both books are flawed, both suffer from that biographical compulsion to tell all. Drabble's book is too long, Bedford's is much too long—worse, *Aldous Huxley,* which was published in two volumes in England, appears here as a single book so large it is impossible actually to want to open it. In each case, the trouble is not the length as such but the effect that the length has on the biographer's control over her material and on her final view of the subject. Still, each does its essential job, each makes biography into an enabling act, and Drabble at her best makes it a noble art as well.

Bedford's *Huxley* takes its shape from reminiscence. By 1930 Huxley had written the satirical novels for which he still probably is most admired; he was a husband and a father, established as a writer, thirty-six, partially blind, a Huxley and an Arnold both and gradually becoming aware of the effects of having had such ancestors and such traditions behind him. At this point, living in the south of France, he met Sybille Bedford, and we are on p. 232. The remaining years, which most people think of as the California years, the Huxley of fads and causes, take Bedford another 509 pp. The book is not Bedford's memoirs, or anything like that, but still, the Huxley she knew is the one she wants to write about. The early years she deals with in scraps and vignettes, done rather as she does her small scenes in her novels; years go by very quickly, and one watches in dismay as a full-grown Huxley is etched in without our having any very clear sense of what he was like, how he came about. For a book this long and full, the early pace seems hurried, fitful, and it isn't until later on that Bedford, as if pleased somehow to have gotten Huxley to the point where she first knew him, slows down, fills in, and by this time the Huxley that many, and perhaps most, of her readers most want to know about is all gone by.

Nor are the difficulties over then. Perhaps the best way to indicate Bedford's stance is with an example. It is 1937, and she is describing a London dentist:

> On Monday morning Aldous went to his surgery. I wish I could recall his name because, as I repeat, he was a very pleasant man, but more to the point proved to be an extremely competent and up-to-date dentist. It was Tregar or something near it. He discovered abscesses at the roots and had to extract three more teeth. The whole job was done brilliantly; Aldous was very pleased and recovered quickly.

Some will not like such a manner no matter what; it is breezy, absorbed with trivia, and the biographer is intrusive. Maybe; though I, for one, am not dismayed. But then, fifteen years and two hundred pages later, we have this in a footnote:

> "The very pleasant young man," whom I called T., who was Aldous and Maria's neighbour at the Mount Royal Hotel in London during that spring and who rescued Aldous from the consequences of the botched operation on his jaw in Paris, did not entirely agree with the article and said so to Aldous. Aldous told T., who is of course Mr. Boris Trainin, the Harley Street dental consultant and analytical psychologist. . . .

Between the first and the second volume as they appeared in England, Bedford found out who T., or Tregar, was. Again, some may object that she should then have done some tidying up, but we can let that pass and come right to the telltale and incriminating "of course": how stupid of me not to remember his name, "of course" we all know Boris Trainin, "the" Harley Street consultant.

Here, in miniature, is Bedford, the insider who too often and at too great length defines "the world" as Fielding said it was defined by people of fashion: "the people of one's acquaintance." Sybille Bedford lives in "the world," Aldous Huxley lived there, and "of course" so too does Boris Trainin. Bedford evokes names and places as though they were all perfectly familiar; she discusses houses and furniture and domestic habits or servants and mealtimes as though of course these are as important as any but the few really important things in life. Most important, she treats Maria Huxley as though she were as important as Huxley himself, because many who knew them both felt she was, and because Bedford wants to tell those for whom she seemed less important that that was only because Maria was such a beautiful arranger. At its tacky worse, we get this, Maria's handling of Aldous's affairs with other women:

> The logistics were largely Maria's. "You can't leave it to Aldous," she would say, "he'd make a muddle." She did it with tact, unbreachable good manners and a smile (ironic). She sent the flowers. Not actual flowers, that wouldn't have been Aldous's style, she saw to it that he sent a book. This he might inscribe with an elegantly turned allusive stanza of her own composition (in French: he still enjoyed *d'être un peu scabreux*). Maria did up the parcel. She did more than that. In a very subtle way she prepared the ground, created opportunities, an atmosphere, stood in, as it were, for the courtship. . . . She did not really mind, Maria took what I should call the aristocratic view of sex.

I suppose this is amusing, and Bedford brings it off pretty well, but one is far from nodding "of course" to the idea that Maria's arranging of Aldous's affairs is a mark of her "unbreachable good manners." Worse, though Bedford is willing to say what she can about these affairs, she will not make an effort to bring the sexual life of the Huxleys into focus, so one is left with: after the birth of their son, the Huxleys could have no more children; after that, Aldous had affairs that Maria helped arrange. Is that all one knows or needs to know? Bedford should either have told more or less, should not have left the Huxleys seeming grossly naïve and impossible, Maria in her "aristocratic view of sex," Aldous in his dinner and bed with various women whenever he got to England.

Yet Bedford has many virtues of which these are the defects. She *is* a woman of the world, an aristocrat of sorts, an accomplished novelist, and a skilled reporter. Having chosen to include the entire Huxley acquaintance, perhaps so no one's feelings might be hurt, she managed the cast with great skill and

tact. She is able to show the attractions and shortcomings of people as diverse as brother Julian Huxley, Frieda Lawrence, and
guru Gerald Heard; she shuffles the quotations from letters and
memoirs in and out with great skill. And, unless one is over-
whelmed by the sheer profusion of detail, she offers a very precise way to see parts of Huxley. Start with whatever image the
satires of the twenties give of their author, add the bit above
about the affairs. Now this, Bedford's description of the Huxleys
in California as she saw them in the summer of 1940:

> I found Aldous and Maria very changed. There was of
> course Aldous's new sight—there he was without his spec-
> tacles, walking, reading (still holding the print close to his
> eyes), but this was not as impressive as it might have been
> because of his looking so drawn and strained, like a man
> with a great burden of unhappiness severely locked away. I
> had often seen him look ill or withdrawn or quietly sad, but
> even during the great insomnia of 1935 he had always kept
> his air of equanimity. . . . It was of course a deeply un-
> happy time for most of us, but it seemed to me that the
> Huxleys were almost deliberately, if not consciously, put-
> ting themselves under the greatest possible strain, submit-
> ting themselves to some rigorous process of repression; a
> process, I thought even then, that must have been of longer
> standing, must have ante-dated the catastrophic news of the
> last weeks.

The move to America had not released Huxley, and for all his
productivity his work had done little to help himself, "the
world," or the world as a whole. Bedford's picture is just what is
needed to show a man approaching a crisis, though when one has
become as adept at repression as Huxley, the crisis may be both
long in coming and long in working itself out.

The article Huxley had written that Boris Trainin had not
liked was on hypnosis; his eyesight had been much improved
with the help of the "professionally" not entirely creditable Bates
method; in the years before 1940 Huxley was deeply involved
with Gerald Heard in the Peace Pledge Union. Huxley had been
getting "into" things that others, many of his friends included,
find to be fads or boltholes for neuroses. When Bedford saw him

in 1940, nothing had helped, except the Bates method. And Huxley went on getting "into" things: massage, occultism, séances, parapsychology, educational theory, Eastern philosophy and religion, global thinking and ecology, LSD and mescaline. Those who like to think so can claim that all Huxley needed was the move to Los Angeles to bring out all his naïve susceptibility to any cause or cure.

Bedford tells another story. Huxley knew he was a "sensitive if under-emotional man," knew he wanted to change his life, knew he could not repudiate his intelligence, rationality, and irony even had he wanted to. Three books, none near the top of most people's Huxleyan Parnassus, tell the story: *Grey Eminence* (1941), a biography of Father Joseph, a devout priest who became Richelieu's chief henchman; *The Devils of Loudon* (1952), a study of an episode of fanaticism, exorcism, and sanctity; *The Doors of Perception* (1954), a little book about Huxley's first experiments with mescaline. Taken together with Bedford's account of these years, Huxley's efforts to wash away the aridity of his life, to open its repression, to overcome if not eradicate his lack of natural piety, are absorbing and moving. He tried so many different things because nothing by itself worked, and the more he worked the more he saw he had to do. "Now the treasure [in Aldous] is flowing in torrents of gaiety and openness," Maria wrote in 1952, and if that overstates its point, it does not misplace the emphasis. "It's a bit embarrassing to find at the end that one has no more to offer by way of advice than 'Try to be a little kinder,' " Huxley said some years later, and if that understates the point, it too does not misplace the emphasis. Lawrence had said many years before that there were many nicer Huxleys than the one who had written *Point Counter Point*, but that knowledge was more available to Lawrence than to Huxley himself; it wasn't until years after *Point Counter Point* that he could begin to be someone truly different, less measuring, less mottled with meanness of spirit. He went on working hard at living his life, at trying to accept a self he did not like, and the effort is impressive.

Bedford offers all the evidence one needs, pours out vignettes, stitches quotations, and comments skillfully, but I wish she had insisted more that to love Huxley was not just to love his efforts during these later years but to admire and applaud his successes. Bedford, creature of the European "world," seems at times a little too worried that we might associate her with Taoism, or séances, or drugs, and there is no need for that. For me, and I hope for others, she makes the later Huxley a fine man, a struggler rather than a pilgrim, and I think she could have endorsed the efforts more strongly and decisively had she insisted that what was important was the work, not the goals. She never loses sight of Huxley, but she lets herself be content with chronicling where she should have been a decisive storyteller. Still, I liked the book much more than I thought I would, given its length, given the falling off before this in Bedford's own career, given my inability ever to warm to Huxley. And those three books of the forties and early fifties that I mentioned earlier really should have more readers.

Arnold Bennett, on the other hand, is someone I have always felt warmly about; so too is Margaret Drabble, though I hadn't realized until now that perhaps the sources of these warm feelings were similar. Bennett was from Stoke-on-Trent, Drabble is from Sheffield, and while both eagerly left home and never wished to return, Bennett in his major novels and Drabble (in part by her reading of those novels) realized the hold these industrial Midlands cities still had on them. There is a moment, in *The Summer Bird-cage*, I think, when a Drabble heroine at a party or a fancy London pub finds herself thinking that the real London is not where she is but in the Long Acre, where the fruit and veg people work. Most of Bennett's life was like that; he wanted to be at the party, on the yacht, in the nightclub dancing, but real life, he knew, was elsewhere, in the Five Towns, in the Long Acre, or Sheffield. When Drabble discovered these qualities in herself, she knew how much Bennett had articulated them for her, and in this book she wants to pay homage to what he did for her and others like her. Given the special nature of Bennett's life—a hugely industrious (one almost wants to say industrialized) writer, immensely successful and quite wealthy, yet able to write at his best only about his grim home county—biography hardly seems the right form. The farther he got from the Five Towns, the more he enjoyed himself, the kinder he may have become, but the less there is to say about him. Drabble realizes this, says at the outset she will concentrate on "Bennett's background, his childhood and origins," which she does, but still, the great things here are all in the first part. After Bennett becomes a public success Drabble keeps at it, but it is work, for her and her reader. Until then, however, she does magnificently. It is like a Bennett novel, warm and detailed, rich in its sense of the past, unstinting in his exposure of meannesses and failings, yet fully assured that the truth will set free both subject and biographer.

The great mark of Drabble's assurance is her almost total lack of needless self-consciousness. She knows all her material is relevant somehow, and trusts it, so that the early chapters are filled with commentary on *The Old Wives' Tale* and the *Clayhanger* trilogy, used as illuminations of places, people, and feelings of Bennett's life; she knows, and so never needs to question, the way art is and isn't life, the way Bennett is and isn't Edwin Clayhanger, his father is and isn't Darius Clayhanger, his mother is and isn't Auntie Hamps. Likewise, she knows her own life is relevant here and brings it in easily and gracefully, again in perfect trust that she is right to do so. Because the result is so very much like one of Bennett's novels, which rely on accumulation of detail and so are practically impossible to quote from tellingly, I can only hope a couple of quotations can hint how it all works. First this, about Bennett's mother:

> She must, like most wives in this district at this time, have been much subdued; certainly she had none of the troublesome "superior" qualities which Lawrence's mother possessed, and which produced many of the conflicts which turned him into a writer. Bennett owes her no such doubtful debt. She may have been ambitious for him, but she didn't show it. Arnold was to remain an attentive and affectionate son—for years he wrote to her every day and sent a constant flow of postcards, on one occasion (31 August 1904) sending as many as seven postcards on the same day. No wonder he criticizes the neglect of the feckless Cyril Povey, in *The Old Wives' Tale*, who forgets to write home.

The equipoise is admirable: "subdued" playing off against "troublesome," in ways that raise a problem without trying to settle it; the simple shift from "Bennett" to "Arnold" as the writer turns for a moment into the son; the glance at Cyril Povey that shows

how passages in novels come to be written in ways that otherwise
are not accountable. Now this, much later, about the death of
Auntie Sarah Hamps in *These Twain*, a scene written shortly
after the death of Bennett's mother:

> The death of Auntie Hamps is magnificently described: it is,
> as Bennett makes us well aware, the death of an era. Thrifty
> Auntie Hamps, who wore black silks, jet ornaments and
> seal-skins, had presented a glorious front to the world for
> years, but Edwin, in penetrating the defenceless fastness of
> her bedroom, finds all her "squalid avaricious secrets" re-
> vealed. Did he find his own mother's bedroom similarly
> squalid? Probably he did. Her appearance, her dying
> vagaries, her final meannesses about coal on the fire, her
> unwillingness to relinquish power, are all ruthlessly de-
> scribed: he has no pity on her. And even at the end, Edwin
> cannot help speculating on the conundrum at the heart of
> her being: did she really believe in her own hypocrisy or
> not? Did she actually believe in the God whose mottoes
> adorn her bedroom wall? Did those who spoke at her fu-
> neral actually believe she was a saint, and an absolutely ir-
> reparable loss to the circuit? There is no answer. The se-
> crets of the bedroom can be exposed, but not the secrets
> and duplicities of the Wesleyan Methodist heart.

The ruthlessness of hero and son and writer denies neither the af-
fection nor the mystery; Drabble knows, Bennett knows, Edwin
knows, that you can't prove that a Wesleyan Methodist is not a
believer by exposing hypocrisies no matter how deeply ingrained;
nor can you thereby cut off all love or loyalty you may feel for
such a person.

These may not be the highest of novelistic truths just as Bennett himself may not be among the greatest of writers. No matter. What Drabble wants to do, what she succeeds admirably in
doing, is to tell the story of the life so that it re-creates the sources
and circumstances of the major novels, and so that, in turn, the
novels can do the same for the life; and she does this by implicitly
insisting that we ask ourselves all over again the terms by which
we value writers we may value more highly than Bennett. The
major explicit comparison she asks us to draw is with Virginia
Woolf, for obvious reasons. It was Woolf who put Bennett down

in her famous speech about Mrs. Brown, and when he is put down to this day it is usually in Woolf's terms; it was Woolf who represented, or at least seems to represent, a standard of social awareness and sensitivity whereby Bennett could be judged as a provincial stammerer; it is her novels whose air of the importance of private intensity seems designed to make Bennett's seem external and thingy; it is Woolf about whom Drabble herself wrote movingly a few years ago, as a sign that she had finally come to see the virtues of a writer whose social class and novelistic manner had hitherto seemed to her remote and overrated.

The second half of *Arnold Bennett*, as I have said, is replete with details of Bennett's life and works that Drabble herself cannot pretend to care much about, and her defense of the later novels, with the exception of the finely done *Riceyman's Steps*, is ritualistic and tepid. So the comparison of Bennett and Woolf, when it comes, is especially welcome as a means of regaining a focus that has been only fitfully maintained:

> Which of them was worldly, which unworldly, Bennett with his yacht and his well-cut suit, Virginia with her snobbery and her migraines? Did she suspect the physical tension that had made Bennett suffer for most of his life, and did she in any way connect it with her own physical manifestations of neurosis? Both of them were highly strung, but his was the sensitivity of a deprived working-class child, not of an upper-class aesthete. Both were melancholic. How could Virginia Woolf have seen him as "coarse . . . glutted with success . . . a shopkeeper's view of literature . . . yet with the rudiments of sensibility. . . ." How could one ascribe to a man who had been rendered *inarticulate* by sensibility merely the rudiments of it? His stammer embodied, physically and unmistakably, his response to life, but she was incapable, through class, of seeing it as anything other than an impediment to his rather dull discourse.

Then, turning to a comparison of their works:

> She accuses him of being interested only in the externals of daily life: in fact he writes magnificently of the little movement of the spirit in its daily routine, just as she does, of the soul within a drab housemaid's exterior. He accuses her

of failing to invent character, but her characters—Mrs. Dalloway, Mrs. Ramsay, Eleanor Pargiter—are as distinctive and enduring as his own. They both wrote of the inner dramas of ordinary events—a holiday, a marriage, a child's sufferings in an adult world; they were both adept at social comedy. But there was something in her, some really fundamental recoil from groceries and shops, that blinded her appreciation of both his subject matter and of his meaning. Her recoil was an involuntary movement of class. She did not like the *nouveau riche*. The sensitivity manifested in a stammer, in insomnia, in gastric disorders, was something she could not translate into her own terms.

Finely said, finally said. Drabble is of course on Bennett's side, but she knows what the other side is about even as she stresses its limits.

As I hope the quotations show, Drabble's great virtue is her way of making Bennett a novelist, a man most alive in his fictions, without using biography simply as a coatrack for criticism, so that her plea for a kind of fiction is also her plea for a kind of human being. Bennett could be extremely artful, but he had no art, and only the most simple kind of professional guile; in addition, after he had found his métier in a few novels, he could not sustain it because the life of the Five Towns did not continue to interest him, even as memory. He was cut off from his past and never tried, as Aldous Huxley did, to break the mold of his life after it had once been formed, and he could not, as Trollope did, go on writing one big novel after another because of the terms his life established. So be.

A further comparison between Bennett and Huxley, along the lines Drabble offers for one between Bennett and Woolf, is not without merit. The great virtue of Huxley, as I see it, is that, born with all the advantages, suffering therefrom, he sought to alter the terms of his life, to make himself not only a better person but a somewhat different one, and in doing this he did not so much repudiate his Huxley-Arnold-Oxford past as severely place its limits and continue to use its rationality as a check against folly. Throughout his life he was a professional writer, and during his last thirty years a sufficiently successful one that he could live more or less as he pleased. But he has no masterpiece, no work or group of works one can turn to and say, "There." His early novels, although immensely clever and witty, are not only a little thin and dated, but really mean-spirited, sometimes in ways Huxley recognized, sometimes in ways he did not. The essays are terribly good as occasional pieces, and one can read most of the *Collected Essays* with pleasure, but, unless I'm mistaken, there's not a one that can be said to be truly decisive. I've not read more than half the total corpus, but I would expect to find even his most offhand things to be of some interest and even his most seriously thought-out works to be distressingly inarticulate in final effect. So too it is, and perhaps for that very reason, with Sybille Bedford's biography; the book is so long because Huxley's was an interesting life; but the life finally seemed not to have shape, and so Bedford let the book spin out, intelligent, well-written, but never quite in focus.

Bennett, on the other hand, with all the disadvantages and suffering therefrom, the man from the north who successfully became a London hack and man of the theatre, might have been only that, exploiting his intelligence in thin, impersonal, lucrative ways, had he not somehow continued to see himself as someone who was fascinated with the world he had left. Drabble rightly sees *Anna of the Five Towns* of 1902, five years after his first novel and thirteen after he had gone to London, as crucial; it isn't very good, but it was his first novel about home, and the remarks of his London friends convinced Bennett they could not see the passion he knew he had created in the little dramas of the Tellwright family. He was of the Midlands still, able to use all the distance London had given him to see how to celebrate that fact; the result was *The Old Wives' Tale* and the *Clayhanger* books, and one can point to them and say, "There." One reason is that there is not a breath of mean-spiritedness in them; the life of the Five Towns, of Constance Povey, Edwin Clayhanger, and Hilda Lessways is too confined and Bennett too repressed for them to rank with the greatest novels, but they are irreplaceable, wonderfully rereadable books. Margaret Drabble therefore could come from the north two generations later, go to Cambridge, become a fine novelist, and use the distance that gave her to pay her homage to her forebear. *Arnold Bennett*, thus, has a centrality of purpose, an illumination of conviction and intent, that makes it a finer book than *Aldous Huxley*.

A final note. At this writing, in this country almost any book by Huxley one might want is still in print, and not one of Bennett's better or best books is. Since most reprinting is tied to the college and university market, one presumes that not even *The Old Wives' Tale* is being taught. A shame; one could make a long list of much worse books that haven't suffered thus. One feels inclined, in such circumstances, to congratulate Harper & Row for doing so well by Huxley.

KURT VONNEGUT, JR.

Kurt Vonnegut is one of the most popular novelists in America, and his popularity seems to be increasing. His latest, *Slapstick, or Lonesome No More!* [1976] has a first printing of 150,000 for the hardcover edition and that may be close to a record. Unlike most extremely popular novelists, furthermore, Vonnegut attracts a following that includes serious people who take fiction seriously. Yet there has always been resistance to his popularity and, since one Vonnegut novel is very much like another, the resistance also is likely to increase. As one who resists, I must try to say why I find *Slapstick* flashy, clever, and empty; I must also try to explain the popularity.

Slapstick opens with a typical Vonnegut cynicism about America having become a place of interchangeable parts, so that Indianapolis, which "once had a way of speaking all its own," now is "just another someplace where automobiles live." I can't speak about Indianapolis, but one thing I resist in Vonnegut's books is that they seem formulaic, made of interchangeable parts, though this is one quality which may endear him to others. Once Vonnegut finds what he takes to be a successful character, motif, or phrase he can't bear to give it up, and so he carries it around from novel to novel. Thus Eliot Rosewater, Kilgore Trout, and Vonnegut's fellow Hoosier humorist Kim Hubbard, having done a stint in *God Bless You, Mr. Rosewater*, all unblushingly reappear to fill a few pages of *Slaughterhouse-Five*, and Trout then takes over *Breakfast of Champions*. *Slapstick* picks up a clever lawyer from *God Bless You, Mr. Rosewater*. Vonnegut had so much fun sprinkling "So it goes" all over *Slaughterhouse-Five* and "And so on" throughout *Breakfast of Champions* that he couldn't bear to leave *Slapstick* innocent of such confetti. Well, as Eliot Rosewater once said in an idle moment, "Hippety Hop." But Vonnegut, older now, and more wan, contracts that to "Hi ho" for *Slapstick* and leaves very few pages uncluttered by the phrase. Of course, such standard Vonnegut equipment as the notion that there are many people who would be better off dead appears in every novel, though in *Slapstick* there is a new wrinkle; being dead isn't much good either, indeed resembles nothing so much as being on a turkey farm. Leaving Indianapolis at the opening of *Slapstick*, Vonnegut tells his brother that writing is painfully difficult for him, and always has been. It can't possibly be the writing itself that's hard—nothing could be easier, surely.

The story in *Slapstick* is part *Cat's Cradle*, part *God Bless You, Mr. Rosewater*, part Kilgore Trout, part Thomas Pynchon, all about an inexpressibly ugly and apparently idiotic brother and sister, Wilbur and Eliza Swain, born to hugely wealthy parents who confine their dreaded children to an estate in Vermont. The kids discover that they form a genius when together, capable of the only ideas that the Chinese, who are taking over the intelligence of the world, find America worth ransacking for. As adolescents the children try to make their intelligence known to their parents who, horrified, separate them, at which point they become ordinary Vonnegut dullards. They also discover they are passionately in love with each other, but feel sinful together in bed and so agree to separate.

All this is told by Wilbur, many years later, from a room in the abandoned Empire State Building on an almost abandoned Manhattan Island. Vonnegut wants it this way because in *Slapstick*, he says, he is "experimenting with being old," though that never concerns him more than the occasional remark that "the years flew by." It seems the Chinese have been raising and lowering the density of gravity, also producing something called The Green Death, and so America gets reduced to rubble. About this time, Wilbur, who alleges he has spent years as a pediatrician, is elected President of the United States—there is also a King of Michigan and a Duke of Oklahoma, and I bet we haven't seen the last of them. The sister, meanwhile, tries the new condominiums in Peru for the wealthy non-Chinese, is buried in an avalanche on Mars, and finally speaks to her brother from the turkey farm.

What is there to say about all this? There's this: Eliot Rosewater drinks a lot; Billy Pilgrim is drugged by his endless time traveling; Wilbur Swain spends his mature years on a drug called tribenzo Deportamil; Vonnegut likes to tell us in his autobiographical beginnings that he drinks a lot. There's this: Vonnegut is now getting almost as rich as the Rosewaters and the Swains. There's this: all his novels flit about in time as pointlessly and arbitrarily as Billy Pilgrim does. Then there is this, Vonnegut's description of how novels are written on Tralfamadore (in *Slapstick* the Chinese take over the role filled by the residents of this imaginary planet in other novels): "There isn't any particular relationship between all the messages except that the author has chosen them carefully, so that, when seen all at once, they produce an image of life that is beautiful and surprising and deep. There is no beginning, no middle, no end, no suspense, no moral, no causes, no effects." Vonnegut imagines himself a Tralfamadorian novelist; if his books have no beginnings, middles, or ends, no suspense, no moral, no causes or effects, they thereby will produce an image of life that is beautiful, surprising, and deep.

Vonnegut is the best selling of the imperial novelists who, at a whim or in a frenzy, commandeer the world of their fictions so completely that nothing except their own voices can be heard. His appeal, so far as I can see, is to the slightly laid back, rather dropped out, minimally intelligent young. He bears about the same relation to the great imperialist, Pynchon, as Mrs. Henry Wood bears to Dickens. Where Pynchon's mania leads him into huge soaring flights of paranoic fantasy he calls the history of our century, Vonnegut's easy, sentimental cynicism leads him into endless parading of the dumb notion that life isn't much good in America because we're all stupid, unloving, or both. It takes stamina, determination, and crazy intelligence to read Pynchon's two enormous novels; it takes nothing more than a few idle hours to turn the pages of *Slapstick* or any of the others. Pynchon is responsible to the integrity of his terrible paranoia; Vonnegut is responsible to nothing except the ease of his cynicism. Here is a perfectly typical self-enclosed Vonnegut moment:

> Not only did Vera have to put up with shells and bullets whistling over the kitchen tent. She had to defend herself against her husband, too, who was drunk. He beat her up in the midst of battle.
>
> He blacked both her eyes and broke her jaw. He threw her out through the tent flaps. She landed on her back in the mud. Then he came out to explain how she could avoid similar beatings in the future.
>
> He came out just in time to be skewered by the lance of an enemy cavalryman.
>
> "And what's the moral of that story, do you think?" I asked her.
>
> She lay a calloused palm on my knee. "Wilbur—don't ever get married," she replied.

Since this comes late in *Slapstick* we already know these are toy bullets, shells, tents, people, and jaws. Thus, when it all is rolled up into the efficient window shade of the closing conversation and disappears, we can hardly be surprised at its pithy pointlessness. Although everything is repeated in Vonnegut's novels, he sticks with nothing long enough to imagine it, give it breathing space and air.

"Hi ho," thus, is not just a bored grunt that disclaims all responsibility for having to look at something; it is a gesture of contempt for all writers who are willing to be responsible for their creations; for all readers who long to read real books; for anyone whose idea of America is more complicated than Vonnegut's country of interchangeable parts full of poor people with uninteresting lives.

Which makes him an ideal writer for the semi-literate young who are slightly too hip for *Jonathan Livingston Seagull* or *The*

Little Prince, because he offers the great assurance that there is nothing worth caring about. While still a genius, Wilbur-Eliza wrote a book on child care called *So You Went and Had a Baby* and, Vonnegut adds, it become the third most popular book ever written, after *The Bible* and *The Joy of Cooking.* That's it, snap it off, never ask what could have been in the book because that might not be easy to say. Books should never pose hard questions.

If my sense of Vonnegut is at all accurate, how can one explain the serious attention he has been given? My hunch is that the mistake is a generic one; people like him because they enjoy the *kind* of novel he writes. When *God Bless You, Mr. Rosewater* was published a little more than ten years ago, the imperial novel was just beginning: *Crazy in Berlin, V., Catch-22,* Vonnegut's own *Cat's Cradle.* It may have seemed then that Vonnegut was as good, or might become as good as any of the others, but where Thomas Berger went on to finish his interesting trilogy, where Pynchon and Joseph Heller took seven and twelve years trying to get *Gravity's Rainbow* and *Something Happened* right, Vonnegut just became formulaic. I would be very much surprised if Tony Tanner or Robert Scholes or others who once expressed fondness for Vonnegut admire him as much now as they used to. Books that are self-confessed verbal constructions simply need more earnest and witty inventing than Vonnegut has shown himself capable of.

I think I would be less bothered by Vonnegut were it not that one of my major tasks is to try to pose hard questions for the semi-literate young, and thereby to convince them that semi-literacy is a phase all literate people pass through. It is not easy to become literate, but it really takes no more than energy and the curiosity that allows for persistent bafflement. Then along comes a writer like Vonnegut, who makes semi-literacy seem not only irremediable but a perfectly comfortable state, careless, indifferent, easy. So rather than tell him he has missed the boat, let me give him a tip: make "I missed the boat" the motto of the next book.

It works like this. The semi-literate is being told something, asked something, a serious something, that may force a change of heart or mind. The youth doesn't "get" it, and may not even "get" why the saying or asking is being done at all. The trick at this point is not to say "I don't get that" or "Run that by again," but "I missed the boat." This turns the asker of serious questions into a capricious maker of boats and schedules who is very fond of saying the boat has just left. Since disappointment and resentment are inevitable on anyone's road to literacy, it seems to me quite wrong to put the blame on the semi-literate young who almost certainly lack the sophistication to see how cynical and destructive is the phrase "I missed the boat." But Kurt Vonnegut has plenty of sophistication, and so should be able to make wonderful use of the awful phrase. Blame him, too, for doing his bit to convince people that learning, and life, are only a matter of catching or missing boats because the game is rigged, and life is uninteresting anyway.

THE GOLDEN AGE
OF THE AMERICAN NOVEL

The novel is alive, of course, was never even close to dead, and seems now to be enjoying something very much like a golden age, a period that people in fifty or a hundred years can look back on as we now do in Victorian fiction, or English Renaissance drama. Since I cannot possibly prove this, however, I can only try to say what I think such later evaluators might find in our fiction to praise or even to envy. In doing so I am not going to try to quarrel with detractors of our fiction, or even to arrive at some kind of balanced assessment of the achievement. Rather, I want to try to locate two modes in current fiction, both relatively new, and also related to each other in ways I don't think anyone has tried to describe. I call these modes "imperial" and "realistic" for the sake of contrast, but since the perpetual tendency of the novel is never to stray very far or for very long from realism, later critics may see more exactly than I can how all the novels of the period have been realistic, as we now can with Dickens, or *Moby-Dick*, or *Huckleberry Finn*. What I'd like to suggest is that the great vitality of the novel at present does not lie simply in those novels which are distinctly different from earlier novels, but in its way of being "realistic" as well, so that the plainest and most straightforward realistic fiction of the last fifteen years or so can be seen as being both distinctly different from earlier realism and allied to the more obviously unrealistic imperial fiction.

The whole idea that the novel is dead or dying was born and had its life in the period when it was also presumed that the novel could not survive as a realistic form. That is, in the years between about 1920 and 1950, people applauded or condemned the fact that fiction no longer seemed realistic or life-like but was, instead, experimental, a self-conscious medium concerned in narrow ways with its form, its language, or with an idea of life that was itself self-conscious, verbally reflexive, and essentially static. If the novel was to be such an experimental medium, then many people felt it was doomed. Since the novel has gone on to new life, we might ask why these two ideas—that the novel was dying, that its future was experimental—occurred simultaneously. The key figure here, then and now, is Joyce. Between *The Portrait* and the final version of *Ulysses* Joyce seems to have convinced some, including perhaps himself, that he had moved the novel irretrievably beyond the nineteenth century by committing it to a self-conscious experimentation with form. Ford's *The Good Soldier* and some of the novels of Virginia Woolf may have done their bit to help foster this impression that concluded from the fact that the novel was no longer like nineteenth-century fiction; it was therefore doomed to self-conscious experimenting that would take it farther and farther from its bearings as a realistic or mimetic medium.

In fact the novel has undergone many changes between 1920 and 1975, but not, I feel reasonably confident, because of Joyce, *The Good Soldier,* Virginia Woolf, Lawrence Durrell, Samuel Beckett, Vladimir Nabokov, John Hawkes, or William Gass. These writers have done amazing things, but they seem to me feats of skill, unrepeatable virtuosi exercises, analogous perhaps to the plays of Congreve, or the symphonies of Bruckner, or the Petrarchan sonnets of Sidney. In most of these cases there is a marvelous absorption in technical problems, in the demands and limitations of the medium itself, but what might have seemed like fresh starts has turned out to be close to the opposite. New paths have been broken and explored all the time, but not by people who began by trying to break new paths, to master a medium. The great novelist of the "experimental" period is Faulkner, and the great Faulkner, I am convinced, is the writer who could barely sustain an entire novel but who, in comic bursts of ten to fifty or sixty pages created and peopled an unforgettable American South. But even Faulkner did not lead to anything more than imitation Faulkner, the sentimental South of much of the work of Robert Penn Warren, Andrew Lytle, Madison Jones, Reynolds Price, and others.

If there is one clear and remarkable fact about more recent American fiction it is that there is no one dominating figure, no Joyce, no Faulkner or Hemingway. In the early 1960s a group of books appeared: *Catch-22*, *Crazy in Berlin*, *V.*, all first novels, followed by *An American Dream*, *Why Are We in Vietnam?*, *Armies of the Night*, *Herzog*, *Mr. Sammler's Planet*, and *Humboldt's Gift*, *Portnoy's Complaint*, *The Great American Novel*, *The Breast*; Alan Lelchuk's *American Mischief*, Thomas Rogers's *Confessions of a Child of the Century*, Alan Friedman's *Hermaphrodeity*, E. L. Doctorow's *Ragtime*. I hope I have named enough to indicate that what these novels share isn't anything that detracts from the originality of any one. I call them "imperial" because their demeanor is individual and commanding: "I call the shots here," says the imperial novelist in every sentence, "and I will not conceal for a minute who I am, though I have no intention of telling you anything more than I choose to." The book can leap time, place, and circumstance in a single bound, as in Pynchon, or Kurt Vonnegut, Jr.; it can proclaim personal agony to be a national problem, as in Bellow, Roth, and Mailer; it can transform a few jokes into a vision of the whole world, as in Heller. Underlying it all is a huge assertion of personal power, which leads to aggressive showmanship, plots used as feats of narrative skill, marvelous flights of fancy—in other words, style used as a badge of personal authority, and personal authority having the ability to invent and master whole worlds. One sees some of this in Faulkner, of course, and in a couple of books at least, of the fifties, like *Invisible Man* and *The Adventures of Augie March*, but one needs no strict definition of imperial fiction to be

able to distinguish it from the cooler fifties, the fiction of Salinger, Vidal, Willingham, Bowles, Buechner, Capote, Morris, as
they were in those years.

My aim in using the word "imperial," of course, is to suggest
an analogy between these writers and their period, and to say
that while most of these writers detest the American empire,
they were in fact also expressing it, and deriving some of their
enormous energy from it. The phenomenon is American because
this country has the empire, and with few exceptions this kind of
writer is not to be found in countries that have no empire—one
might call Dickens an imperial novelist, but not Iris Murdoch or
Kingsley Amis. These writers share with the empire a ruthlessness in their imaginative assertions, and a tendency to sweep
aside or to subsume such external objects as other human beings.
Patient realistic writers tend to dislike the imperialists; one could
not expect to find Morris, or Buechner, or James Welch, or
Thomas Savage, among the fervent admirers of Pynchon or
Mailer. The lions and the lambs do not here lie down together.
To illustrate why, let me quote a passage from the stunning opening of Pynchon's *Gravity's Rainbow*, the sort of thing that seems
to me imperialism at its best:

> Now there grows among all the rooms, replacing the night's
> old smoke, alcohol, and sweat, the fragile musaceous odor
> of Breakfast; flowery, permeating, surprising, more than the
> color of winter sunlight, taking over not so much through
> any brute pungency or volume as by the high intricacy of
> the weaving of its molecules, sharing the conjuror's secret
> by which—though it is not often Death is told so clearly to
> fuck off—the living genetic chains prove even labyrinthine
> enough to preserve some human face down ten or twenty
> generations . . . so the same assertion-through-structure
> allows this warm morning's banana fragrance to meander,
> repossess, prevail. Is there any reason not to open every
> window, and let the kind scent blanket all Chelsea? As a
> spell, against falling objects . . .
>   With a clattering of chairs, upended shell cases,
> benches, and ottomans, Pirate's mob gather at the shores of
> the great refectory table . . . crowded now over the swirl-
> ing dark grain of its walnut uplands with banana omelets,

banana sandwiches, banana casseroles, massed banana
molded in the shape of a British lion rampant, blended with
eggs into batter for French toast, squeezed out a pastry noz-
zle across the quivering reaches of a banana blancmange to
spell out the words *C'est magnifique, mais ce n'est pas la
guerre* (attributed to a French observer during the Charge
of the Light Brigade) which Pirate has appropriated as his
motto . . . tall cruets of pale banana syrup to pour over
oozing banana waffles, a giant glazed crock where diced
bananas have been fermenting since the summer with wild
honey and muscat raisins, up out of which, this winter
morning, one now dips foam mugsfull of banana mead . . .
banana croissants and banana kreplach, and banana oatmeal
and banana jam and banana bread, and bananas flamed in
ancient brandy Pirate brought back last year from a cellar in
the Pyrenees also containing a clandestine radio transmit-
ter . . .

As a certain kind of writing I doubt if this can be bettered. It is so
assured, so replete, so eager and able to follow its own path as far
as it can go, so strong and piquant at once, that one might claim
that such writing is, if not justification for the American empire,
at least the beginning of an apology for it.

Pynchon insistently creates his own reality, rearranging the
objects and people to suit himself; if we say he uses the material
of the real world to make his extravagant fiction, we are saying
little more than that his language is American English. But he is
not, on the other hand, an experimenter in the old-fashioned
Joycean sense; he has no theory to guide him, not of language or
of the novel as a form, or of life as history, to keep him away from
the real world on principle. He has structures and plots based on
his ideas of rockets, entropy, bondings, and paranoia, but he really runs on energy: these passages start out, go where they will
go, stop when they are tired. Thus he can be tasteless, vulgar,
boring, indulgent, and inhumane because he runs out of fuel and,
like most imperialists, is not very intelligently self-reflective. In
the imperial novel there is usually a putative form, so we know
rather what the end is going to be like, but the real form is the
thrusts of the energy through long and often magnificent flights
and swoops: Mailer walking around the Washington Monument

in *Armies of the Night*, or describing guns in *Why Are We in Vietnam?*; Sammler on New York seen as though viewing another planet, or the moon; Charlie Citrine contemplating what his brother Julius does out there in Texas; Heller on Major Major Major Major, so silly and so funny; Portnoy's first meeting with The Monkey, Roth's laugh-a-minute description of his baseball team in *The Great American Novel*; Pynchon at the Christmas vesper service in Kent, meditating on toothpaste tubes and death. Often in these passages, as with the bananas above, the essential grammar is nothing more than a list, the propelling gimmick a simple joke, because it is not the material but the novelist's delighted exploiting of it that gives these passages their splendor.

When one runs on energy, swagger, and inspiration, what happens when they begin to run down? Sometimes what happens is just another willful whipping of the tired imagination, to be sure. Sometimes, too, since these writers are all men occupying something close to one-person worlds, there will be a search for a victim one can then blame for the running down of energy, the bondage that prevents further flying. But surprisingly there often can be something else, a touching down, and into something quieter, softer, more elegiac, often done with something like realistic writing, certainly something that is not at all an advertisement for oneself or one's empire. I'm thinking of much of the Valetta section in *V.*, the closing scenes of *Herzog*, back in New England and Ludeyville, Yossarian's last conversation with Nately's Whore in *Catch-22*, Portnoy's reminiscence about the Sunday morning softball games of the Jewish men that he watched as a boy. In all these there is, for a moment or a cluster of moments, some kind of acknowledgment of something that the imperial touch cannot quite master, create, or control.

Here, for instance, is a moment from near the end of *Gravity's Rainbow*. Slothrop has been wandering in the Russian sector of Germany after V-E Day, 1945; he is not quite all there, and he is being chased as a deserter by perhaps two armies or their agents. He comes to a village celebrating a festival and he is feted, dressed up in a pig costume, which gives him at least a momentary disguise. Pynchon describes the day with loving care, and at the end Slothrop is lying next to a young girl who, he knows, wants to run away with him:

Both of them on the run. That's what she wants. But
Slothrop only wants to be still with her heartbeat a while
. . . isn't that every paranoid's wish? to perfect methods of
immobility? But they're coming, house to house, looking for
their deserter, and it's Slothrop who has to go, she who has
to stay. In the streets loudspeakers, buzzing metal throats,
are proclaiming the early curfew tonight. Through some
window of the town, is a kid for whom the metal voice with
its foreign accent is a sign of nightly security, to be part of
the wild fields, the rain on the sea, dogs, smells of cooking
from strange windows, dirt roads . . . part of this unrecov-
erable summer.

Like most realistic writing, this demands a larger context than
I've been able to give it. We have been with Pynchon for so long
during this summer, followed him through so many pages of the
bizarre and the unlikely, seen him so insistently challenge the
limits of possibility by his painstaking penchant for accuracy of
detail, that when he touches down here, and reduces his perspective to Slothrop, the girl, and the kid who will remember
1945 as the year of the loudspeakers and the foreign accents, one
feels the writing is not fanciful but precise, the key word being
the redundant one at the end—it has indeed been an unrecover-
able summer. At such moments the energy is yielded up, not as a
sign of mastery but as a mark of limitation, and it can then return, as in realistic fiction, with no need to apologize, to a sense
that our home is the world after all. Indeed, part of the appeal of
the imperial novelists at their best is that their brutality can carry
with it raggedness and tornness, and a moving acknowledgment
of vulnerability and necessary incompleteness.

Most of the books I have mentioned thus far were written
five or more years ago, and it does seem true that the imperial
impulse as it was felt in the sixties may not long survive the Vietnam aftermath. Two facts are notable here: the great and obvious
flaw of imperial fiction is its piggishness, its nigh scandalous treatment of women, and a good deal of the continuing American
energy in this decade has come from women who have, in the
case of Erica Jong, produced imperial fiction no more interesting
than that of Vonnegut or Kesey, and who have, in the case of

Anne Tyler, let imperial modes mar otherwise good realistic fiction, and who have, more generally, not written novels as good as
the major imperialists. Given the excitement and freedom generated by the women's movement, one cannot imagine this state
of affairs to last for very much longer, though when new important women writers appear, they almost certainly will not resemble Pynchon, Mailer, Roth, or Bellow.

There is reason to believe, however, that writers of both
sexes in the next decade or so will derive more from imperialist
fiction than they perhaps will want to realize or than is easily rec-
ognizable. This is very much the case with realistic fiction generally in the last five years. In general, the realistic writer tends to
think there is something gratuitous, even childish, about the imperialists, but that fact need not deter us from seeing, first, that
imperialist fiction and realistic fiction in the last fifteen years have
made a conscious reaction against the fiction of a generation ago,
and, second, that the imperialists have, willy nilly, taught the
more realistic writers a good deal. I don't see much of this in the
work of some older writers, like Morris and Buechner and the
old-young Updike, who have tended to go their own way—and in
the case of Morris and Buechner, at least, it has been a very good
way indeed. But it is evident in many excellent realistic novels of
the seventies: Robert Stone's *Dog Soldiers*, James Welch's
Winter in the Blood, Theodore Weesner's *The Car Thief*, Toni
Morison's *Sula*, Larry Woiwode's *Beyond the Bedroom Wall*,
Richard Price's *The Wanderers*, Maureen Howard's *Before My
Time*, James Alan McPherson's *Hue and Cry*, Thomas Savage's *A
Strange God*. Most of these writers are under forty, good, not imperialistic, yet employers of a power similar to what I've been
calling imperialist. In a realistic writer power is usually felt as the
confidence that this tale of these people matters, and of course
one finds that here. But there is more to it than that.

Let me look at a passage from Weesner's *The Car Thief* to
show one kind of instance of what I mean. It comes early in the
novel; Alex Housman, sixteen, has recently stolen his fourteenth
car; he spends the earliest pages of the book driving aimlessly
around, going to school but leaving quickly, going home and falling asleep on the couch. The phone rings; a girl he has picked up

and given a coat he found in one of the stolen cars tells him she was forced to tell her father where she got the coat, and the father has called the police:

> Stepping over to feel the wall for the light switch, he discovered that his hand was weak. The flourescent lights came faltering on. He squinted. By the wall clock it was nine or ten minutes after ten. The day was refusing to die. He stood still a moment, not knowing what to do. He remembered the call again as if he had already forgotten. They had found the coat. He was thinking she should have said they had found her wearing the coat, and he was thinking he should have thanked her for calling—he had not—and he should have apologized for the other day. A yawn took him then and made his eyes water with exhaustion. He exhaled to nearly collapsing, envisoned the blue-uniformed police, and felt far too tired to fight, or to run, or to think, felt no more than a thought away from anything.

The style of realistic fiction, since it seldom calls attention to itself, is often hard to identify at all. But when one makes actual comparisons, one sees how distinctive Weesner's writing is, because of the pressure it places on its own details. Here is an apparently climactic moment, but Weesner acts as though it weren't, or as though if it is a climax it must not therefore be rendered differently from any other moment. "They had found the coat"; a realization, surely, but of what? "He had been thinking," Weesner goes on, as though the realization that they had found the coat can both direct and not quite interrupt Alex's train of thought about what she should have said, or what he should have said to her. "A yawn took him then, and made his eyes water with exhaustion." A remarkable yawn, that, not at all to be confused with a sigh of relief—at last the cops are coming and we'll get it over with—not that at all; the thought of the cops "felt no more than a thought away from anything." Something has indeed ended, but Weesner keeps insisting on what for him is most important: how much hard work it is for Alex to live his life, how far away he has placed everything—the girl, the car, the coat—so that even as they press upon him he does not quite know where they are in relation to him.

Weesner can put his pressure on his words because he does not do what almost any other writer would do. He never simply adopts Alex's point of view, because to do that would be to soften, to excuse, and he never sees Alex only as the main figure in his world, because to do that would render him susceptible to explanations sociological or psychosexual. Weesner's prose is the writing of short stories where the pressurized writing says something is about to happen, the prose of Grace Paley, for instance, about extraordinary changes at the last minute. Of course what is about to happen is only the next sentence, in this case the next minute in Alex Housman's life. But to keep that up for hundreds of pages is a daring thing to try to do; it is something like the realistic equivalent of the imperialist effort to make a whole country out of a single sensibility. He solders his sentences together as closely as he can, thereby to keep the pressure intense: "It was nine or ten minutes after ten. The day was refusing to die. He stood still a moment, not knowing what to do." The wonder of Weesner is that he can do that, he can keep insisting that trying to say that something is about to happen is all he can or needs to say to give this life whatever shape it can be given. There are, during the course of the novel, some fairly relaxed places, but for forty-, fifty-, sixty-page stretches Weesner presses, presses, presses, so that any understanding of Alex that he gains as the story unfolds does not release him from the next minute or from acknowledging its importance.

Thus, while there is no surface resemblance between *The Car Thief* and the imperialistic fiction, there is an underlying daring—confidence is what we'd call it with an imperialist, faith is the word with Weesner—that he shares with his contemporaries. I know of no influences of other writers working on Weesner, and I assume his similarity to the imperial novelists is only a shared historical pressure leading to a similar abundance of energy and a willingness to risk. Read for a few pages only, *The Car Thief* will seem as though it wants to be a transparent eyeball, but when Weesner keeps the pressure on for whole sections of his novel one sees that it is as much a written book as *Mr. Sammler's Planet*. Other realistic fiction has asserted its power in a quite different way, in a way perhaps more obviously analogous to that of imperialist fiction. One notices in most contemporary realism gaps between sentences such that sentences Weesner would write get left out, and such that the reader is made to leap from one bit or fragment to the next as the writer asserts: this sensibility, my own or my narrator's, is strong enough to make leaps, to need little in the way of ground transportation. It is not a voice asserting, "Watch me," like an imperialist, and the leaps are something we do as readers, not something we watch the author do as a thing of beauty or athletic feat. To get over the gaps, to keep jumping, to keep wondering where one now is, is to be aware of a writer asserting a kind of strength that, especially in its cumulative effects, is very strong indeed.

There is a moment in Judith Chernaik's *Double Fault* that might help us illuminate the point while at the same time indicate the difficulty of so doing. Chernaik's heroine, a novelist, is speaking to a group about the problems of writing novels these days:

> I propose that a serious writer today is going to find himself inevitably tempted to play with the conventional narrative mold, to break it, finally to abandon it; specifically, to abandon the past tense for the present, chapters for short paragraphs, or none, or few; the narrator's point of view for no point of view, a write-your-own point of view. But this temporary difficulty, this impulse to break up form, order, meaning, is not a matter of free choice. The writer is in the grip of larger historical and linguistic forces, angels as it were who direct and inhibit consciousness, who seize the writer's pen in midair, as he is about to write: Toward the end of the month of October, 1829 . . . and compel him to write instead: Who am I? What right have I to compel you to listen to me?

That was written in 1975, but it reads a bit as though it might have been written any time shortly after the end of the month of October, 1829, or at least any time after Henry James. Since *Double Fault* is about a novelist writing a novel, indeed the novel we are presently reading, one quickly compares it to *The Counterfeiters*, but the moment we do, we can see that what it has meant to abandon conventional narrative mold, or past tense for the present, or chapters for short paragraphs, has constantly been

changing during this century, so that the novel Chernaik ends up
writing is light years removed from Gide's cunning controlled
meditation on the relations of life to art to being a creator of art.
For her, like so many contemporary realistic writers, breaking up
the conventional mold is not to abandon realism, not to develop
an experimental theory that will match up Our Time with a brand
new art form. It is to be assertive, to force the reader into the
narrative and thus into the imagined lives. In Chernaik, or in
Maureen Howard, or Larry Woiwode, it is to make leaps; in
Winter in the Blood and *Dog Soldiers* it is to watch character and
plot insistently refuse to take shape; in *A Strange God* it is to
create a destiny and then to imagine a life fully enough to fulfill
it. The methods and tones of course vary, but the underlying insistence is always there, unstated, pulling us in.

Maureen Howard's way is to create a kind of magnetic field,
and then to see what will get pulled into it. Start with Laura
Quinn, wanting to talk to Jim, her nephew, who has come up to
her comfortable affluent Boston home from his "Siberia of weed
and concrete" in the Bronx. She wants to talk to him:

> It came to me as we sat in the driveway on the brink of a
> lovely June evening, that he didn't intend to listen to any of
> it. Not to be heard is death. Not to be loved, not to have
> the feel of a man with you, not to have children or a home
> or a purpose for your days is tragic, but not to be heard is
> final and it is death. See how I punish myself with rhetoric
> and it will no longer serve . . . But I know that I've always
> asked too little of myself, been content with contrived ideas
> turned into delicate tales and though it takes me where I
> don't want to go, to places in my own heart that I hear, I will
> be heard.

Now, if possible, take all that along back down to the Bronx,
where Jim has a twin brother and sister, and the girl, Siobhan,
feels that her early adolescent attractiveness and her mother's
will are separating her from her brother, Cormac, who is oblivious to all that is happening to them:

> One Saturday Fred Monahan, whose pencil holder she
> placed beside her bed each night, called up and asked for

her, asked if she would like to come play baseball over in his street. Siobhan who would normally have jumped at the chance said no she couldn't, that she and her brother had to go out. Monahan said, "See you in church." She was awkward, put the receiver down abruptly, yet would like to have talked on to him. All week she'd noticed Fred Monahan's flesh. He had lots of moles on his arms which she liked, but none on his face. The skin of his face was pure and unblemished, darker than any boy she knew. His mother was Italian though his features were Irish and his eyes were blue. Blue was her favorite color. When she turned round from Fred Monahan's telephone call she said to her mother and Cormac, "It was nothing," and, head in a whirl, went straight to the pantry for a handful of Hydrox cookies though it was only nine in the morning.

Now if one wants an explanation for Siobhan's wolfing of Hydrox cookies one can say simply that she is making herself unattractive so she can continue sexless and remain Cormac's twin thereby. But if one asks why one is reading about Siobhan Cogan at all in a book that starts out to be about Laura Quinn, then leaps off to Laura's brother, then to Jim and Siobhan's mother's past, one is not quite so sure, and the little leaps one makes reading Howard's sentences become symptomatic of the biggest leaps one takes with her narrative. "I will be heard," Laura has said, "not to be heard is death." So too will Siobhan be heard, but in no way comprehensible to herself, her brother, or her mother. She too is asking too little of herself, and is here being content with Hydrox cookies as a substitute for Fred Monahan, and is thereby going places in her own heart that she fears.

I don't mean, in saying this, that Howard works as foolish critics of Shakespeare have been known to allege he does, by stating themes and bringing parts of her book in line with them. I'm suggesting, rather, that what allows Howard to leap about in her narrative is her assurance that the forces at work on one character are like those that work on another, and she needs only the signature of a title, *Before My Time*, to say how this is. This lets her leap, and lets her characters remain distinctly different from each other, and lets her get along with a very loose structure for a book that any reader knows, often without knowing how that knowledge came about, is leaping with clear and present intent, the leaps the mark of Howard's assurance that the looseness gives her freedom without making her incoherent. The prose is as much unlike Theodore Weesner's as it is unlike Pynchon's, but the confidence of the darting and leaping writer is the same. Howard's leaps express the power of a writer who can say: "This is all I can give you, purposeful leaps rather than narrative mold, but it is much after all, even when the book is mostly about people before their time." Life, in such a book, is continually inadequate to the human spirit, but it is adequate indeed to the art of the realistic novelist.

My suspicion is that one reason realistic fiction has never received the attention it deserves is that it is not easy to describe its ways and means, and that the more obviously eccentric, experimental, high-flying fictions often make and keep their lofty critical status because they are easier to describe and appreciate. One is always tempted to say that a realistic novel is just there. Thus the technical feats of *Catch-22*, in which the same stories are told over and over, is something anyone can see even after one reading, and it can be enjoyed, furthermore, after a number of rereadings. If one asked, however, why the grimness of Stone's *Dog Soldiers* is not empty or disgusting or cynical and enervating as ostensibly grim books so often are, one might not easily see, or care to inquire. In fact, I think Stone does it by keeping his characters always at approximately the same distance from each other, starting with Converse talking on a park bench with an evangelical missionary, where one expects to find considerable distance, and continuing onto his conversations with Hicks, his partner in heroin smuggling, and then onto Hicks's partnership in heroin addiction with Converse's wife; the scene moves, the action takes shape, but the characters can never get closer or further away from each other. In the hands of someone like Sartre or Robbe-Grillet this technical fact would be the whole point of the novel and the presumed point about life, whereas in Stone's more powerful and even more civilized hands this technical fact is only the way we come to know and care about his helpless and unlovable people.

If the imperial novel runs down when its energies are exhausted, the realistic novel runs down when a plot unfolds that is too shaping for its sense of life. In some cases, like Welch's *Winter in the Blood*, plot appears only as a slight grace note near the end; in *Before My Time*, plot as such never appears but Howard does begin to play her chords more loudly near the end. But the realistic form usually has to take some kind of shape in order for the lives it describes to become clear for us, and unquestionably many very strong realistic writers, Stone and Weesner included, have found the action of their novels exerting too strong a control for their most powerful effects to be sustained. I tend to think that Philip Roth, after he had written *Letting Go* and *When She Was Good*, and E. L. Doctorow, after he had finished *The Book of Daniel*, despaired of the problem of plot or story and went into imperialistic fiction as a recourse, since in that mode one can offer the most gargantuan and grotesque plots and see them all as part of the show. That is, it is terribly hard work for the realistic writer to conceive lives both boldly and patiently, and plot is always beckoning as a great simplifying temptation. The comic writer has a somewhat easier time of it because most comedy will allow for coincidence and well-engineered turns of storytelling, whereas the more somber writer has usually got to keep plugging, to make these lives take their strange shapes as though they themselves were directing them, and in such cases plot often just gets in the way.

If I now say that *Middlemarch* has a plot that gets in the way of George Eliot's most original realism, that Hardy was cursed by his plots from one end of his novelistic career to the other, I don't really mean to imply that Theodore Weesner and Robert Stone are anything like that good, no more than I mean to say that Bellow and Pynchon are as good as Dickens. It seems to me needless to worry about what is truly and lastingly major when dealing with the work of one's own lifetime; the point is the obvious riches, because it is not so much undoubted masterpieces as abundance of wonders that makes a golden age anyway. One could, if one wished, claim that the long supposed age of giants that preceded the present one has yielded us little more than *The Great Gatsby*, *The Sun Also Rises*, and Faulkner, but that too would be unfair. I have not meant, here, to begin to assess the greatness of Saul Bellow, who I persist in thinking our finest living novelist, and I have not mentioned John Barth, Bernard

Malamud, John Cheever, John Gardner, Stanley Elkin, Evan Connell, Richard Stern, the author of *Confusions*, the author of *Faith and the Good Thing*, plus Lord knows how many others; recently I read a review by an intelligent writer which claimed that John Casey's *An American Romance*, published last spring [1978], is the best American novel of our time. No matter the pertinence or impertinence of the judgment; just remember the riches implied in the possibility of its being made at all.

When I look back over my own relatively brief career as a reviewer of fiction, I can only feel fortunate. In the first review I wrote, in 1961, I was youthfully restless and unsatisfied, though I had to add that there were some quite good books that had recently appeared—*Acrobat Admits, Mrs. Bridge, Golk, The Hours Together* were on a list I made to illustrate some point, as I remember. But in that same review I also had to respond to *Catch-22*, and I at least had wit enough to see that this was something different, something I called "a genuine neanderthal American threat to civilized novel writing." As indeed it was, and *V.* and *Herzog* soon followed. No one need like all these books, or their successors. The power of America, known and hated and dizzying, has made vital almost a generation of fiction, imperialist and realistic, funny, manic, surging with power even when subdued in tone, experimental only in the sense that anyone trying to respond to self and world with full energy must experiment. Some of these books will fade from view, and some will not—so be. It is enough to say that in what has sometimes seemed the worst of times these novels may well be that time's best achievement.

CRITICS

RENÉ WELLEK

In the last fifteen years, René Wellek has become established as the premier historian of modern literary criticism. Before this, though he always spoke mildly and judiciously, Wellek seemed to have an eager eye out for enemies of his favorite ideas: that criticism needs a coherent philosophical base from which to work, that impressionistic criticism and historical relativism are dangerous, and that extrinsic material is usually irrelevant in the understanding of a given work. But since he began work on his massive *A History of Modern Criticism,* the third and fourth volumes of which are now at hand, Wellek has slowly become convinced that he is really unopposed, and so he has ascended to a height from which he is able to view contemporary criticism as though it were ancient scroll work and still receive increased adulation rather than scorn as his reward. He calls Earl Wasserman's books "turgid," he speaks of M. H. Abrams's *The Mirror and the Lamp* as a "booklet," he blandly announces that the aims of Northrop Frye's "Polemical Introduction" to *Anatomy of Criticism* are "doomed to failure." It seems that heresy, even when it speaks the truth, can be received in the scholastic establishment with equanimity—when uttered from very high elevations.

Wellek has achieved this eminence almost exclusively by one method: knowing more than anyone else. Blessed with a prose style no one would describe as better than adequate, equipped with a literary sensibility that strikes few as being superior to their own, possessed of an intelligence that reveals no originality and seldom more than judiciousness, he has simply blown competitors from the field with erudition. He is conversant in at least seven modern languages and commands a staggering knowledge of their respective literatures. In the *History*, he quotes in English, provides the original in the notes, and does almost all his own translating. These notes also contain large bibliographies of their subjects while the text itself ranges over history and literature of the last two centuries without pausing for breath. In the sweeping reviews of modern scholarship now included in *Concepts of Criticism* he handles up to four major authors per page. If anyone can claim to have read everything literary and philosophical written since 1750, Wellek is the man. The *History* was originally announced in four volumes, but four have now appeared and the twentieth century is still untouched; maybe it can be finished in two more. It is a huge mine of a work, ranging almost as widely as anyone could wish yet spending much of its time scrutinizing the major figures. Beside it, Brooks's and Wimsatt's *Short History of Criticism* seems both narrow and narrow-minded, and many more specialized literary histories do not do as well as Wellek in surveying and examining the assumptions of a critic's work. A number of the individual treatments of separate authors are the most sensible these authors have yet received, at least in English. With all this, no one could possibly claim the *History* is a bad book. But it certainly is a very disappointing one. One finishes the fourth volume with the feeling that amidst the great concern to cover and do right by everything, Wellek has not asked the relevant questions about literature and criticism.

There is, first of all, the theoretical inflexibility. Wellek means this to be here, to be sure, but it hurts nonetheless:

> [In England around 1830] the idea of a coherent literary theory disappears almost completely and with it any technique of analyzing literature and any interest in form. The nature of literature is misunderstood.

Readers of the earlier volumes will remember that Wellek takes Dr. Johnson to task for "misunderstanding the nature of literature." We have all been here before: the genius of English literature and criticism is not congenial to a Continental philosopher like Wellek. Wellek thinks the words "coherent" and "consistent" are synonyms, and one need be no Arnoldian to see how much English criticism will be distorted under the weight of *that*. The critics in the generation after 1830 are Carlyle, De Quincey, Hunt, Mill, and Ruskin; only Hunt is well handled while the important ones, Mill and Ruskin, are wrestled into contorted positions and then pronounced inadequate. Mill's early and extravagant "What Is Poetry?", written shortly after the crisis, is laid out elaborately and then refuted. But the really interesting literary fact about Mill is his constant mediation between his Benthamite training and his love of Wordsworth, and this is passed over, presumably because it appears to best advantage in *Dissertations and Discussions*, "non-literary" essays that reveal on every page that Mill did not "misunderstand literature." The instance of Ruskin is worse, for Wellek knows Ruskin is a great writer, yet he is also sure he is "the most obsolete and remote of all the Victorian 'sages.' " Ruskin is a scattered and derivative theorist, something hardly worth showing again at this late date; yet Wellek can comment exasperatedly:

> Much of *Modern Painters* does not concern itself with works of art at all, but for long stretches discusses cloud formations, tree shapes, rock surfaces, etc. quite apart from pictures. . . .

As though that were the end of the matter, as though some of these descriptions were not magnificent and did not contain in them a striking "theory" of vision.* Wellek can say Ruskin has "little use for Dickens" and ignore the wonderful note on *Hard Times* in *Unto This Last*. He can refer to Ruskin's famous assertion that the great scenes of nature are "all done for us, and intended for our perpetual pleasure," as "naïve," as though the passage came not from *Modern Painters* but perhaps from the *The World as Will and Idea*. Again and again Wellek distorts as he finds "positions" for his authors and attempts to hold them in some timeless solution, as he shakes his head at the refusal of the English to know what they were doing.

* See, for instance, some fine paragraphs on this by Hugh Kenner in "The Experience of the Eye," *The Southern Review* (Autumn, 1965).

But the objection must be made more deeply. Wellek is opposed to treating his subjects biographically, and, given the limitations of space and the usual irrelevance of such biographical work, the choice is perhaps wise. But, beyond this, he seems not even to conceive of them as men that were or writers that are. That these critics ever struggled with the world, that the mind may grasp fitfully yet wonderfully, that understanding literature is a precious and difficult occupation, that readers may find these nineteenth-century monsters both exasperating and fascinating—one can look in vain through hundreds of pages without finding more than fitful recognition of these things. Wellek is a large-minded and sympathetic man, yet there is something fundamentally disrespectful about his habit—it amounts almost to an insistence—of never quoting a writer at length and then discussing the quotation, of almost never going through a piece of writing to locate not only its outlines but its motion and sense of motion, its characteristic twists and turns. Wellek, hunting for theoretical assumptions, quotes only words and phrases and sentences, and often these are gathered from different works written years apart. We are told each critic's preferences in literature, we learn what everyone thought of Goethe or Shakespeare, but seldom do we get a description of the constellation of this taste or the pressures and contradictions at work in a given writer that formed the taste. Quite a few are denigrated as impressionistic with only passing worry given to the question of the excellence or tastelessness of these impressions.

Some day, someone is going to talk about Arnold's touchstones not as though they were carved on Mount Rushmore but as though they were embedded in some of Arnold's most closely argued and carefully considered prose. Wellek, though, is content to rely on the traditional notion that the touchstones are "all in a note of sadness, melancholy, and resignation," categories that hardly fit the passage from Milton and Satan, barely fit Henry IV's expostulation to sleep, and certainly do not fit Chaucer's "O martyr souded in virginitee!" He seems only partly aware that the touchstones are used to enforce Arnold's idea of high seriousness, another idea that deserves more sympathetic attention than Wellek gives it. It has been years since anyone asked if Chaucer is limited the way Arnold says he is, and Wellek should have looked into the matter, remembering the while that one name on most of Arnold's lists of the greatest authors is Molière. But Wellek does not look freshly because he places his authors rather than seeks them out. There is, more generally, a certain complacency in Wellek about his own taste. He says, for instance, that Courbet's paintings "appear to us conventional and mediocre"; that "nowadays" Keats, Shelley, and Coleridge "seem much greater poets than Byron"; that "it is hard to believe Stephen's criticism can be made to speak to our time"; that Robert Buchanan's attack on Rossetti has "arrogant moral pretensions." That these judgments seem extremely near-sighted is not quite as important as the way they show Wellek's refusal to find merit in anything flamboyantly vulgar or solemnly moral, which means, in effect, that Wellek is left with very little genuinely to admire in the nineteenth century.

This brings us to Wellek's whole idea of historical study, but before considering that, we should mention some smaller matters. First, the Continental writers tend to be better handled than the English and American, and the reason seems to be that they fall more often into the class of the fully theoretical, like Dilthey and DeSanctis, or the fully untheoretical, like Heine, Flaubert, and Anatole France. On both groups Wellek is excellent—on the first because he is very good at laying out a system, on the second (Heine, by the way, called Hugo's *Les Burgraves* "versified sauerkraut") because the absence of theory throws Wellek back on those native sensibilities he so seldom trusts otherwise. Even better, or at least more surprising, are the fine sections on Taine and Pater, with neither of whom Wellek agrees but both of whom he explains delicately and carefully. Finally, it should be added that throughout both volumes he is consistently good on the really minor writers who do not demand elaborate treatment; he can allow himself to say what he finds good about them without worrying about their shortcomings.

But the result *is* an encyclopedia, not a history. At one point Wellek describes Ludvig Uhland's idea of literary history: "Mere description of work according to genres, or explanation of the conditions and influences from which the works arose, or even critical appraisal, is not sufficient." Wellek seems to approve, but does not see he has in fact here described his own method. It is the result, almost certainly, of his need to discredit something he variously calls "historicism" and "historical relativism," which seems to mean anything from genuine historical insight such as that of François Brunetière to belle-lettristic sinking of writer and work into "period." Wellek can speak highly of Brunetière's idea that

> "At all times, in literature as in art, it is the past which presses with heaviest weight upon the present." What is to be established is the inner causality. In literature—after the influence of the individual—"the greatest operating force is that of works on works."

Yet he cannot see that his own volumes have almost no sense of "inner causality" or "the operating force" of "works on works." The nearest he comes to understanding is in a rather pathetic "Postscript" to the fourth volume. "Is it correct to say," he asks, "that we have written a history?" He then, really, gives it all away by showing what he thinks a history would be if it sought to be "beyond the chronological order of exposition." He says he has attended to external influence:

> The change from the idealistic Hegelian atmosphere of the early 19th century to the prevalance of empirical positivistic, or materialistic allegiances and terminologies is too obvious to be missed. The profound impact of science. . . .

That, for Wellek, is history: an endless flow of *isms* within and across boundaries of countries and disciplines: an eternal fountain of psychologism, organicism, historicism, conceptualism, intellectualism, comparativism; a profound aversion to treating human beings as the unit of historical description and analysis. Finally, for Wellek, history is either "the chronological order of exposition" or "a reflection of the social, political, philosophical or even literary-historical conditions of a time." That such a position is terribly impoverished, in fact and probably in theory, let one instance attempt to show.

In the second volume of the *History*, Wellek discusses Shelley and Keats without trying to show that both have considerable critical intelligences. For instance, both knew Wordsworth was a

great poet, and both knew they scorned the Wordsworth still
alive in 1818. A nice problem for two brilliant young poets, and
they handled it in two documents that, characteristically, Wellek
never considers: Shelley's *Peter Bell the Third,* Keats's letter to
Reynolds about the Mansion of Many Apartments. Wordsworth
had, and decisively, made his own experience the matter of great
and long poems, his mind the haunt and main region of his song.
Yet the song had died out and the singer had become crabbed.
Shelley and Keats were driven to see Wordsworth's life critically,
as a story. Not biographically in any narrow sense, but as the history of a poetic development and decline:

> He had as much imagination
>   As a pint-pot;—he never could
> Fancy another situation,
> From which to dart his contemplation,
>   Than that wherein he stood.
>
> Yet his was individual mind,
>   And new created all he saw
> In a new manner, and refined
> Those new creations, and combined
>   Them, by a master-spirit's law.

The tone is admiring and scornful, but Shelley can honor both
feelings by seeing Wordsworth not just as a self, but as a lifetime.
So too Keats, who sees Wordsworth in the dark passages beyond
the chamber of Maiden Thoughts, lost yet grand enough to make
him a poet deeper than Milton. One hesitates to tell Wellek this
is the first time in criticism that major emphasis is placed on a
poet's career as a means of measuring his achievement and limitation, though Wellek mentions no one doing this before Rudolf
Haym in 1856. Yet the emphasis placed by Shelley and Keats is a
terribly important one to us, and is the major barrier between us
and a sympathetic reading of the biographical method of Dr.
Johnson—he saw the facts of a life, the character, and the works
all in separate compartments; Shelley and Keats saw a career.
Theirs is criticism, romantic criticism, a contribution at least as
great as all that Coleridgean "organicism."

But in order to see this one needs an idea of history more

responsive to relevance than is Wellek's; one has to see writers not just being "influenced" in some unreal thematic way, but also invented, as Shelley and Keats invented Wordsworth. What these younger men were doing with their master is what Eliot did with LaForgue and Donne, what James did with Hawthorne, George Eliot, and Turgenev. It is what Eliot meant by tradition, what Brunetière meant by history, what Wellek does not see and therefore cannot use to save his book from the reference shelf.

HUGH KENNER

The Counterfeiters was published a year ago [1968], and has been received rather as all Hugh Kenner's books have been, with silence punctuated by an occasional burst of respectful incomprehension. It is a delightful book, and has in it more exciting sentences than anything Kenner or anyone else has written for years, yet it stands even less chance than Kenner's earlier ones had of gaining decent recognition because it is hard to say what it is about. Kenner himself is perhaps a little too pleased with its multiplicity of "subjects" and begins with a list of them that smacks of the undergraduate joke: "Buster Keaton (stoic comedian); bad poetry; Albrecht Dürer; Joyce; Swift, Pope; closed systems, mathematical and mechanical; Charles Babbage and his Calculating Engines; the late history of Latin abstract nouns; Andy Warhol; Gödel's Proof; horses, computers, games; a clockwork duck that suffered from indigestion; and a man who wore a gas mask to ride his bicycle." That is admittedly daunting, but in itself is far from an adequate explanation of the book's shabby reception. More plausible, one feels after sampling published commentary on Kenner, is the never very clearly conceived notion that the man's politics are very Right—he was poetry editor of the *National Review*.

In most circles, however, a man's politics do not in themselves condemn him. Kenner's master, Eliot, was also of the

Right, but his classicism, catholicism, and royalism have always been treated with no less than respect and disbelief; Leavis is also a Tory (if any label will do), yet no one has ever attacked him for *that*. One no more hears attacks on, say, Cleanth Brooks for his politics than one hears slurs on Father Ong for his religion. But there is something about Kenner's manner that sets people off, and because with him the politics and the style are integral, casual observers easily mistake their dislike of one for their unease with the other. Kenner has set himself as his central task the recasting of Eliot's central insights, but because he is doing this fifty years after "Tradition and the Individual Talent," at a time when many others seem trying to pretend Eliot never existed, and in a place six thousand miles from London, Kenner has evolved a style which must risk the charge of complacency in order to avoid the pompousness and the self-pity that usually characterize the Eliotic. The attempt to regain the insights and the past they imply must not tempt one into any displacement from the present. The style, then, is cool, breezy, witty, free of academic jargon, relaxed but capable of great precision, and above all, knowing. Kenner acts as though there were nothing he could not make part of his subject, nothing he could not transform with his style, and people don't like that.

Before *The Counterfeiters*, Kenner devoted most of his energy to the great Tory moderns, though his three textbooks make clear how widely he can range. Kenner deals with the momentous events of 1910–1940 as though they were simultaneously ancient history—and thus capable of being treated with unimpassioned rightness—and happening yesterday—and so affording intimate glimpses of these writers at work. He does little with biographical material as such; he works, rather, with the public self or selves, the circumstances of publication or the format of a work, always implying that his favorites are as knowing, confident, and careful as he is himself. Anything about them about which he cannot speak with perfect assurance he simply does not mention. Perhaps if others were as intelligent, sensible, and subtle with these authors as Kenner, others who were also more inward or personal with them, then we might say that Kenner's method is merely flashy. But such others do not exist. Most Joyceans, for instance, try to overlook Wyndham Lewis's complaint about Joyce's style that it is all cliché, and thereby leave themselves defenseless against the charge of the unbeliever that Joyce is a mean-spirited wordbag. So Kenner opens up Joyce and says: look at all those clichés, how flat and flaccid the writing is, how ironic, how detached, how exquisitely comic. No wonder Kenner sets people's teeth on edge—he acts as though he were trying to put everyone else out of business.

The Counterfeiters has some passages about Joyce, Pound, and Eliot, as well as some wonderful ones about their contemporary, Buster Keaton, but mostly it is about "an astonishing half-century, 1690–1740," and it is unlikely that the caretakers of Augustan literature are going to be any happier about this book than the specialists in modern literature have been about the others. They cannot complain, however, that Kenner does not know enough or that he ignores "the eighteenth-century point of view." He does speak, however, for all his careful footnotes and acknowledgments to earlier writers on the period, as though he were the first to examine this material: "Appearance, appearance: and the world is perhaps a congeries of appearances, imperfectly observed? (David Hume was to think so)." The repetition, the colon, the word "congeries," the rhetorical question, the aside about Hume—this is not R. S. Crane or Irwin Ehrenpreis—it is all gesture, designed both to place us "back then" and to insist that we are not then, but now:

> Observe one appearance with care, and record the observation: you have a Fact. A dog with eighteen ounces of water pumped into its thorax grew short-winded. Record another: a dog injected with opium, brandy, and water, died. Another: a die swallowed by a dog was excreted after twenty-four hours, its weight halved but its shape and spots retained.

Within a few sentences we are in a typical Kenneresque limbo. The writing is whimsical, yet clear, intent, effortless, obscure in its direction:

> All these were noted at the Dublin Philosophical Society in the 1680's, when Swift was an undergraduate. Do they help us know what a dog is? A dog is perhaps partially defined as

that animal which is inconvenienced in one way by water in the thorax, but in another way by brandy in the jugular, and has the power of halving the bulk of dice. Or granted that these conditions are insufficient to specify dogginess, what conditions are? Is there such a thing as dogness, as a dog, or do we merely triangulate shifting points? Dogness, horseness, manness: *caninitas, equinitas, humanitas:* such terms, denoting stable essences, men in the seventeenth century were learning increasingly to view with suspicion as being part of the empty terminology of the schools.

We have heard about "the influence of the Royal Society," but not in this way. Kenner is more interested in the investigations themselves than the writers of textbooks usually are, yet the detached, Cheshire-cattish air implies some larger purpose. By 1738, we learn, Jacques de Vaucanson "has exhibited in Paris a mechanical duck which could waddle and splash, beat the air with detailed feathered wings, wag its head, quack, pick up grain, ingest this with swallowing movements, and eventually excrete the residue." Did Vaucanson make a duck? No, a counterfeit. Deny duckness, though, and the question arises as to how we can tell a "real" duck from Vaucanson's.

Kenner here makes a typical leap, Nijinsky-like in its casual implication that he is doing nothing more than developing the argument along obvious lines. If a duck has not essence and can be imitated by a machine, what happens to ancient authors:

> For grant the principle on which counterfeiting rests, that a man is knowable only in his behavior, and, when he is dead or otherwise out of sight, only in the traces his behavior has left; grant that, and the authority of the Ancients, doughty men whom we had been accustomed to treating (Tully, Maro) with the familiarity we accord living eminences, dwindles to a problem in the evidential consistency of scraps of paper. . . . Our civilization is nourished by a strong vein of wisdom running from remote antiquity. And the comfort of contemplating this *vis perennis* Bentley destroyed, by asserting that nothing of Aesop's was extant and that Phalaris' letters were a manifest hoax: for he mentions towns which were not built, and quotes books which had not been written, and uses a dialect unknown until five cen-

turies after he died. Being flayed, Phalaris' person is altered
greatly for the worse. . . . In an age which looked to antiq-
uity not for books but for men, Bentley was asking inconve-
nient questions.

Bentley did with Phalaris what Vaucanson did with his duck, he
stuck to appearances, The Evidence, facts. Homer and Milton, in
Bentley's version, waddle, splash, quack, and pick up grain:
"Hence (Alexander Pope foresaw) a long twilight, a vertigo of
classicism into fuddyduddy chaos and lexicographic catatonia:

How parts relate to parts, or they to whole,
The body's harmony, the beaming Soul,
Are things which Kuster, Burman, Wasse shall see,
When Man's whole frame is obvious to a *Flea.*"

The movement from dog to duck to Bentley to Pope is completely fluid, as though anyone who could see the eighteenth
century clearly would see how closely related are various things
which we, in our specialized ignorance, have allowed to become
disparate. Pope was and is scorned for qualities rather like Kenner's and for his insistence that the dunces indeed sought to
make man's whole frame obvious to a flea. Pope too was "reactionary," "presumptuous," either wicked and obscure or else obvious and repetitious, because he knew that the then new (but
now triumphant) scholarship and new empiricism were killing
any idea of being human that could not be counterfeited.

This Pope, however, is partial because ideological and partisan, so Kenner offers another perspective in order to make him
funnier, more literary. If animals and ancient authors can be
counterfeited, so too can poets, as witnessed by *The Stuffed Owl,*
the anthology of bad verse edited by D. B. Wyndham Lewis and
Charles Lee. These editors start with Cowley but don't really
know why: "To read their preface is like watching Galileo fail to
discover gravitation." Kenner-Newton then goes to work on an
absurd ode of Cowley's which Lewis and Lee had put early in
their anthology without seeing that Cowley's way of being bad
was "a wholly new way for poetry to fail, so that failure becomes a
kind of positive quality." The poem is about Harvey's discovery
of the circulation of the blood, and has lines like "But Harvey,

our Apollo, stopt not so./Into the bark and root after her did go."
Kenner says: "This is what comes of the Restoration emphasis on
clarity; it leaves nothing whatever for the poet to do but strike a
bardic posture and elevate his language." Before Cowley bad poetry had been simply boring or incompetent, but beginning with
him, poetry, under the pressure to be clear and reasonable, also
becomes capable of being perfectly silly: "Spade! with which Wil-
kinson hath tilled his lands." "Observe that when you are perpet-
ually diagramming the reasonableness of what you are doing, it is
open to any reader who has not fallen under the spell to wonder
why you should be doing it at all."

Under such circumstances the difference between a good
and a bad poem is not that one is written better or employs different techniques, and first Dryden and then Pope had to find
ways to be serious without being laughably bad: "The price of poetry, [Pope] was almost alone in understanding, had come to be
eternal vigilance." Cibber's relation to Pope is exactly analogous
to the Vaucanson duck's relation to a real duck. As long as poetry
is a matter of obeying the rules, getting the form right, keeping
the tone decorous, making the statements clear, then there is no
sure way to tell the real from the fake. The poet who knows his
own *humanitas*, who sees the world suddenly filled with counterfeit poets, becomes beleaguered in his relations with the world—
"Shut, shut, the door, good John, fatigu'd, I said"—and reliant on
vigilance and taste to succeed at all; the mockery of the mock
heroic becomes a grim business indeed. Pope, like Kenner, must
be a Minute Man.

Kenner follows with a splendid demonstration that Pope's
"To Augustus" is the first work of Pop Art because just by looking
at the lines you cannot tell if they are the insolent work of Pope
or the excited incompetent work of Ambrose Phillips: "Pope's signature does not merely accept responsibility for the libel, it
creates the libel." Unfortunately, it is too long to work with here.
It is not hard to see, however, that Kenner's way of seeing the
human and the real in the light of the counterfeit opens up rich
possibilities for readers of those ancient mariners Robinson Cru-
soe and Lemuel Gulliver; Gulliver becomes a kind of Vaucanson's
duck, a figure so clear and reasonable and devoted to examining
appearances that he has a difficult time explaining to the King of

Brobdignag and the Houyhnhnm master what it is to be human.
Part of Kenner's summary must suffice:

> Many things have been said about Augustan civilization.
> We can say one thing more, that related as it was to a phi-
> losophy which detached appearances from realities, a
> science which was learning to read the gone Past by looking
> at mute present objects (as Edward Gibbon looked at the
> ruins of Rome), and a cultivated class preoccupied with
> knowing simulacra of the prestigious, it was engaged as men
> were never to be again with massive experimentation on
> the relation of fear to fraud.

What is fascinating here, as so often with Kenner, is the way the
style sees everything in an historical moment as expressive: the
philosophy, the stance of an historian, Timon's villa. The effect is
to make us see that nothing is too small to consider if we know
how to consider accurately:

> Perhaps its principal masterpiece is a forged travel book,
> complete with forged maps, introduced by a cousin of the
> nonexistent author who discusses the principles upon which
> he deleted from the manuscript thousands of words that
> were never written; we learn from it what horses talk about,
> and how men make shift to counterfeit horsey virtues, and
> are frightened by its genial implication that our world is
> more excremental than a horse's. The man who conceived it
> earned the undying gratitude of his countrymen for expos-
> ing, under an assumed name and in an assumed character, a
> scheme for flooding Ireland with counterfeit half-pence, and
> in his will he endowed a mental hospital.

The tone is whimsical, eccentric, insistent itself on "appearances," the author an ironic Gulliver, an undisturbed Swift.
Therefore: "We cannot wonder that eventually the cult of sincerity had to be invented, to give us breathing space before Andy
Warhol." There it all is: we can move to the "Digression Concerning Madness," to the lepidopterist in *Dunciad IV,* to Pea-
chum in *The Beggar's Opera,* to Pamela's difficulties with words
like "honor" and "honesty"; from there down a generation to the
massive skepticism of *Rasselas* and to Gibbon, to the Romantics

and the cult of sincerity and right down to Warhol and ourselves. The past is lucid, helpful, and the historian is, for all his impassive detachment, invigorating, stirring, urging us to see it all as something we can see better than we have. To care about the past one perhaps needs to be a reactionary, but one need not give in to nostalgia, antiquarianism, specialization, or other forms of self-pity.

Of course reservations can be made, and, once one has said this much, are perhaps in order. A style that implies that there is nothing it cannot transform is one that must, if it is honest, leave much alone. At the beginning of his next-to-last book, *The Stoic Comedians*, Kenner sets his heroes—Flaubert, Joyce, Beckett—off against the writers of the Great Tradition—Tolstoy, Dostoevsky, George Eliot, Lawrence—and as he does so acknowledges that the writers he does not treat are in many ways more important than those he does. But such a disclaimer does not say enough. One way of praising *The Counterfeiters* is to say that its major authors, Pope and Swift, are greater and more in need of careful attention than Kenner's later comedians, and he does magnificently with them, making them superbly aware and intelligent and controlled about matters of crucial importance. The Swift is so good it scarcely can be improved upon, but Pope is not. Kenner's Pope is too much like Swift and too much like Kenner, and so cannot move us as does the author of the portrait of Flavia, the tale of Sir Balaam, the vision of triumphant Vice in the first *Epilogue to the Satires*. No one can recover for us the conditions that made Pope urgent and desperate better than Kenner does, but Kenner cannot show us why Pope is among the supremely great writers, as Swift is not, as the later stoic comedians are not. Kenner does not risk, and cannot treat those authors, those works, those aspects of life that demand risk-taking, courage, lurching into doubt or despair. The aloofness of Kenner's wit, cleansing though it is, seals him and us off from anything that might make us sadder or more joyous; the man's sympathies, especially compared with the breadth of his knowledge and the precision of his prose, are narrow. He is not a philanthropic writer, and no acknowledgment that we do not ask most critics to work out of love for man can make us overlook that.

But given the occasion provided by *The Counterfeiters*,

given the dreadful treatment generally given this singularly intelligent critic, that is no note to end on. Kenner offers us a way of being historians that allows us to be better about literature than we were, and he also reminds us that the alternatives to being better readers lie all around us, symbolized in this book by the soup cans that were never signed by Andy Warhol. To the soup cans we might add: those Minute Men not named Kenner and who reportedly use the gulches of Santa Barbara for shooting practice; the Party of Youth; its adversary, the Party of Money. Against the forces represented by these things it is not always clear what we have to muster, and in such circumstances Hugh Kenner is invaluable. We eat soup from cans, to be sure, are ourselves Minute Men of sorts, love youth, make money, we live in what Kenner calls the "different and less accessible universe" of things untouched by art. Kenner is able as few are to show us a style, a signature, a way of being literary that can transform the world of soup cans and dead authors "into a sort of world, totally inexplicit, totally assertive, inexplicably permanent."

LESLIE FIEDLER

At the end of the second huge volume of Leslie Fiedler's *Collected Essays* is "Chutzpah and Pudeur," a very good and very characteristic piece about two impulses that Fiedler sees lying behind a great many works of art. On the one hand, the *chutzpah* of "I sing" or "I am Walt Whitman," the brazen impulse, oral and loud; on the other, the *pudeur* of "Let me restrain" or "I must qualify," the impulse of hiding, anal and cultivated. The essay is characteristic of Fiedler because it ranges widely and easily in its learning and presumptions, and because it seeks new ways to tell old truths. It is good because it finds these ways, as perhaps this shows:

> It is characteristic of aggravated *pudeur* that it tries to disguise even itself, pretending it is piety rather than mere

bashfulness and shame and guilt; but the hermetic tradition, as it passed from Arnold to Eliot to Leavis and Cleanth
Brooks, is revealed finally as mere gentility, i.e., *pudeur*
bereft of *chutzpah*. . . . Without an adequate faith to justify it, any venture at defining a canonical literature, like
any attempt to separate a sacred language from a profane, is
revealed as one more spasm prompted by the castrating
shame which has been haunting Western Art ever since the
first Western artist set out to sing of sex and the "I."

That is recognizably Fiedler, filled with *chutzpah*, brazen, sing-
ing an old tune with some new lyrics.

It is a little surprising, though, that someone who has always
set out to tell us the truths we *pudiques* have tried to hide should
produce his *Collected Essays*, as though he were not youthful, assertive, gay, but dead, dying, or so established as to become almost Official. Certainly there is no sign in the more recent essays
that Fiedler has gone gray; the jacket photograph shows him
swinging a cigar as though he were a labor leader played by Lee
J. Cobb, and his work of the last two years shows him as energetic and as ravenous to read and write as he ever was. Yet here
are these immense volumes, complete with an "Introduction to
the Collected Essays," and introductions to each volume, Fiedler
treating himself as a fact of history, all just as though he were
another High Priest of *pudeur*, like Eliot or Leavis.

But the paradox can be explained, Fiedler has always been
delighted to hurl himself into the immediate moment, not just to
live that moment but to rewrite history or politics or mythology
from the perspective of that moment. He obsessively defines the
characteristics of recent historical periods, not just content with
setting off the fifties from the sixties or having one lead to the
other but making minor demarcations everywhere: the *early* thirties, the *middle* sixties, etc. Fiedler never tires of setting out a
current problem or issue, comparing it to something else a decade or a generation ago, redefining the problem given the context of the past, then projecting from that redefinition.

When you do things this way, and also write a lot, you inevitably change your mind a good deal, and Fiedler has never been
one to try to hide his many shifts in opinion and emphasis over
the years. Though the *Collected Essays* look monumental and
imply settledness, in fact they describe the history of a sensibility

as it leaped and darted through the last twenty years. For Fiedler the important task has always been to be abrasive, to say "No! in Thunder," and in as many different ways as he can.

The shift from the *chutzpah* of being a truth-telling and sometimes naughty *enfant terrible* to the *chutzpah* of one who wants his essays collected and enshrined can be explained by Fiedler's apparently recently acquired sense that he has found an audience that does not revile him, as he used to hope would happen, but that listens gratefully, as he now delights in thinking. In his introduction to the second edition of *An End to Innocence* he says of the "trilogy" that begins with *Love and Death in the American Novel:* "These books have become for a new generation of teachers in universities, colleges and high schools, the basis for a new understanding of our classic books and of our culture in general, as well as the model for critical studies which do not even bother to acknowledge their source." So Fiedler is now our guru, and sounding rather like Leavis at that. No wonder, then, that he collected his essays.

There is reason to believe it was not an entirely good idea. It is perhaps unjust to complain about such collections that there is a great deal of repetition in them, but in this case it is more marked and more revealing than in most. Fiedler has certain subjects—being a Jew in America, American Jewish writers, liberal politics and taste, the mythology of chaste homosexual relations at the center of classic American literature—to which he returns over and over, and about which he has had, essentially, one idea. He has gone on liking the idea, and gone on giving himself contexts in which it can be used. The two best essays in these two volumes are "Negro and Jew: Encounter in America" and "The Eye of Innocence." In each case the idea has appeared in earlier and rougher versions, is then polished, given classic status in these two essays, and then rehashed and reworked again and again.

Well, none of us has enough good ideas to avoid this kind of thing, but the format of a *Collected Essays* ruthlessly exposes it. Whitman and Nathanael West and Henry Roth and Alger Hiss appear in a dozen contexts in these pages, and it is always the same Whitman, West, Roth, Hiss.

After a while one begins to feel uncomfortable. It begins to seem that Fiedler is constantly plunging himself into the present, into some apparently new context, in order to avoid his or our seeing that he has a rather small stock of ideas. Worse, Fiedler now feels so secure that he no longer cares if this fact is revealed in a collection. But if he has exposed himself to this charge, it is unfair nonetheless, and one feels like trying to save Fiedler from himself. He has never pretended to be rich in ideas, but he has meant to be profuse in contexts and challenges. If we have, to go back to the original example, grown accustomed to thinking of Eliot as haughty and Leavis as scornful, then Fiedler can do us a service by charging them with a lack of *chutzpah*. Here is still another example:

> The critical interchange on the nature of the novel to which James contributed "The Art of Fiction" and Stevenson "A Humble Remonstrance" memorializes their debate—which in the thirties most readers believed had been won hands down by James's defense of the novel as art; but which in the dawning seventies we are not sure about at all—having reached a time when *Treasure Island* seems somehow more to the point and the heart's delight than, say, *The Princess Casamassima*.

One need not agree with a word of that, or relish the prospect of the seventies if it turns out Fiedler is right, in order to be grateful and happy that the scrappy and tireless author of these sentences is around. It is not an idea, only a reshuffling of our received notions of James and Stevenson in the light of new tastes, but it is good to have.

The real point about Fiedler, which we can make praise or blame as we choose, is that he is always a political writer, always putting himself into situations where he is speaking against this fashion or that obsolescence, deriding some official line, jockeying for some new position. He always acts as though we might be deceived by some other hawker of myths and contexts if he did not set us straight, and he loves doing this so much that he will take any opportunity that presents itself to keep us informed, protected, reminded. But he also just plain loves to hear himself talk, too, and as long as he is excited by an idea he will go on saying it.

This means not only that he repeats himself but that his relation to literature remains essentially impure, and that, in turn, means that much of what he writes dates rather quickly. Because he is most interested in his own ideas, he doesn't quote enough, or find enough other ways to treat books on their own rather than on his terms. He tends to make contexts control works rather than the other way around, which leads not so much to distortion, because Fiedler is a good and therefore honest man, but to overrating whatever will fit his context.

In a few years, for instance, Fiedler almost certainly will be able to say what should be clear now, that Ken Kesey is a sentimental writer, but at the moment Fiedler is willing to override his own good taste because he and Kesey are at present both interested in the mythology of the Indian and the Old West. That kind of relation to the present inevitably leads to datedness. Also, when we look back at the Fiedler of fifteen or twenty years ago we see that even where he still seems right he also seems wrong because he exaggerated the importance of whatever was news and got in the habit of making everything he wrote too long, too laborious, too liable to need revision later on.

It is hard, finally, to admire Leslie Fiedler as much as he deserves, as much as his best work needs. That best may consist of no more than a dozen essays or chapters, but it is work of a high order. It is unfortunate that the *Collected Essays* will probably not gain him new readers or convert old ones into greater admirers; it is not a good format for him. Perhaps the penchant for battle and for immersion in the present tense need not always be at odds with the penchant to tell truths, to be wise and impersonal. They are not always at odds in Fiedler's work. But the *habit* of battle is a punishing one, as is clear to anyone who finds himself becoming a little weary of Fiedler's otherwise splendid and necessary *chutzpah*.

LIONEL TRILLING

Lionel Trilling is probably as famous now as he was twenty years ago, but unless I am much mistaken, his reputation is nowhere near as high as it was in the fifties, the years of *The Liberal Imagination* and *The Opposing Self,* and the little essays for the Reader's Subscription. Back then, if this country had a leading literary critic, or, more precisely, a leading literary spokesman, it was Trilling. He was at the center of a number of concentric circles important to the literary intellectual life of the country. He was a famous and respected teacher at Columbia. He was widely known in American universities, and perhaps was the only critic frequently read by historians, philosophers, social and natural scientists. He was one of the best-known "New York intellectuals," by which was usually meant "Columbia" or "the *Partisan Review* crowd," a group sufficiently coherent in its cultural and political centrality that its enemies, especially the younger ones, always knew who to attack when they wanted to strike their father dead.

Those days are long gone. Liberalism no longer has a near monopoly on intelligence; the *Partisan Review* is just another journal; the categories "Jewish intellectual" and "young Jewish novelist" no longer are rallying terms of hate, respect, and envy; teaching by means of the formal lecture is much less prevalent and is considered much less desirable, and courses that assume the centrality of Western Culture no longer dominate the curriculum. All these facts serve in varying degrees to deny Trilling the place he once had. His is not a voice that one could expect to adapt itself easily to the sixties, and now that the sixties are almost as dead as the fifties, no one seems to be rediscovering him, finding out that he was right all along, or doing much more than vaguely wondering if he is still alive. A dozen years ago I gave a group of undergraduates some passages from Trilling's *Matthew Arnold* for comment. There was, as I remember, a shuffling of voices and feet. Well, yes, Trilling didn't do very much, and Arnold seemed mostly a hatrack on which Trilling was neatly piling the sombreros of all the best-known names in the West. But no one could say that straight out, or even directly agree with it, and under my prodding the students got sullen with me rather than articulate about Trilling. Last year I gave a group of graduate students—people temperamentally much more cautious and respectful—the same passages, and they just hooted, not with the glee that one associates with the discovery that the emperor is not wearing clothes, but with the more casual derision that accompanies the question, "Who does this guy think he is, anyway?"

Well, admittedly *Matthew Arnold* is not the best Trilling. After that book he never again attempted to sustain a long consecutive argument, and he discovered that perhaps his most congenial form is the lecture. The voice of *The Liberal Imagination, The Opposing Self,* and *Beyond Culture* speaks from a lectern: here is a subject, a problem, a matter for an hour's serious thought, let us see what we can say about it. His latest book, *Sincerity and Authenticity,* is an attempt to carry on a single argument through a series of lectures given at Harvard a couple of years ago. The voice is still strong, sure of its centrality despite the events of the last twenty years, and if reading Trilling in bulk does bear certain affinities with eating a meal consisting entirely of Thousand Island dressing, it cannot be said that the years have really taken much toll. Trilling is calm, measured, judicious, generous, as always, and he continues precisely to make the kinds of distinctions he was always most interested in making. One need feel no embarrassment—such as one feels reading the later Eliot, Leavis, or C. S. Lewis—while reading *Sincerity and Authenticity;* whatever he was good for, Lionel Trilling is good for still. That last sentence implies a question I must try to answer later; but first, a look at these lectures.

Anyone who teaches the literature of the last few centuries has had to talk to students about the question of "sincerity." Is Cleopatra "sincere" when she offers her hand to Caesar's messenger to be kissed? Is Marvell *ever* "sincere"? When Clarissa says she wants only to submit to the reasonable will of her father, does she mean it? Etc. Trilling's opening answer is good:

> We cannot say of the patriarch Abraham that he was a sincere man. That statement must seem only comical. The sincerity of Achilles or Beowulf cannot be discussed: they neither have nor lack sincerity. But if we ask whether the young Werther is really as sincere as he intends to be, or which of the two Dashwood sisters, Elinor or Marianne, is thought by Jane Austen to be the more truly sincere, we can confidently expect a serious response in the form of opinions on both sides of the question.

The rest of the opening lecture is good too. When "society" was invented, when Machiavels traipsed stages of theatres and countries, when villainy became associated with duplicity, when plain speaking became possible and plain speakers could be applauded or laughed at, the question of "sincerity" became a real issue. The more some people simulated selves, and others dissimulated "sincere" selves, the more threats there were both to the society and to the individual attempting rightly to perceive the world around him.

One ideal that such an age will foster is that to be found in Shakespeare's late plays:

> The hope that animates this normative vision of the plays is the almost shockingly elementary one which Ferdinand utters in *The Tempest*—the hope of "quiet days, fair issue, and long life." It is reiterated by Juno in Prospero's pageant: "Honour, riches, marriage blessing,/Long continuance and increasing." It has to do with good harvests and full barns and the qualities of affluent decorum that Ben Jonson celebrated in Penshurst and Marvell in Appleton House. . . .

But as society became less whole and real, that ideal tended to become the lynchpin of a reactionary, hypocritical, "insincere" aristocracy, and the ideal that replaced it became more fragmented and confused, given to multiple and complicated tones in order "sincerely" to respond to society. In the second lecture Trilling is at his best. True, he consistently uses his familiar lineup of Big Names—Rousseau, Diderot, Hegel, Goethe—but Trilling knows these figures well, and he is very convincing at outlining the shifts they show us in moral consciousness. Empson, writing about the history of the word "honest" in the same period, is perhaps better than Trilling at this kind of thing, because he can catch more odd and partial tones, but Trilling is always assured and accurate when he retells the history of High Culture, and if such a history can show us the modern consciousness becoming born, Trilling can do the showing.

But at this point Trilling relaxes just when he should have been most cautious and vigilant. When he comes to the nineteenth century he conveniently shifts the focus from the "sincere" to the "authentic," and this allows him to go skating over ponds where the ice is never thin. He carries on from his earlier essay on *Emma* as pastoral idyll, he gives us Emerson on the English authentic virtues, and Conrad's Marlow on the authentic cruelty of Kurtz. We have all been here before, and a good deal of the time Trilling himself has been our guide. What the opening lectures beautifully set us up for is something much more interesting and difficult: the fate of "sincerity" from the time when Jane Austen could tell us who is the more "sincere" Dashwood sister down to the time in this century when "it all depends on your point of view." The most serious writers of the nineteenth century wrestled with the problem as if their lives depended on it. If the Machiavel survives in a figure like Morris Townsend in *Washington Square,* the hard questions about sincerity do not concern him but Dr. Sloper. We sit and stare at the narrations of Esther Summerson and Nelly Dean, and their very innocence and lack of self-consciousness leads us to wonder at their "sincerity." Perhaps most interesting is Thackeray and Becky Sharp. Trilling puts Becky at the end of a list of duplicitous characters, wolves in sheep's clothing, like Tartuffe and Blifil. But Becky, plotter and schemer though she is, at the crisis of her life claims she is guiltless of Rawdon's charge that she has been unfaithful with Lord Steyne, and Thackeray knows he does not know what to answer. "What *had* happened?" he asks, "Was she guilty or not?" The questions are not coy; Becky is living on Lord Steyne's money, or, more properly, living well on nothing a year; the morality that can label her "whore" (and therefore duplicitous and insincere) cannot easily operate when transactions are a matter of credit rather than cash. There is sufficiently little difference between Becky's relations with Rawdon and with Steyne that Thackeray cannot say, and knows he cannot say, with whom she is "wife," with whom she is "mistress," to whom she is false or true.

The pity is that the questions I have just raised are right up Trilling's alley, precisely the sort of historical, moral, and literary problem he enjoys most. But instead of asking these questions Trilling sets up the deeply sincere but fundamentally inauthentic command of George Eliot to do one's duty and plays it against the really authentic command of Oscar Wilde to be as artificial as possible, and he does this, presumably, because he knows how to do so, has done so before. But the argument is familiar, to say nothing of doing injustice to George Eliot. This lapse into the familiar, furthermore, continues right through the lectures on the twentieth century: Marinetti's attacks on Ruskin—which, by the way, may be characteristic of early modern attitudes, but are not in themselves worth serious consideration—and a long discussion of Freud that is only slightly different from earlier ones in *The Liberal Imagination* and *Beyond Culture*, ending with predictable, if salutary, slaps at Marcuse and Laing.

At the very end, though, Trilling speaks out with full resonance, and we can perhaps use his closing sentences as a means of locating what is best and most limited in Trilling's liberal faith. He is responding to Laing's invitation to all of us to go mad, and Trilling calls this mere cant:

> And when we have given due weight to the likelihood that those who respond positively to the doctrine don't have it in mind to go mad, let alone insane—it is characteristic of the intellectual life of our culture that it fosters a form of assent which does not involve actual credence—we must yet take it to be significant of our circumstance that many among us find it gratifying to entertain the thought that alienation is to be overcome only by the completeness of alienation, and that alienation completed is not a deprivation or deficiency but a potency. Perhaps exactly because the thought is assented to so facilely, so without what used to be called seriousness, it might seem that no expression of disaffection from social existence was ever so desperate as this eagerness to say that authenticity of personal being is achieved through an ultimate isolateness and through the power that this is presumed to bring. The falsities of an alienated social reality are rejected in favour of an upward psychopathic mobility to the point of divinity, each one of us a Christ —but with none of the inconveniences of undertaking to intercede, of being a sacrifice, of reasoning with rabbis, of making sermons, of having disciples, of going to weddings, and to funerals, of beginning something and at a certain point remarking that it is finished.

There is much that can be said of this passage, but the most obvious is its conviction, its sincerity and authenticity; the voice that intercedes, that reasons with rabbis, that here comes to an end, knows that for whatever else the mantle of reasonable discourse is to be discarded, it will not be for the chicness of a sentimental madness. And I for one find the patriarchal quality of that list at the end quite moving.

But the passage also reveals the way Trilling's prose is his own worst enemy. In the first sentence it gains nothing to redefine "don't have it in mind to go mad" as "assent which does not involve actual credence," because all it yields is the repetition of "the intellectual life of our culture" as "our circumstance," and to a repetition of Laing's doctrine at the close of the sentence. Having thus wrapped himself in his own thick phrasing, Trilling can only go on saying where he quite obviously already is, and the second sentence, full sixty words, adds absolutely nothing, leading neatly, in the final sentence, to still another repetition of Laing. The man, it must be admitted, just loves the sound of his own orotundity. Nor is my example unfair; the heaviness, the repetitiveness, is everywhere in Trilling's prose, and has been there from the beginning. When one says Trilling's writing can be flexible, one does not mean that it is not ponderous.

What the prose shows in every gesture, of course, it reveals about the mind. Trilling treats himself as an institution, and so he can never speak with anything less than full assurance. It never occurs to him that we may not want to know what is on his mind, or that we might entertain an idea of Western culture different from his, or that we might approach it in different ways. Trilling does not think the history of the last five centuries is fully recoverable, but he unfailingly does think he can recover enough to make it relevant for any question that happens to be pressing; all you do is make patterns, continuities, trends, emphases. That way you seldom have to go one-on-one with an author, or to wish you knew more, or, occasionally, less. He never gives the impression of having read anything for the first time, of being surprised, confused, delighted, enraged, or captivated by anything he has read. That the past can rebuke the present is clear enough to him, though he never takes this idea seriously enough to think that perhaps now is not the best time to say something.

The impulse is to be masterful, to make sermons, to have disciples, and anyone who has ever taught or written knows it well. But since it is an impulse that easily can blind us to what we have not said, it is one which anyone of conscience and intelligence must guard against. The easiest and best way to keep the guard up is to quote, to quote a lot, to quote at length, because, unless one does this in the spirit of a copyist, one is forced to face the fact that the subject is another mind, one is forced to try to make one's prose responsive to the words of another, even if the response is scorn or laughter. Trilling quotes, but almost always in a summary way, so that what he is quoting can easily be folded into Trilling's argument and Trilling's demeanor need never alter. The point is not that Trilling is René Wellek or A. O. Lovejoy or George Steiner or someone else whose impulse to mastery leads to mongering the humorless, the absolute, or the fashionable. The point is, rather, that for all his serious and generous intelligence, he shares with these and similar writers the quality of seeming much better in the reading than in the memory. The way he seeks to gain himself, to be the master, is a way that tends to mean that he loses us because he never fully lets his subject live separately from him.

One suspects that for the average reader Trilling will be most admired for his utility in speaking to and perhaps even settling issues where literature is only part of the subject: "Reality in America," the essays on Freud, "The Meaning of a Literary Idea," "On the Teaching of Modern Literature," "The Two Environments," etc. The advantage Trilling enjoys is that he is a thinker, he is generous, but he is no theoretician, and as a result these essays have and probably will continue to find their way into anthologies; they are useful, if one admits their subjects to be anything like as interesting or crucial as Trilling takes them to be. But for me these essays reread very badly, and for two reasons: the subjects themselves tend to date, and the whole idea of being plumply judicious about subjects of concern is one which has seen better days. There is no better way to see this than to look at the references to individual authors and works in the essays where the subject is a general one. The Dostoevsky, the Proust, and most devastating, for me at least, the D. H. Lawrence that Trilling speaks of when he is not thinking directly and carefully about those writers are all caricatures, and worse, caricatures that appeal to the most fully received clichés about them. If the occasion to respond to the Leavis-Snow affair or new fashions in psychoanalysis is going to lead someone as learned and thoughtful as Trilling into these caricatures, then the occasions themselves perhaps had better be avoided.

Trilling is better than this, I think, when forced to address himself to a particular writer or work. This focus is no guarantee of success, but then it never is, and when quotation is what is called for and Trilling won't quote, the results can be damaging, as in his failure to note how flaccid Wordsworth is in the first half of the *Intimations Ode*, or to see how very good is Vernon Parrington's description of Hawthorne, even though his estimate of Hawthorne is much lower than Trilling thinks it should be. But even here Trilling is really interesting; if he cannot settle subjects, be truly decisive with individual works, he can almost always be counted on to ask good questions, to open something up: the essays on *Emma* and *Mansfield Park*, the appreciation of Keats's letters, the piece on *The Bostonians*, the sections on Diderot and Hegel in the present volume—give Trilling a subject where his penchant for generalizing is called for, and he is a careful and fine critic. One wonders why he has never done more than allude to the late Augustan writers—Fielding, Johnson, Gibbon, Burke—for surely here, if anywhere, is his real métier, the sober, the wise, the ironic, the heroically reasonable and learned. Trilling needs centrality of concern to be himself central; he cannot respond well to quirkiness and eccentricity, to slippery surface texture, to unargued assertion, to prejudice or mere opinion. He might feel he can twit Leavis about Leavis's apparently insistent moral tone, but he could never have written with Leavis's delicacy about Jonson, Carew, and Pope.

If Trilling's moment of highest fame and respect has passed, it is not likely to return, because he just does not write well enough, care enough for words, to outlive the world he received and in which he flourished. If we are to maintain our link with the European past we will have to do so more fugitively and eagerly than Trilling has done, and with a more urgent sense that we are liable to lose it if we fail to speak in our own voice, our ignorant voice, our American voice. Trilling wanted to be Matthew Arnold, and there was a time when that was taken as a wonderful thing to try to be. Trilling filled the role well. One might complain that he chose the wrong model, that Mill, or Ruskin, or George Eliot are more worth the effort. Perhaps the better complaint is that we had best be done with models, that we can keep the past alive not by imitating or emulating it but by reading its words aloud and by answering them in whatever authentic voice we have, wildly, loudly, or in hushed tones.

ALFRED KAZIN

Yes, the bright book of life indeed, not just the novel, as Lawrence said, but the American novel of the last thirty years, as Alfred Kazin now says. It has all the necessary qualities of a great form gaining and sustaining its energy in an historical period, like the Elizabethan drama or the eighteenth-century satire in couplets: it is distinct, it has produced some great works, it has proven sufficiently powerful and attractive that many minor writers have been given a voice they might otherwise not have had.

Here is Kazin, too, who has been following the American novel the entire time, offering us one good capsule sentence after another of its best-known practitioners: of Hemingway:

> The circumscribed narrow world, the tightening of nature to design as in painting, the handling of weapons, the prize ring, the arena, the making and unmaking of camp, the use of any moment to show only the ultimate responses to life, the line of words in Indian file that is exciting because it conveys the ordeal of consciousness to itself.

of Updike:

> Brightness falls from the air, thanks to the God on whose absence we sharpen our minds. . . . The world is all metaphor. We are not sure *who* is thinking these brilliant images in *Rabbit, Run*. Need Updike's fine mind be so much in evidence?

of Bellow:

> The process of self-teaching thus becomes the heart of Bellow's novels, and the key to their instructiveness for others. One could compile . . . a whole commonplace book of wisdom in the crisis era that has been Bellow's subject and opportunity.

of Nabokov:

> Its self-celebration slops all over the planet. Nabokov has certainly not saved himself. Nor has he wanted to. But he has saved *us* from being always at the mercy of the age.

One need not agree, of course, in order to see that Kazin is constantly at work, trying to state in these capsules what is characteristic and central in each of these writers. It is not reviewing, but it is the fruit of reviewing, of forcing oneself to try to say it all, or most of it, in a few sentences or a paragraph. There are good sentences on more than a dozen writers in *Bright Book of Life*, and on one or two the best I've seen. Even on Hemingway, about whom few people want to hear any more for a while, the sentence above seems to me as precise about what makes him appealing and limited as any writing on him that I know of.

So here is a fine subject, apparently, the contemporary American novel, perhaps just now becoming capable of coming into focus, and here is Kazin, a thoughtful and patient observer and a writer of some fine sentences. The sad shock is that the book is terribly disappointing, not dull, but enervating, self-defeating. It's hard to say just why without seeming merely to outline the book one would have written oneself, but the effort must be made.

There are two obvious ways to put together a book such as the one Kazin wants to write, and had Kazin refused either of the two he could have justified himself easily enough, but instead he has refused both. The first way is like Lawrence's in his book on American literature: sustain all opinions and differences in authors by means of a vision of the country and its history. Kazin refuses this, on grounds of temperament or prudence, and with the sure knowledge that most people who try to do it Lawrence's way end up with what in academic circles is called an "idea" but what is really a gimmick, a way of sacrificing authors for the sake of scheme. The second way is to look only at those authors about whom one has strong feelings, and really go at them with all the intensity and freshness one can muster. This is the way, say, of Leavis's *The Great Tradition,* or of Kenner's books on modern authors. Kazin refuses this, too, presumably because he wants to avoid the appearance of making contemporary fiction into his sandbox of favorites.

Having made these choices, however, for whatever good reasons, Kazin seems not to have seen what an odd book would be the result. Here are, besides the authors mentioned above: Faulkner, Taylor, McCullers, O'Connor, Percy, Mailer, Jones, Heller, Vonnegut, Cozzens, O'Hara, Cheever, Salinger, Pynchon, Malamud, Roth, Porter, Sontag, Plath, Lurie, Oates, Didion, Capote, Baldwin, Ellison, Burroughs, Barthelme. I want to offer some comment later about that list, but certainly it is not one that can be faulted on grounds of crankiness or parochialism; the only obvious omissions are Hawkes and Barth. But thirty authors in a book of three hundred pages, about each of whom one tries to say the most important things, means in effect that it is authors that are treated, not books, and authors treated rather summarily at that.

It is one thing for Kazin to assume we have read all these books, another to assume we all agree on what is in them, and that Kazin need not describe, or evoke, or *lean* on the books. There are precious few quotations here—and unfortunately they are set off in tiny italics so as to resemble the words on tombstones—and that has the effect of making Kazin *only* a summarizer, only a writer of capsule sentences. It's as though quarrels, worries, doubts, quirks, preferences about contemporary fiction were all behind us, as though literature were not something that always must be looked at freshly.

Furthermore, because of this encapsulating habit and the lack of any unifying web or tissue, a chapter called "The Absurd as a Contemporary Style," to take one example, begins with Ellison and goes on to "black humor" and its usual accompaniments, but by the time we get to Barthelme ("We have been cut off by the words hanging over our heads; our poor little word-riddled souls are distributed all over the landscape") and Pynchon ("The key to Pynchon's brilliantly dizzying narratives is the force of some hypothesis that is authentic to him but undisclosable to us") we have totally lost Ellison. I tried to construct that last sentence to indicate the kind of effect that is achieved; here is a subject, and everything is seemingly in place, but the conveyor belt quality of its sense of place prevents anything from staying in the mind after it has been dropped from immediate attention.

What is asked to serve as construction here, as connecting tissue, are the all too obviously arranged chapters: "The Secret of the South," "The Decline of War," "Professional Observers," "The Earthly City of the Jews," "Cassandras." Though Kazin intends nothing of the sort it is almost an insult to his writers to put them in such slots, so that we know the moment we are done with Bellow and Malamud we are soon to be on to Roth and Mailer; finish Cozzens and can O'Hara, Salinger, and Updike be far behind? It might have worked better had Kazin really taken these categories as anything other than conveniences, had he sought to come up with something new about Southern or Jewish or absurdist or WASP fiction. But he doesn't because he isn't interested in the categories so much as in the authors, with being good about them. Except, to come back to that, they don't have time enough to breathe and be themselves as they are hustled along down the conveyor belt.

Since I'd hate to treat Kazin as summarily as I've just accused him of treating his authors, let me offer one extended quotation:

> Bellow has found fascinating narrative forms for the urgency of his many thoughts. He has been clever in finding a distinct *style* for so much silent thinking—from Joseph's diaries in *Dangling Man* to Herzog's equally incessant meditations and finally old Mr. Sammler's haughty soliloquies, where the style is one of the lightest, feath-

eriest, mental penciling, an intellectual shorthand (here involving brusque images of the city) that answers to the traditional contractedness of Jewish thought. The favorite form for Jewish sages has always been the shortest, and Bellow's best fictions are his shortest. V. S. Pritchett, who admires Bellow for powerful descriptions of city life rare among "intellectual" novelists, thinks that in his long books Bellow "becomes too personal. There is a failure to cut the umbilical cord." Bellow's more lasting fictions will probably be those whose personae are not *exactly* as intelligent as he is—*The Victim* and *Seize the Day*.

Let me praise Kazin's "clever" as a signpost that it is precisely not the discovery of styles for silent thought that he admires most in Bellow; praise too the "haughty" and "mental penciling" that describes Sammler; praise him for not going on long about the favorite form for Jewish sages, and for the Pritchett quotation; praise him, most, perhaps, for an opinion which I do not share, but which is suggestively offered and may well turn out to be right.

But what do we get next but one paragraph, about the length of the one just quoted, on *The Victim* and *Seize the Day*. That is simply a terrible misappropriation of space and energy. We are left with the outlandish notion that these novels must be Bellow's best because the forms for Jewish sages have always been the shortest; with logic like that, who needs grubby novels, Leventhal and Wilhelm? Of course Kazin does not need to try to prove his assertion, but he should treat it honorably, being both his and interesting, instead of going on from his pathetic handful of sentences about these "best" novels to *Sammler,* to which he gives more space than he gives to these two combined, and then on to Malamud, whose "best" novel is *The Assistant* and Kazin will give *it* only one paragraph, too.

At one point Kazin offers us the accurate statement that "novels seem more expendable these days than ever, but *novelist* is still any writer's notion of original talent." Here he is accounting for Capote's strange desire to call *In Cold Blood* a novel, and the situation he describes is, however true, deplorable, as he well knows. Yet if he is not going to treat the novels he most admires with any more care than he has done in *Bright Book of Life* then it's no wonder that people of less intelligence and with less interest in fiction are going to end up chattering away about novelists whose works they have read only casually and partially.

That such a thoughtful and scrupulous critic can be accused of such oversights as these seems odd, I know, and I wish I knew how to account for it. My only suggestion is that we might return to Kazin's original choices for subjects and note the almost antiseptic absence of quirks in it. At one point he offers us two pages about William Eastlake's *The Bamboo Bed,* at another two on Jane Bowles's *Two Serious Ladies,* and those are the only places where he looks, however cursorily, at writers who wouldn't necessarily be on one's list of those one had to discuss if one meant to give a complete account of contemporary fiction.

The point is not that Kazin has only read books he had to read, and the point certainly is not that he somehow hasn't read enough. It is, rather, that contemporary American fiction is for him already a *received* subject, something he has lived with for so long, perhaps, that he cannot work with it except in his thoughtful, summarizing way. If he seems to have no enthusiasms of his own among the countless other writers he might have allowed to intrude into his company, he seems to have lost or mislaid his enthusiasm for *The Victim, Seize the Day, The Assistant,* and other books about which he wants to say they are their author's "best" or "most brilliant" and have done.

Could it be that this is what happens to someone who makes contemporary literature into his main subject of interest? That he teaches and writes and lectures about it so much that he finds it difficult to get back into that frame of mind in which he originally read because it was a novel and he was a man alive? If so, then it is a powerful argument indeed against letting "contemporary literature" be a subject to teach or be the subject of wise retrospective lead essays in journals. The last thing one needs in dealing with any literature, but especially our own living literature in its own most vital parts, is grayness, and I'm afraid that for all its intelligence and its author's care *Bright Book of Life* is a gray book.

IRVING HOWE

Irving Howe has had a long, admirable, and increasingly enviable career. An academic who is never musty and a journalist who is never merely quick or content with flash, he seems to have grown over the years, and his prose is sharper, his insights more precise and flexible. Of course he loves polemical situations too much, and a taste for battle born in the days when the Old Left was new has never left him. So here, in his tenth book, *The Critical Point,* a collection of 14 recent essays, he begins and ends with two inferior pieces, scoldings of the New Left and Kate Millett, both of which choke their efforts to be capacious with that old embattled assurance that there are two sides here, mine right, yours wrong. But in between these two is a good deal of vintage Irving Howe, and two or three essays rank among his very best, which is to say among the best criticism now being written in America.

The bad news first, the stale bread, as it were, that is asked to encompass this wonderfully filled sandwich. Howe really only wants to say to the young revolutionaries and the women that Daddy Knows Best, which is hardly an attractive pose, and one made worse by Howe's attempts to be dispassionate and wise about subjects that arouse strong and too deeply entrenched feelings in him. That Kate Millett, for instance, seemed a few years ago a suitable target for attacks on the women's movement is unfortunate but understandable. That Howe can cut her up pretty easily is even more unfortunate, because his demolition of *Sexual Politics* leads him to stop wondering what the shouting is all about. There *are* differences between men and women, he keeps insisting; *of course* women have it hard, but so do men, especially in a capitalist society; women are often more *interesting* than men. All Howe can reveal here is not so much prejudice as experience that turns out to be more limited than Howe has any intention of admitting, and so his taste for polemic leads him to fight when he should be more patient and attentive.

But such a defect is common among old warriors, and the good news, to repeat, is that this is far from all that Howe at present is or represents. Perhaps the most surprising essay in the book is on Edwin Arlington Robinson, a poet I thought I had done with, and that Howe would never have touched, though Howe's excellent book on Hardy should have been a tipoff: "Robinson's language seldom achieves the high radiance of Frost, and few of his short poems are as beautifully complexioned as Frost's 'Spring Pools' or 'The Most of It.' But in Robinson there are sudden plunges into depths of experiences, and then stretches of earned contemplativeness, that Frost can rarely equal."

Anyone who can find such a right phrase as "high radiance" to describe Frost, and who can then name two of what indeed are his most "beautifully complexioned" poems, has earned our attention when he tries to say what Robinson can do better than Frost. So turn to "The Pity of the Leaves," "Hillcrest," and "Eros Turannos," and you'll see it is just as Howe says. It is better than discovering a poet; it is the warming and chastening experience of recovering one.

Only slightly less dazzling are the measured estimates of Saul Bellow and Philip Roth. Here we all know what we think, so the going is tougher; but Howe earns the right to his slight underrating of *Herzog* and considerable overrating of *Mr. Sammler's Planet:* "Of all the 'American Jewish writers' of the last few decades Bellow is not merely the most gifted by far, but the most serious—and the most Jewish in his seriousness. In him alone, or almost alone, the tradition of immigrant Jewishness, minus the *Schmaltz* and the *Schmutz* the decades have stuccoed onto it, survives with a stern dignity. Sammler speaking at the end is something like a resurrected voice: experience fades, explanations deceive, but the iron law of life is the obligation we owe one another."

That is not exactly news, but "stern dignity" is just right for Bellow in his crucial moments, and right because there is for him at least one law made of iron. Only the best critics are generous enough to find the right words for their authors. It is the force of Howe's sense of Bellow, furthermore, that gives him his key to what has always limited Philip Roth and what has gone wrong in Roth's recent books:

Roth, despite his concentration on Jewish settings and his acerbity of tone, has not really been involved in this tradition. For he is one of the first American-Jewish writers who finds that it yields him no sustenance, no norms or values from which to launch his attacks on middle-class complacence.

Thus the eventual turn to vaudeville in *Portnoy* and to the horsing around he has done since then. It is perhaps worth noting, too, that when Howe was criticized by Wilfrid Sheed for this essay, he did not immediately rush out with a counter-argument. Only some things, after all, are worth fighting about, and one hopes Howe simply realized that "Philip Roth Reconsidered" is pretty close to a definitive statement, not in need of defense or amplification.

These three essays seem the best of the current gathering, but an introduction to Zola's *Germinal,* a review of Dostoevsky's notebooks, a "partial dissent" on Sylvia Plath, and a fine devastation of George Steiner are only slightly less good. One is tempted to say, given his current successes and few failures, that Howe is better when his subject is more literary: but that, I think, is a partial way of putting it. When one feels embattled, as the editor of *Dissent* has and must often feel, one's prose becomes a blunter instrument than it otherwise might be. Lay aside the question of whether Howe should have felt so embattled, should have fought all those fights. What needs celebrating here is his ability to do something other than this, and to make his writing full and precise when these qualities—rather than strict arguing—are most needed. Howe seems to be trusting his human and literary instincts more than he once did, and that trust is repaying him handsomely. Perhaps his own world has indeed and finally grown more attractive. If so, it is a blessing that the result has not been relaxation or complacence but this richer and more precise prose.

It is no longer the fashion, and probably rightly, to worry about keeping up our lists of the best at this or that—the three best novelists, the finest writer of stories, the best commentator on politics, etc. But I did marvel at a number of these essays and did ask myself who is as good as or better than Irving Howe, especially among our older critics. What interested me was the realization that Howe's political and polemical engagements have always kept me from considering him simply as a critic, and perhaps his tendency to write pieces like the first and last in this book has contributed to that prevention. In a sense it seems almost impertinent to insist that Irving Howe is awfully good. But he is. *The Critical Point* is a very rewarding book. One can only expect and hope for many more.

MARVIN MUDRICK

Marvin Mudrick published his first essay for *The Hudson Review* in the fall of 1954, and since then has almost *become The Hudson Review;* by my rough count his fine essay on Dr. Johnson in last summer's issue [1970] was his fortieth contribution. This is probably a record of some kind, one that seems especially remarkable because Mudrick does not make his living as a writer and because he never writes a bad piece. Rereading the whole run, I was struck first and most strongly by the high quality. Mudrick, we know, is learned, witty, grim, quick to scorn and delighted to praise, but also, all these qualities are at work and at play all the time. A second, correlative impression is that when Mudrick is not writing he must be reading; there simply are not enough hours in the day for anything else. Not long ago the man whose office is next to mine, David Wagoner, had his fifth novel reviewed by Mudrick in *The Hudson Review.* Mudrick had not liked the novel very much, but, not content with that, he had gone back and read Wagoner's first four before describing his opinion of the fifth. Wagoner was understandably not very happy at Mudrick's dislike of his novels, but more than that he was dumbfounded by Mudrick's procedure. I could only tell him that this was just like Mudrick, and also that I too knew no one else who would read five novels by a man in order to be able to level against one in just the terms he wanted.

Readers of *The Hudson Review* cannot help knowing Marvin Mudrick, but it is not clear just who else knows him or what impression they have. Back in 1952 he published *Jane Austen: Irony as Defense and Discovery*, which is rather too convinced of itself for me but which also was just about the first good book ever written on Jane Austen; later Mudrick edited a collection of essays on Conrad, and he seems at one time or another to have been working on books on Chaucer and Colette which were never finished; his "The Originality of *The Rainbow*" has been reprinted often enough by now to be known at least to most Lawrentians. Still, it must be that it is for his essays and reviews in *The Hudson Review* that Mudrick is best known, and it should be added at once that anyone who feels that herein lies a falling off because reviewing is at best high-class hackwork has not read Mudrick in sufficient bulk.

The question of collecting one's reviews and incidental essays, though, has always been a ticklish one, and while Mudrick is at least as aware of the dangers as anyone else—see, especially, his "The Possibility of Criticism" in *The Hudson Review* for Autumn 1962—he does not seem altogether to have solved the problem in compiling *On Literature and Culture*, a gathering of seventeen essays and reviews, eleven of which first appeared in the *Hudson*. Lots of people collect their essays, and lots of reviewers discuss the rights and wrongs of so doing, but for a number of reasons Mudrick's collection presents somewhat special problems. One way of stating them is to say that those reviews on which the reviewer has to work the hardest are the fiction chronicles, yet these are the ones that can seem the most ephemeral ten years later. Mudrick has written many of these over the years, and almost every one has something special about it that makes it seem worth remembering, but one can understand why they do not seem to fit in a collection in a book. Omnibus reviews depend greatly on the books being reviewed, and the most one can do is to quote honestly and judge quickly; if the books themselves are not, in the light of later reflection, worth even the five hundred words per book that can be spent on them, then there is not much the reviewer can do about it. So, in making *On Culture and Literature*, Mudrick has kept out all his omnibus fiction reviews, and instead offered a book which, the jacket copy says, moves "from Lady Murasaki and Chaucer to Casanova, Tolstoy and Shaw, from Eliot and Hemingway to Haggin, Bellow, Oscar

Lewis, Mailer and Harold Rosenberg." If one assumes that some principle of selection had to be found, then Mudrick was probably right to choose his work on those authors who are much more likely than the average novelist to remain themselves of interest. But an admirer wants to cavil, to say that the book represents his best work and reflects his greatest virtues only in part.

To call Marvin Mudrick a great reviewer is not just to say that he writes great reviews. It is to say also that certain qualities which he exemplifies better than anyone else, qualities which are absolutely essential to a reviewer but not as important in others, obtain in Mudrick's prose whether or not he is writing a review. A reviewer needs, most of all, good taste and the ability to say a lot in very few words. He does not need, and indeed is probably better off doing without, the capacity to construct an independent argument; we all know and distrust writers who use reviews as occasions to rehearse their own ideas on a subject. The work under consideration must be judged, but it also must be allowed to exist independently of the reviewer's judgment, and at allowing books so to exist there is no one better than Mudrick. A great deal of this skill involves the capacity to quote well, which means choosing for quotation not only those passages which are useful for proving the reviewer's point but choosing those passages which are honestly representative of the whole book. An omnibus review by Mudrick is often more than half quotation, which is in itself not perhaps a good thing, but which, when one sees how quickly and well Mudrick can shepherd his quotations into a tasteful judgment by adding just a little of his own, seems exactly the right way to do it.

When the book being reviewed is a novel, such quotation and comment often are enough. When the book is about another book or subject, however, the conditions of reviewing may often impose limitations on the reviewer which may be necessary but also regrettable. When Mudrick reviewed John Bayley's book on Tolstoy, for instance, he rightly chose to focus on Bayley and to let his ideas on Tolstoy remain a matter of inference and of quickly stated perceptions. But when the review is put into a book, and becomes, as it were, a chapter, not called "One Bear Too Many" but "Tolstoy," the result is deflecting. One wants Mudrick on Tolstoy, and Mudrick on Bayley seems a less adequate substitute than it did when the piece was published as a review. So it is with the pieces in this book on Shaw and Eliot; the reviewing conditions seem too limiting. Interestingly, Mudrick has made some real and important changes in his review of Hemingway's *A Moveable Feast*, because, he says, that book "no longer seems to me so wonderful a recovery of Hemingway's powers as it did then." But he need not have apologized that way, because in praising early Hemingway stories directly rather than inferentially, in saying why he thinks Hemingway should be considered primarily as a writer of stories, he has changed a good review into a good essay, which is something quite different from modifying one's earlier views. I wish Mudrick had tried similar transformations with other reviews, not because any change of heart is called for, but just because the possibilities offered by the different format could have been acknowledged to the advantage of both the books and their critic.

One reason Mudrick did not try to change more essays when he began compiling his book is that temperamentally he is so completely a reviewer that he may not have seen what more he could do; and in most of those essays which were not originally written as reviews we can see his reviewer's habits at work nonetheless. In one case, the essay/review of Casanova's *History of My Life*, the difference between one critical genre and another can barely be felt; here is an author about whom there is little to do except celebrate, and so Mudrick quotes, wonderfully and often, celebrating. But in other cases more of an argument seems to be called for, so that when Mudrick's essay on Lady Murasaki turns out to be really a long review of *The Tale of Genji*, one feels disappointed that Mudrick keeps himself under wraps. That Mudrick knows that often the acts of evocation and judging are not enough is most apparent in this volume in his very short essay, "Chaucer's Nightingales," which evokes a great deal and which praises Chaucer wonderfully, but by means of building up an argument about Chaucer and "nature" in comparison with *King Lear:*

> What Lear discovers after catastrophe and madness Chaucer has been continuously instructing us in by an unillusioned examination of image and metaphor from the beginning: that nothing—no power or vanity of language or

of temporary human comfort—can save man from the recognition of his own solitude and eventual powerlessness. Tragedy is beyond sulphurous and thought-executing fires, as it is also beyond larks and nightingales.

These are big sentences, not like those of most critics, and not easily possible in a review, and when I say their point and power cannot really be grasped without reading the whole essay which they conclude, I am saying that here Mudrick has built an argument as he so seldom does. Drawing back from such arguing is characteristic of most Mudrick, just as the overarguing and reducing of literature to a scale altogether too manageable is characteristic of most criticism. It is as though Mudrick were reacting against such a tendency to murder by dissecting and, in doing so, restricted himself too often to performing the reviewer's essential tasks of quoting and briefly judging. In reviews, of course, this is no defect at all, but in independent essays it can be.

Another way, perhaps, of making the same point is to come at it from the opposite direction, and to say that in making his selection he has not only exposed his general unwillingness to build up large arguments but also has excluded too many of his great short bursts. Many of these come when he is talking about an unimportant or even a downright bad author, but they are in their way terribly good and, furthermore, almost Mudrick's way of stamping the reviewer's task as his own. I would like to quote some here just to show the kind of thing I mean, and to try to move thereby to some further assessment of Mudrick that *On Culture and Literature*, when taken by itself, does not really allow for:

> . . . but he isn't bashful, he carries on without a blink, authoritatively elucidating the sheer horror of thinking.

> . . . nothing so naked as a surface or an animal could survive the armored-car redundancies of Mme. Bree's *Yale French Studies* prose.

> Mr. Price seems determined to prove that for Southern writers every sex act, as a matter of phallic principle, confirms the superiority of the male, infallibly fertilizes, and must be celebrated in the smuggest and most simplistic agricultural metaphors.

Sergius himself, appointed by Mailer to survey the mystery, is a grand lacuna into which whole chapters topple and vanish.

With a little luck, it may yet turn out to be the worst novel ever written.

Of these five, only the fourth appears in *On Culture and Literature*, about which omission more can and should be said than more's the pity.

One has heard the objection to this kind of writing many times: it is Style, it calls attention to itself, it celebrates the reviewer at the expense of the book or author reviewed, etc. Those who take this line will admire *On Culture and Literature* because, given the bulk of Mudrick's work, it contains relatively little of this kind of thing. Worse still, they may take this fact as a sign that Mudrick in essence agrees with them, and recognizes that in deciding what should be permanently enshrined in a book, it becomes time to put away childish things like those swinging, slambang sentences I've quoted. Marvin Mudrick has read more bad novels and as many good novels as anyone I know or can imagine, and he has read them with at least as much attention as most of them warrant. When he says about Françoise Sagan's *Aimez-Vous Brahms?* "With a little luck, it may yet turn out to be the worst novel ever written," I feel that he may well be right and that he is even expressing his own kind of hope, even optimism, in saying so; it would be wonderful to think that the worst novel that was ever to be written was now safely behind us. The point is truly expressive, not only of a judgment but of that judgment's capacity to articulate a sense of life. Rather than trying to make more of one incidental sentence than perhaps should be made, however, let me consider another example of greater length.

In one of his very best reviews, of the Richard Ellmann and Charles Feidelson anthology, *The Modern Tradition*, Mudrick offers the following list of what the book includes, about which I am sure that it could and has been claimed that Mudrick is only exercising his sense of superiority to the anthologizers:

The editors throw in something for all tastes: Vico because Joyce was a Viconian; stale chestnuts like Arnold on the fu-

ture of poetry and I. A. Richards on the pseudo-statement;
Santayana in his role as aesthete of Catholicism (There is no
God, and Mary is His mother); Paul Tillich stuffing mean-
inglessness into meaning, disbelief into piety, hats into rab-
bits; Proust of course with his soggy madeleine; Malraux on
the "museum without walls"; Henry Adams scared to death
by the new and American century of profane power.

One must hope that Ellmann and Feidelson, reading that and
feeling Mudrick was shooting at easy targets, liked the phrases
about Tillich; still, if that list were all there was to Mudrick's
judgment they might be right in feeling misrepresented by their
reviewer. But the point is that Mudrick's voracious energy, learning, and taste are all at work, just as they are in the sentence
about Françoise Sagan; he is not just having fun. He quotes the
passage from Henry Adams in question—it is the opening of the
last chapter of *The Education*—then closes his review with this:

> Perhaps Adams was on the right track, the editors might
> have taken a tip from him: that the modern is America, un-
> bounded centrifugal energy spinning away from the totem
> of history. Take as epigraph from Donne's Elegy XIX the
> line, "O my America! my new-found-land," which denotes
> the naked body of his mistress as he explores it for its own
> sake and his: no spiritual preparations, no coyness, no faint-
> ing spells, no Don-Juanish palaver; pure profane activity in
> a new world, out of bounds. For an introduction, Law-
> rence's *Studies in Classic American Literature* (which the
> editors don't see fit to use in *their* book on the modern) will
> do very well, and is more entertaining than Vico. Then
> forget Europe and see how far you can go without stum-
> bling on its ubiquitous relics. Anyhow it's an idea, which is
> more than Messrs. Ellmann and Feidelson, for all their
> impressive labors, have come up with.

There is an air about that last sentence which implies the whole
thing has been tossed off, but of course, it hasn't been.

One can, for example, take that sentence about Donne's line
and do three things with it, and it works each time. Take it first,
and almost irrelevantly, as an evocation of Donne's tone in the
poem. Take it second in the context of the list of ubiquitous Eu-

ropean relics quoted above, and read Mudrick's phrases as criticism of the objects on that list that is much more accurate than snotty. Take it third as an evocation of America as we all know it; suddenly the country seems both as wonderful as Donne's line and as scary as Adams's passage. And—as familiar as the world around us. The result may not be what is usually called an idea, but one begins to see how much thinking lies behind it.

The point, then, is that Mudrick earns his tones, all of them, and that it is in reviewing that he has found a wonderful way to move his tone around gracefully, wildly, carefully. *On Culture and Literature* is disappointing because it does not really reveal this, because perhaps no collection selected with certain principles in mind could reveal it. It is not simply a matter of variety, though that does seem important when one places the collection of essays beside the whole run of Mudrick's work, but also a matter of stance. The reviewer always must implicitly accept the world because he does not choose his subjects, really, and while this often is a curse it creates advantages too, especially for someone as restless and energetic as Mudrick. The tone must be constantly capable of shifting, and when it can do this it can also persuade that the tone used at any one moment is precisely the one called for. The reviewer may master his tones, but that mastery is in itself an acknowledgment and celebration of the fact that the world cannot be mastered. His power of evoking is a sign of this, his refusal to argue at great length is a sign of this, his flexibility in judging is a sign of this, his endless willingness to pick up a new book is a sign of this. To put the matter this way is not to make reviewing something totally different from other kinds of criticism; it is only to suggest why it might be that though *On Culture and Literature* is not as good a book as *Selected Essays*, T. S. Eliot was not as good a reviewer as Marvin Mudrick is.

So I think Mudrick was in something of a bind when he came to make his book. He could have included the review of *The Modern Tradition* all right, and the wonderful "The End of the World or Else," which ends with stunning quotation-and-comment on R. Buckminster Fuller, but the difficulty would still be there: so much of what seems finest about Mudrick comes in bursts, in phrases that seem at times almost incidental, in comments that come after long quotations from which they cannot be torn loose and which may not in themselves be worth a great deal. Mudrick's solution was to make himself a little more solemn than he is, and less restless and insistent. He is himself such a good writer on the novel (and surely it is not accidental that in his forty contributions to *The Hudson Review* there is not one poetry chronicle or one essay which treats a poet primarily as a poet) because the novel, like Mudrick, knows no rules, is wary of allegory, and is eager to take the next thing that comes along on its own terms. Yet this is not something he could have gotten in any book shorter than his complete works. Its essential quality is to exist for the sake of the particular novel he is writing about, and to convey only cumulatively his sense of the variousness of the novel as corresponding to the peopledness of life, each one in need of a care expressive of the uniqueness of the individual work. Given that care, he is often dour, severe, disappointed; novels make him feel that way just as people can, and Mudrick knows why he wants to take one as our best sign of the other:

> There are no longer any communities, or religions, or emblems, or spirits. But there are persons; and so fiction—all that prose which drives out devils—is still with us and will have to do.

"All That Prose" is the title of this omnibus fiction review; "Man Alive" is that of another; "Is Fiction Human?" that of still a third. Perhaps the best way to praise Marvin Mudrick is to say that, like a great novelist, in producing the first of these he creates the second and so answers the third affirmatively, and in ways that make *now* matter.

CITIES

Eight years ago, having spent my life in small towns in the East, I moved to Seattle. There was nothing extraordinary in that, people do it all the time, but I came here in order to live in a city while most people don't come to Seattle at all but to some place called the Pacific Northwest: mountains, forests, fresh and salt water, great fishing and climbing, etc., anyplace but a city. As a result, when I wandered around trying to find out what kind of city Seattle is, I found few people to talk to. I was given the impression that others thought if I really wanted to live in a city I should have stayed East, or gone to San Francisco. Then I found Jane Jacobs's *Death and Life of Great American Cities*. It was, and is, a rather staggering book, not about urban design or renewal, not swamped in the sentimental notion that all major decisions in cities are made by bureaucrats and insurance companies, really about what one could see if one opened one's eyes. Quite simply, Mrs. Jacobs believes that cities are intelligible, and she shows over and over what makes one city park fail and another succeed, why short blocks and old buildings are important, what happens when you change two-way to one-way streets, how city neighborhoods can gain or lose power. What made it particularly fascinating for me was that in Mrs. Jacobs's terms Seattle wouldn't seem to qualify as a "great American city." It is large enough, perhaps, but it appears to follow suburban rather than urban schemes of living; I live in the central area, on the edge of the ghetto, but as I write I look out onto lawn and a hedge, a holly tree where robins eat berries, and the roof of my neighbor's house. Thus a great deal in *Death and Life of Great American Cities* had to be translated into Seattle terms. But because the book is not only staggering but immensely sensible, the translation could be made, and once made, Seattle became understandable and patterns of living and dying emerged. I spent long hours walking and driving around, flabbergasted and pleased at how much I could learn.

I soon learned also that here and throughout the country Mrs. Jacobs was being reviled. Of course she had her cheerleaders, but they too were thought of as nuts, quaint and nostalgic seekers of some long gone golden age when city life was safe and interesting and pleasant. I remember a review that compared the author and her followers to a scene in a Grace Moore movie where Miss Moore drives down a street, stands up in her car to sing something like "That's Amore," and soon shopkeepers and passersby are coming in on the chorus. The allegation always seemed to be that Mrs. Jacobs likes the corner candy store and doesn't like supermarkets or housing projects, and obviously anyone who thinks that way is unqualified to comment on twentieth-century disasters like American cities.

Now, eight years later, the pattern seems to be repeating itself, for me, Mrs. Jacobs, and her critics. I am on sabbatical, trying to write a history of Seattle, which to many seems absurd because Seattle is to them not much more than a large huddle of houses barely a century old, and which to me seems simply very hard. As if to show me that and even how it can be done, Mrs. Jacobs writes *The Economy of Cities,* shorter and more analytical than her first book, but if anything better, more challenging and releasing, because if there is anything people are really cynical and unthinking about it is economics. So I have spent the last few months seeing how Seattle's economic history is describable in Mrs. Jacobs's terms, and along the way I note that it looks as though this book too will be misunderstood and shunned. The reviewer in *Commentary* says that though it is closely and densely argued, which it certainly is, it really is a kind of economic pastoral, which it certainly isn't; the man in *The New York Review of Books,* though claiming to approve, can find no better term to describe Mrs. Jacobs than the evasive and misleading "anar-chist."

For better or worse, what Mrs. Jacobs is is a vitalist; her key words are "growth" and "stagnation." She is not in any usual sense of the term an optimist—"In human history, most people in most places most of the time have existed miserably in stag-nant economies"—but because she is a vitalist her sense of his-tory is not linear and so she believes that processes of growth can begin in all but the most moribund and despairing economies. Seeing possibilities for life, however, is not the same as pretend-ing they exist where they don't, and a good deal of the book is taken up with showing how cities stagnate. For her the great wrecker is coagulation of power and money, usually as the result of some earlier wonderful success, in the hands of those who make even large cities into company towns because they are un-aware that they are changing the city they bleed from a living body to a turnip to a stone. A city needs constantly to be devel-oping new work from its old work, and if it only goes on making its old work more efficient, it will eventually atrophy when other cities begin to make what it makes or other products and pro-cesses render its work obsolete. Like ancient Harappa, which went on turning out, in greater and greater quantities, solid wheels and one-piece weapons and implements while other cities were learning to make spoked wheels and ribbed instruments and thus lighter and stronger vehicles and tools. Like medieval Dinant, which concentrated on making wonderful brass vessels and so declined when London and Paris began making them too. Like nineteenth-century Manchester, which Engels and Disraeli saw as the city of the future, but which stagnated because it tied everything to its textile industry. Like modern Detroit, which is dying from a surfeit of cars. Like Seattle, which triumphed over other cities on Puget Sound and then over Portland because in its early years it was creating all kinds of work that was not simply logging and shipping, and which has "grown" into a company town where everyone's job and psyche is tied up with the for-tunes of the Boeing Company. Efficiency not only makes slaves, as we have always known, but it is in itself a form of slavery for cities.

The stories Mrs. Jacobs tells about these cities are too long to be quoted in full, but let me paraphrase the one about Detroit. The city began, as all cities do according to Mrs. Jacobs, as an exporter, in this case of flour, and everything else it made—candles, shoes, hats, whiskey, soap—was only for local consumption. Around the flour mills and the docks grew up machine and repair places—Detroit's first instance of making new work from old—then parts manufacturers and shipbuilders. By the 1860s some people who had started out in the mills had broken away and were making marine engines, and Detroit became a major exporter of both engines and ships. In turn these new enterprises began to support new businesses, suppliers of parts, tools, and metal. The biggest of these were refineries of copper alloys made from local copper ore, and soon the exporting of copper and copper products became Detroit's biggest business. Then the copper ore ran out, and had the city's economy been dependent completely on this one industry, it would necessarily have begun to stagnate. Instead Detroit moved into the period of its most explosive growth, and grew from 116,000 to 285,000 people between 1880 and 1900. What is even more remarkable is that Detroit did this without finding one big new industry to take the place of copper refining, so that it looks as though Detroit was growing explosively without having anything to sustain it. But part of the growth was the result of having generated a host of other exports—paints, varnishes, steam generators, pumps, lubricating systems, tools, store fixtures, stoves, medicines, furniture, leather for upholstery, sporting goods; part was the result of making for itself more of what hitherto it had had to import, and "import replacing" is a city's major means of creating great and diversified growth. To replace an import is to create new local work and is also to create the conditions whereby this new work may thrive, as will happen whenever the product or service, once imported and now locally made or done, is developed into a new export.

It was, thus, no accident that the automobile industry was successful in Detroit, because Detroit was already making all that Henry Ford needed:

> He bought from various suppliers in Detroit every single item he needed for his cars—wheels, bodies, cushions, ev-

erything. The Dodge Brothers, young mechanics who had been producing transmissions for Olds in their machine shop, expanded to make Ford's engines. They were adding work. The first Ford factory was a wooden building in a coal yard, financed by the carpenter who built it. . . . Ford's first significant innovation of any kind—and one of the most important he was ever to make—was to promise customers that they could get a complete stock of repair parts for Ford cars. At first he bought these parts from his subcontractors, the same people who supplied the original components. But then he began making repair parts himself, beginning with those that proved to be most in demand. Thus little by little, he added to his assembly work the manufacturing of part after part. By the time he was ready to put the first Model T into production, late in 1907, he was capable of much of its manufacture.

This sequence of Ford's early activities is the great sign of the vigor and health of Detroit's economy. The point is not that it couldn't have happened elsewhere, but that a relatively small city was sufficiently diverse in its manufacture to supply Ford with all he needed.

But this very success was a danger sign, and one that no one in Detroit read rightly:

The Chinese ideogram for "crisis" is composed of the symbols for "danger" and "opportunity"; just so, a very successful growth industry poses a crisis for a city. Everything—all other development work, all other processes of city growth, the fertile and creative inefficiency of the growth industry's suppliers, the opportunities of able workers to break away, the inefficient but creative use of capital—can be sacrificed to the exigencies of a growth industry, which thus turns the city into a company town.

And so, as Mrs. Jacobs says in another place while showing what goes wrong when capital is exported instead of being used locally, the story ends:

Almost no capital is used in Detroit for developing new goods, services, enterprises or industries there, while De-

troit exports extraordinary amounts of the capital it gener-
ates. Some is exported in the form of the immense philan-
thropies of the Ford Foundation, dispensed from its
headquarters in New York throughout the world. Among
other things, the Foundation has financed many studies of
the "causes" of poverty, and of what is wrong with the poor
in stagnant cities.

Hardly an economic pastoral, and whatever of anarchy there is in
the idea of creative inefficiency, there is no anarchy at all in that
prose; it is hard to think of so strongly latinate a vocabulary being
made so spare and direct.

What is important as an idea is the pattern: a new city exports to an older city, then creates supporting goods and services,
then experiences explosive growth as it replaces its imports with
locally made goods and services and so earns new imports, then
creates new exports out of its new local industries. But, though
this is central to her book, it is not the idea, really, that makes
The Economy of Cities so exciting; it is, rather, the immense variety of examples used to buttress the central terms. One can imagine, for instance, someone at the Ford Foundation reading my
quotations above and snorting at a phrase like "the inefficient but
creative use of capital," because he did not remember or found
irrelevant the very creatively used capital in Detroit around the
turn of the century that made, among other things, the Ford
Foundation possible. Or because he had not read elsewhere in
the book about the way bicycle manufacturing in Tokyo, now an
international industry, began when lots of bike repair shops in
that city began making parts to fix imported bikes; immensely
creative, that, but it would have been much more efficient to
have Schwinn or Columbia just come in and make their own, and
much more regressive too. Or what about the story of Thiokol,
the Kansas City firm trying to make anti-freeze, that was driven
out of town by Prendergast because the smell tainted the bootleg
liquor, and ended up as the first manufacturer of the solid fuels
used in space rockets. Reading such stories gets one in the habit
of finding them oneself. The other day I heard a friend of mine
who works for Cesar Chavez talk about pesticide manufacturing,
and it wasn't hard at all to see that the better and safer pesticides
needed by the farm workers would not be made by the presently

powerful and efficient firms because there is no need for them to
do anything differently unless the political heat gets too much.
Rather, the pesticides of the future will almost certainly be developed by a new, small outfit. Perhaps its people will come from
one of the existing big pesticide firms, perhaps from a company
now not interested in pesticides at all but in perfumes or desalin-
ized water. Wherever they come from, however, they will be
sorely in need of inefficient but creative capital, inefficient because almost certainly the new pesticide makers will not score on
the first or even the fiftieth try—which is why the likes of the
Crocker Citizens Bank will go on investing in the likes of Shell
Chemical—and creative because Mrs. Jacobs is right: the only
way new things happen is by breaking away, starting clumsily,
and doing something most people wouldn't do at all.

That there is something mysterious about all this is part of its
excitement: "All that Birmingham seems to have had, to begin
with, was a good supply of drinking water—no novelty in Renaissance England." But being aware of the mystery not only makes
the examples rich, it also allows Mrs. Jacobs to score repeatedly
against people who are happiest at the drawing board and most
uncomfortable when looking at the real world. In *Death and Life
of Great American Cities* the enemies, cited so often it really
becomes an annoying tic, are the planners and the urban renewal
boys. Here they take more varied forms and are shoved out of
the way in neat, short bursts. On the location theory of cities:

> The mouth of the Connecticut River, the largest river of
> New England, is so fine a site for a depot city that had a
> major city grown there, we may be sure that it would have
> been accounted for in the geography textbooks by its loca-
> tion at the river mouth. But in reality, this site has brought
> forth only the little settlements of Lyme and Old Saybrook.
> . . . Among the best natural harbors in Britain, for ex-
> ample, are those belonging to the settlements of Ipswich,
> Yarmouth, King's Lynn, Sunderland, South Shields, Los-
> siemouth, Shoreham, Stornoway, and Greenock. . . .
> Many cities engaging in enormous trade occupy notably in-
> ferior trading sites. Tokyo and Los Angeles are examples.

On the relation of overpopulation, natural resources, and poverty:

Furthermore, if people cause their own poverty by their own numbers, it follows that if a given population is reasonably scanty to begin with, it will not be poor. Yet countries that have always been thinly populated, and have rich resources besides, are quite as liable to poverty as heavily populated countries. Thinly settled Colombia, has topsoil rich and deep beyond the dreams of Iowa, and high-grade iron ore beyond the dreams of Japan, yet Colombia festers in poverty and economic chaos worse, if anything, than densely populated India.

As I say, all this is very mysterious, in a way that makes you want to look around, to reflect on what you know of elsewhere, to read the yellow pages and the U.S. Census and see it all differently, as if for the first time. You take a sentence out of context and it seems only that someone is riding a hobby horse: "What we abstractly call the dissemination of cultures consists of many exports, some of them amazingly complex, that were first developed within the local economies of cities." But put it back into context:

> The scrolls that went from Athens to the great library of the ancients in Alexandria, the complex work of Roman surveyors and engineers who mapped out aqueducts in the Iberian peninsula and Gaul, the treatises on agriculture and fossils and the musical instruments that went forth from Paris to Thomas Jefferson in Monticello, the periodicals sent from London to Benjamin Franklin in Philadelphia, the medical work being done by teams of specialists and sent forth from present-day Peking—these are not what one could call simple exports.

It's like having a whole new world to think about.

In our making and unmaking of cities lies our great difference from other animals, the humanness of our hopes and awfulness. Because she is so clear, Mrs. Jacobs is also a very stern judge: most cities stagnate, only a few live to earn over and over the process of renewal. But she can show also that our present wantonness with our environment is not simply a matter of original sin, or the necessary concomitant of a burgeoning technology, and also make it clear that we can renew our air and water and find better means of transporting ourselves simply by using the very means we used to create filth and waste. My city has just put a new airplane on the market, one so huge it seems to darken the sky like an eclipse. It will do in some ways better and more efficiently what airplanes are supposed to do, move people great distances very fast. And after the Boeing 747 comes the SST. These planes will probably complete the job of making Seattle into a company town, and almost certainly they will create air and automobile congestion and noise as yet unexperienced. Yet as Seattle lurches—happily no less—to fulfill the economic destiny of Detroit along the urban patterns of Los Angeles, yet it could be that even here someone—not a division of Boeing, surely, or a governmental advisory board, but someone—is now at work on a machine or material that makes engines less noisy or that moves people along the ground in quantities and at speeds analogous to those of the big planes in the sky. The fact that many people, if asked, would guess that such things will be done by the Japanese or the Germans means they really believe them possible. Mrs. Jacobs quotes Alcaeus on Greek cities in 600 B.C.: "Not houses finely roofed nor the stones of walls well built nor canals nor dockyards make the city, but men able to use their opportunity."

That men have at some times and in some places been able to use their opportunity is not a matter of faith but of history. What is at bottom so invigorating about Jane Jacobs, for all that she stresses the way "most people in most places most of the time have existed miserably in stagnant economies," is her strange and wonderful conviction that men love to work. The joy of working, of course, lies in trying to make new things, whether they be truly new, as with inventions or great works of art, or new adaptations of old solutions for new problems and local conditions, like good urban building, or literary criticism, or *The Economy of Cities*, or Japanese bicycle manufacture. That we build from old work is both a sign of the necessity of cultural continuity and of that economic health which makes the present potentially productive and the future possible. The old, if it is powerless, must stagnate and die, and if it is powerful is apt to be conservative, even destructively reactionary. It is for this reason, one presumes, that so many of the world's newer economies are trying to get along without cities because cities for them mean either the old and dying or the old and reactionary, or both. One knows perfectly well why Castro hated the Havana of Batista and distrusts it still, or why Ho Chi Minh might go to war against the dying and reactionary Saigon. But Mrs. Jacobs is surely right in insisting that human beings develop as their cities develop, and that no rural economy can last for long without the renewing power of cities to make new work out of old. Among her bagful of stories are ones about the farcical efforts of the Rockefellers to make a birth control factory in the Indian countryside or the self-defeating aspects of Mao's Great Leap Forward.

There are ways to disagree with Jane Jacobs, but not as many as you might think, because on her own terms she is almost invariably right and the real questions arise when you start to consider what she has left out. For instance, in *Death and Life of Great American Cities* Los Angeles comes in for some pretty solid pasting: the place is unsafe, ugly, and weak in growing those veins and arteries on which the lives of great cities depend. In *The Economy of Cities* Los Angeles must come off much better because it fits all the patterns for explosive city growth that Mrs. Jacobs shows are necessary in the cyclical life of a healthy city economy; indeed, one of her most staggering lists is of all the things Los Angeles started to make in the late 1940s just when its death was predicted because it had lost its wartime airplane industry. There is a discrepancy here that Mrs. Jacobs does not face in either book, which might not be worthy of remark were it not that it leads one to ask if or how the growth of some cities is preferable to that of others even when both are fulfilling Mrs. Jacobs's patterns of continuing renewal, and, conversely, if there aren't some kinds of economic stagnation that are preferable to others. I know that of course Mrs. Jacobs can reply to these questions by assenting to their implied answers and adding that such matters lay outside the scope of her inquiry. But such a reply would be at least a little ingenuous, because Mrs. Jacobs is a vitalist and because she is interested in all forms of life—one of the joys of her book is the way she makes so many things relevant to the economy of cities. I do not think Los Angeles a total disaster because it is so very obviously a triumph, but I also think that what has triumphed there is in many ways frightening.

Let me put it another way. For *The Economy of Cities* Los Angeles and Tokyo are the contemporary heroes because Mrs. Jacobs can show that in both instances a city, without great nearby natural resources, without good harbors, with a severe threat of overpopulation, "just grew" because men have been able to use their opportunity there. We know also that many Europeans, who live in cities we love but which they think are dying, look upon Los Angeles and Tokyo as the great good cities of the future. Let me add that Mrs. Jacobs grew up in Scranton, Pa., a city that never grew beyond its first spurt of explosive activity, and has spent most of her adult life in New York, a great city whose signs of stagnation no one is better at listing than Mrs. Jacobs. It seems to me at least plausible that someone whose life has followed that pattern might be driven to see economic health as absolutely crucial, as it might be for someone who grew up in Manchester or Lyon and moved to London or Paris. In such contexts it is easy to see why one might come to idealize Los Angeles or Tokyo. Furthermore, though I know little of either city, I always feel a strong urge to idealize them whenever I hear them denounced by someone who makes it clear that what he really dislikes is either cities or whatever century he is living in.

Still, there is more to the problem than learning the rhythms of history. To be a vitalist is to believe almost absolutely in patterns, and to do that is to choose to overlook the ways history does not just make patterns and the ways one city is not the same as another no matter how similar their patterns of growth and decay. Though Seattle is fulfilling the economic destiny of Detroit along the urban patterns of Los Angeles, it is very much different from either; in its God-given beauties, in its position on the continent, in its historical period of growth, in tangible things that make living here different from living there, or there. The maker of patterns must stress likenesses, there is no other way, and the vitalist must accept life wherever she finds it. But much of the mystery of cities lies in their differentness one from another, and when she overlooks those differences, for whatever good or obvious reasons, Mrs. Jacobs becomes at least partially kin to those people she rightly dislikes most, the planners and governments determined to make similar things into the same things. From the angle of, say, London, Los Angeles and Tokyo become the same place; from the angle of New York, Seattle and Detroit and Atlanta are one. When you see as well as Jane Jacobs does, you can see a lot looking from such vantage points, but you miss a lot too, and it is the special quality of those who see clearly and well (especially when they are attacked for their greatest virtues) that they tend to take what they leave out and pretend it is not there. Men may live miserably, and many surely do so because they live in stagnant cities, but as our greatest vitalist has said, it is the quality of unhappy households to be very much different one from another.

Perhaps all I am suggesting is another reason why it is in the examples and in the lists that *The Economy of Cities* is most wonderful, for it is there that Mrs. Jacobs gives us, with the density of a great nineteenth-century novelist and the clarity of a splendid revisionist historian, the mystery of and reason for the human achievement that is city life. The Japanese bike makers, the Roman engineers, Los Angeles in the 1940s, the Dodge boys, the Parisian books on fossils exported to Virginia—all in a short book one can read in an evening. And I've not said a word about New Obsidian, or the origin of Route 128 around Boston, or the great future for chemical toilet manufacturers, or the lady who made the first brassiere. To call such abundance anarchy or pastoral is to walk down West Eighth Street or Charing Cross Road and to long for Stuyvesant Town or Welwyn Garden City.

TOYNBEE, ELLUL, SAFDIE, NEGROPONTE

By all rights, these four books on various urban matters should be all wrong. Two are European, somber, gloomy, full of long views taken as though from the long end of a telescope, seeing God and History but seldom anything so complicated, dirty, noisy, or interesting as a city. The other two are North American, young, cheerful, uninterested in history, seeing new ways of designing houses and environments where the cities their projects are placed in appear as through the right end of the telescope. They are full of pictures of things that look as if they're made of origami, without anything so complicated, dirty, noisy, or interesting as a city. On the one hand history is everything, and it moves in long, decisive swoops and whirls; on the other hand, history never happened and the most interesting facts about people are that they like sunlight and privacy. Yet it turns out that none of these four books is worthless, that the perspectives they offer can be useful, and not simply as ways of reminding us of what we always knew.

Arnold Toynbee's *Cities on the Move* is the latest in a spate of books he has published since he finished *A Study of History,* and while Toynbee has not learned much over the years, he is, as always, a cheerful, charming, and learned man. He is one of the world's largest reference libraries, everything is down on three-by-five cards, all carefully cross-indexed. If the category is "The Choice of Capitals for Convenience," Toynbee can spout up Constantinople, Paris, London, Patna, Memphis (Egypt), northern Chinese cities from Chang-an to Peking, Rome in a unified nine-teenth-century Italy, Seleucia and Ctesiphon in Afghanistan, Kamakura and Yedo (now Tokyo), on and on, with side trips along the way to look at capitals created to avoid clashes of power between existing cities and efforts to rule from twin capitals.

The "conveniences" which dictated the establishment of each city are briefly described, then Toynbee flips his card and leaps hundreds of miles or years just by moving on to the next card. If the subject is holy cities, paragraphs will begin with sentences like "Being a charismatic personality's birthplace or being the scene of his subsequent mission are not the only forms of local association with such a personality that can make a holy city" and "Neither a martyrdom nor a tomb is indispensable for the making of a holy city; the belief that the place has been the scene of a miracle can be equally efficacious." The paragraphs that follow such openings practically write themselves.

Toynbee's name appears on *Esquire*'s latest list of the world's hundred most important people, but it is my impression that in the fifteen years since *A Study of History* he has been increasingly ignored by professional historians, and with some reason. His idea of history is so simple, his method so easily reduced to a system, that not only churlish or myopic specialists object to his cheerful, bland leaps across space and time. Yet I often remember, and in reading *Cities on the Move* felt I was right so to remember, that it was while reading Toynbee on Pope Gregory VII that I first felt the thrill of being a historian. The section is called "The Nemesis of Creativity" in volume IV of the *History*; the subsection is "The Intoxication of Victory." Surely the pretentious titles and manner appealed to my own adolescent pretensions, but I don't think that was all of it.

Toynbee's innocence and simplicity can create in him and in his reader the sense that any place and any time can be made into the present tense; he moves from Gregory VII to Harun-al-Raschid, locks into place his correlative comparison of Innocent III and Suleiman the Magnificent, and never pauses for breath. Human beings simply are not mysterious to him, nor are their dwelling places, the distant past is only yesterday. This may be folly, but it can also be exhilarating:

> The highlands of Afghanistan, however, are, in wintertime, even more inclement than Persepolis and the Isle of Thanet, and consequently the Ghaznevids' climatic problem was to escape, not the summer heat of the lowlands, but the winter cold of the highlands. The Ghaznevids were not concerned for themselves or for their human troops; these were hardy; and they could have braved highland Ghazni's winter snows if the maintenance of their rule had depended on enduring these rigours. Actually, however, the Ghaznevids' master-weapon was not their soldiery; it was their elephants; and, for the elephants' sake, the Ghaznevid Court decamped, in the autumn, from Ghazni to Lashkari Bazar, far down the course of the Helmand River, where the winter climate is almost as genial as it is in the elephants' native Hindustan.

Every gesture in that paragraph is mechanical, but those elephants! those October journeys to Lashkari Bazar! Toynbee may be oversimplifying horribly, as the professionals have told us he so often does, but then we have many other places to go to be reminded of the density and insolubility of history.

And if we feel that these glances at the Ghaznevids take us a long way from the problem of cities, Toynbee can show us that part of the reason we do so is that the problem of cities as we tend to think of it is not age-old but new. Up until the time of what Toynbee calls mechanized cities, urban centers could be created and moved about by governmental decision, and those decisions could be based on the desire to find a good climate for the military elephants. Since the end of the eighteenth century, however, cities have become more their own masters, more subject to internal rather than to external change, and considerations of climate or prestige become less important. Constantine or Shah Abbas or Peter the Great could make a great city by command, but after cities became mechanized this could not be done, as Washington, Ottawa, and Brasilia show.

As to what creates internal change in a mechanized city, Toynbee is not only innocent but incurious; the problem is so complex that he cannot even see it. Thus, the closer he comes to the present, the more his simplicity seems defective, and, perhaps sensing this, Toynbee spends little time on his mechanized cities and moves quickly into the future, about which he can once again be grand and simple, via the Monopoly board visions of the Greek planner Doxiadis. The fault is not Toynbee's alone. We will encounter more than once this tendency to avoid casting a naked eye on the relatively recent past and the present, to go to the telescope instead.

The views offered through the telescope of Jacques Ellul are very long, like Toynbee's, but his spirit and temperament are very different. Apparently Ellul is becoming very big as a Protestant "thinker," which may tell us more about the times than about Ellul himself. The Committee of Southern Churchmen has edited a volume called *Introducing Jacques Ellul,* which has contributions by such up-to-date people as Christopher Lasch, Julius Lester, and William Stringfellow, and which stresses Ellul's "social thought." Ellul himself is unsparingly gloomy, convinced of the folly of all liberal politics, anxious himself to become a Jeremiah who insists that the real names for our cities are Nineveh and Babylon. His latest book, *The Meaning of the City,* is filled with passages like the following:

> The first undeniable element in this life is due to the city's nature as a parasite. She absolutely cannot live in and by herself. And this, moreover, characterizes all of those works of man by which he seeks autonomy. Everything takes its life from somewhere else, sucks it up. Like a vampire, it preys on the true living creation, alive in its connection with the Creator. The City is dead, made of dead things for dead people.

This kind of thing really should not be thought of as the latest thing in ideas. Some of the contributors to *Introducing Jacques Ellul* identify Barth and Weber as Ellul's mentors, but most of his tone and manner can more easily be found in the generation of Ruskin and Baudelaire. Which should not seem particularly surprising, because when a late-twentieth-century Christian tries to adopt a biblical mantle, he will probably sound like nothing so much as a nineteenth-century prophetic city-baiter.

Ellul himself, however, tries very hard to avoid any sense that he can be historically placed, just as he wants to insist that we should not try to explain the Old Testament hatred of cities by reference simply to the historical position of the ancient Hebrews:

> In order to understand the history of the city and the situation as it now exists, we must take into account not only its beginning as a human enterprise, but also the curse placed on it from its creation, a curse which must be seen as a part of its make-up, influencing its sociology and the habitat it can provide. This curse is not only that placed on the entire world, but is a special curse on the city, both as belonging to the world and in itself. It is the curse expressed from one end of the Scriptures to the other by "I will destroy, says the Lord."

Ellul's popularity seems to derive from his insistence that God is not only not dead, but is judging us as absolutely as He judged the worshippers of Baal and the citizens of Sodom. Christian apologetics have tended to be rather fancy, liberal, and watered-down of late, and here is someone trying to call us back to the old truths: what is wrong with the city is not its technology, its filth, its sprawl, but its very nature as man's fortress, pride, and home; the builder of the first city is Cain.

What is most attractive for Ellul about his position is its simplicity. Read the old texts rightly and ye shall know. But surely it takes no Gibbon to point out that the Hebrew and Christian God, born (as it were) in exile and nurtured in the shadow of the Egyptian, Assyrian, and Babylonian empires, protected by but endlessly suspicious of the Alexandrian and Roman hegemonies, is not a cosmopolitan deity. For Him cities are where men go to hide from His judgment, where they will try to build a world in which they can do without Him; even the great Hebrew citymakers, David and Solomon, will not be exempt, and if Jerusalem is an image of the Heavenly City which can be man's ultimate reward, it also, as an historical city, is not exempt from God's curse. But if God can never be less than angry with man's cities, His exegetes when they try to sound like His prophets cannot avoid the terrible limitations attendant on God's simplicity.

Any modern lover of cities must live in dread of their wasteful power, must wonder and worry about any future where almost all human achievements are the properties of cities, but he need not therefore be more than mildly fascinated by the fullness and sweep of Ellul's exposition. When, as with Ellul, all cities become The City, when all periods of history become the same moment, when like Ellul we are not interested in any differences between his city, my city, and ancient Nimrod, then Armageddon may be near, but until it comes, man, proud man, dressed in his little brief authority, must continue to try to make distinctions.

Such as were made, for instance, by the Israeli-born Canadian, Mosche Safdie, when he returned to Israel after his spectacular rise to fame as the designer of Habitat, symbol of Expo 67's great success in Montreal. Safdie meets a young Israeli soldier who complains that the trouble with the Arabs is that they are bad soldiers. "That may be," Safdie answers,

> but they build so much better than we do and their towns are so much more wholesome than ours. Their art, their

pottery, their clothes, their jewelry, their music is the soul of this land; there is so much we can learn from them.

Safdie had been raised in a kibbutz and the teachings of that raising had remained with him throughout his career as an architect, yet for him distinctions are still possible: the Arabs built so much better cities than the Israelis. Did not, perhaps, design them better, but lived in them better, and made their cities the expression of that living.

The shame is that this moment is unique in Safdie's *Beyond Habitat;* it took a return to his homeland and a confrontation with Israel's "new housing projects that rape the hills and the landscape" to make it happen. At that moment Safdie is looking at what is and imagining what could be by seeing what has been. The trouble with the rest of *Beyond Habitat* is that it tries to do too many things and so does all of them incompletely. It offers an account of the way Habitat came to be, which is mostly a kind of self-justifying gossip about predictable hassles between designers and contractors and bureaucrats.

What Safdie means to tell us is why Habitat is not the building he wanted, which is fair enough, but he neither explains in sufficient detail exactly what he wanted nor describes what seems to him good and exciting about the building that was built. One suspects that on the one hand all the old wounds caused by the infighting have not healed but that on the other Safdie is no longer really interested in Habitat and is anxious to move on.

The trouble is that he has moved on too fast. He talks briefly about housing projects and designs which could take place anywhere: San Juan, the San Francisco State campus, the deserts of Palestine, Washington, D.C., New York's East Side waterfront. But once again none of the designs is described in any detail, each is reduced to a political and topographical problem, each place becomes any place. The designer has traveled so much that he has become a designer with an idea, reworking that idea in disregard of place. Safdie knows better, knows that Frank Lloyd Wright was a great builder of buildings and a lousy thinker about communities, knows that to build as wonderfully as the Arabs have built one must live long in a place and sink into it. But his early and great and deserved success has prevented him from acting upon this knowledge, or from remembering it in *Beyond Habitat* except occasionally.

Along the way, however, Safdie keeps us nicely abreast of certain facts and problems. He is convinced that proper designing of mass-produced modules can create a much better environment than anyone who knows the usual modern apartment house or prefabricated house can imagine, and despite Safdie's failure to offer many details about what Habitat or his other buildings look and feel like, one can believe him. He is very clear about the advantages of pyramidal structures over those built like houses of cards, about why a frame into which prefabricated units are fit or plugged is redundant, about the terrible and expensive inefficiency and stupidity of modern building as compared with modern airplane and automobile design.

You can't have much modernization in plumbing when it is written into union contracts that all plumbing will be as it was a generation ago. You can't sensibly build bathrooms and kitchens when all research money is spent on tile or stoves or bathtubs and never on whole units. You can, furthermore, design many projects which are much better on the drawing board than in completed fact. Safdie is enthusiastic about all kinds of possible developments in technology, especially in building materials, but he is fully aware that the aim of his designs is not just concrete walls an inch and a half thick or perfectly designed kitchens but places for human communities.

But, unlike the Arabs he rightly admires, he has not yet slowed down long enough to realize how the poet and the implicit historian in him can be genuinely at odds with the designer in him. For long stretches in *Beyond Habitat* human beings are only those odd creatures who like sunlight or play space for their children or furniture and wall colors which "express" them. If the book were more technical, had more drawings and demonstrations of problems of wind stress and concrete, this would be fine, but it isn't, because Safdie means to be wise and perceptive about human problems, and he doesn't often enough compensate for the lack of more technical detail. And when an architect's talk about design is neither technical enough nor sufficiently rooted in the urban worlds he knows, it can seem very self-defeating. In Safdie's case we have an explanation—he simply tried to do too much—and have ample grounds for hoping for better books in the future.

But if Safdie offers us only glimpses of real cities, Nicholas Negroponte's *The Architecture Machine* does not do even that; "design" is everything. Near the beginning Negroponte rightly notes that the architect is not "well trained to look at the whole urban scene," nor is he "skilled at observing the needs of the particular, the family, the individual." It is only "building-size" problems that architects handle at all well, and the result is "urban monumentalism . . . foisted upon us by opulent, self-important institutions."

That is well said, and very much worth saying, enough to justify our going a long way with Negroponte into his labyrinths. Negroponte feels that the architect needs a machine that can correct him, that can discuss with him things he can intuit but cannot satisfactorily realize, that can remind him of all that he enthusiastically leaves out. Well, Mosche Safdie is a very good architect, but he is guilty enough of Negroponte's charge against architects that he, and we, might pay attention to Negroponte's idea of a machine that "problem worries" rather than "problem solves."

To show that this idea is not just fanciful, Negroponte describes at some length a machine he helped design a few years ago called URBAN5. It was developed from an IBM 2250 computer, and worked with both words and graphics. URBAN5, for instance, had a heading called ACTIVities under which it was asked to consider a number of simple design qualities, each one of which had to be explained to it exactly as its makers wanted: age groups, play space, shady areas, times of day, noise levels, etc. When a new activity, like playing football or cocktail parties, was described to the machine, it then ran through all its programmed design qualities and decided whether the activity and the qualities were compatible: Can you play football on a shady veranda? Does the average-sized cocktail party destroy the privacy of the nearest neighbor?

The machine gradually learns a vocabulary and contexts in which its words and pictures can be used in ways that make sense to it. It probably could not learn from what it is told about football and cocktail parties that some people when drunk are likely to start throwing footballs on a shady veranda, but, had it been told this, it could be expected to store this information so that it could bring it to bear in some other context in which people are getting drunk.

I have never seen an IBM 2250 and Negroponte does not stop to explain its mechanics and capacities, so there is a good deal in his descriptions which I simply have to take on faith. Furthermore, URBAN5 was built as a research project and never had any capacity to handle what might be called the real world, for which more sophisticated machines will be necessary. But Negroponte makes quite clear the outlines of what he thinks is possible: a machine that evolves as it comes to learn and understand the human being with whom it talks so that its virtues will not be those we usually associate with machines—computational figuring and reminding—but those we associate with friends or colleagues—anticipation, hesitating, counter-proposing. The task for the architecture machine is to enter into a dialogue with the designer so that nothing is overlooked and hierarchies of fact and value can be established. Negroponte begins his book by admitting that the machines he wants do not exist yet, but he says enough about those that do exist to make clear that their shortcomings lie in their crudities, not in their theoretical incapacities. Machines that can see and hear are with us already, though they are only babies; machines that can show us what we had not known or perhaps even imagined are on their way.

The question is, what *will* they see? For Negroponte the essential problems of "design" are like those raised by Safdie in his lesser moments; they are abstract matters of form and behavioristic amenity. If Negroponte's architecture machine does not see and worry about different problems from these, then we may find we have moved out of the various pasts created for us by the likes of Toynbee and Ellul and into the futures imagined by the likes of Safdie and Negroponte without ever quite knowing where we are now or seeing our urban world rightly.

Ellul creates cities under a terrible but indefinite curse; Negroponte creates dialogues between men and machines intent on designing away everything except original sin. Both past and future seem too simple, too easily reduced to system and drawing board, too oblivious of that which the naked eye can see. All four writers seem implicitly arrogant, though of arrogance in its usual sense only Ellul is guilty. By this I mean a fatal tendency to imagine more is seen and understood than really is. Toynbee and Ellul subject all cities of the past to the same simplifying historical perspective, Safdie and Negroponte look at spaces and shapes and tend to call what they see the world, or as much of it as they will be professionally concerned with. It has taken a great deal of writing like this to make everyone forget what he knows as matters of common sense: cities are dense, massive, entangled, extraordinarily difficult to understand.

The primary antidote to this implicit arrogance is to give up the distant past and the future, the things about which we know so little except patterns that we can be tempted to ignore our ignorance. The recent past and the present do not admit of easy simplification because what we know of them tends to be blurry, contradictory, and bewildering, and because the naked eye can come into play. We are usually confronted with two kinds of evidence, social scientific analysis and personal testimony, patterns and lore, and one trouble with this evidence is that what is often too small, too detailed, too eccentric to be measured in patterns is still too large and confusing to be recorded well in personal testimony.

For instance, I spend three months in London and am endlessly fascinated. This is what a city should be: dense, various, a city where expertise is still a matter of experience rather than a function of the educational system, a city where elegance and plainness can both mingle and sort themselves out, where perspectives offered by different historical periods are endlessly and unself-consciously available. Yes, the man who is tired of London is tired of life. Yet in every newspaper and magazine, from every Londoner and every American who knows the city better than I, comes a clear verdict: London is dying, dead, the whorish queen of an empire gone welfare. So I recoil, and then reply by asking why people don't know the blindness of such certainty. Don't they know that a hundred years ago every intelligent and farseeing man in London was saying the same thing and producing as his evidence Victorian London, a city we now find anything from interesting to priceless? But they are not interested, they have the evidence: London is strangling itself with traffic, its schools are stupid and overcrowded, its housing is deplorable beyond the dreams of Harlem, its governmental machinery puts latter-day Byzantium to shame.

Fortunately, for me and I hope for the pattern-makers too, London is blessed with a writer who really knows the city, and in ways that do not ignore or abjure social scientific analysis or personal testimony. Ian Nairn, author of *Nairn's London,* is practically unknown in this country. Someone who reads Nairn without ever having seen London would not know how accurate are his off-hand, impressionistic descriptions, but he would see on every page Nairn's fascination and absorption with his city, his many ways of making available his sense of history and its cunning passages. One selection is hardly enough to show this, but here is his description of the waterfront at Twickenham:

It begins only a few yards from the clogged shopping centre, down Water Lane or Bell Lane. There was some bombing here, and the area has been left to decay instead of being put on its feet again. The borough council now have comprehensive proposals for comprehensive beastliness: long may they be postponed. Straight away, there is the footbridge to Eel Pie Island, quite an elegant concrete design (1957) that is not wearing too well. Eel Pie Island is one of the private worlds that London excels in and that modern planning abhors. No cars, but boatyards, shacks, every man his own eccentric. One of them, Hurley Cottage, is so pretty and so beautifully painted in blue and white that it would be worth a special visit to Twickenham on its own account. Places like this produced the kind of person that sailed the little boats across to Dunkirk and we'd better not forget it.

Mind and landscape, feeling and history, brought into single focus, on the page and in the scene when one looks at it. One can be delighted and pleased at Toynbee's elephants, but know that knowledge leads to nothing; one can feel in reading Nairn one's own capacity to see and know being challenged and therefore growing.

Not that Nairn need serve as a necessary model; in this context he is offered mostly as a possibility and as an implicit criticism of those who see their cities through telescopes. In this respect many journalists and planners are perhaps even more guilty than the long-range historians and the short-sighted designers, but because most bad journalism is simply ignored while bad planning often leads to bad everything else, maybe the onus should fall most heavily on them here. What Nairn's London offers is also offered by Augie March's Chicago and Jane Jacobs's New York: a vision so dense that we learn why in great cities all planning should be on as small a scale as possible.

Change anything in the city and you are apt to change a great deal; widening a street, putting in a fountain, rezoning a block, all can have considerable consequences, and these things should be undertaken only by people having a genuine claim to knowing the area in question so well they can at least hope to be able to calculate the consequences of a plan. In past years my neighbor's basketball hoop has been a magnet for kids who come from as far away as eight blocks to shoot baskets, talk, and remake their social selves. The kids tended to be both older and blacker than those who lived on the street, and so tended to dominate the street life.

Within the last year the hoop has come down, the street is deserted most of the time, and the kids who live on the street are freer to play there. The black kids who live on the street now go elsewhere to play. The younger among those remaining are delighted at the change, but some of the older ones are not so sure, and I am inclined to agree with them. We have a quieter street, a less bothersome street, but that silence can be ominous. I then turn for confirmation to a neighborhood south of mine, about which, I must confess, I don't know a great deal. I drive in it a lot and know people who live there, but most of what I know is patterns: the burglary rate is the highest in the city, higher than in my own; in the public schools in that neighborhood the affluent have been at war with the poor and the black, again even more than in my neighborhood.

If I accept those patterns, I then can assert that one possible consequence of the loss of the basketball hoop on my street is an increase in the burglary rate. There are no such hoops or their equivalents, at least that I can see, in the neighborhood to the south. That's just the kind of thing there wouldn't be because the hoop provided for a mixing of ages and races and income levels; the mixing was far from being entirely harmonious, but it did work well most of the time.

When the silence on the street seems ominous I may be overestimating the value of such mixing, and I may be accepting too easily the patterns offered me by the neighborhood to the south. But in this context that is of secondary importance. The point is that no one living more than a block away would consider that basketball hoop as a planning matter in the first place, and so they would be oblivious to the possible consequences of its being up or down. And it is precisely this kind of mistake, this failure to see what is and is not crucial in any given area, that I myself may be making when thinking about an area that I "know" but in which I do not live.

The scale on which I am trying to consider things here is terribly small because it seems to me necessary that most of our thinking about planning take place on such a scale. The moment I move very far from my street I am more likely to accept patterns as truth; the moment I move outside my own city I am the victim of the few things I see and the few people I talk to; I suspect the reason I loved Atlanta and hated Detroit in a short visit to both cities was as much the vagaries of the weather as anything else. What is scary is the thought that so much of what is written and planned about our cities is the result of people believing that personal experience of that sort, or statistical analysis, is all we need or can have.

Of course we will have planners, just as we will have mayors and governors and presidents, and we know these men will make decisions on the basis of almost hopelessly inadequate information. For having sought and gained positions almost totally isolated from all that might help them in their deciding and planning, such men earn our occasional contempt, our occasional pity, and our obligation to tell them whenever they seem to have chosen well or ill concerning those few areas about which we really know something. In these matters, "areas" cannot be a metaphor, because cities take place in literal space, because each one must be known slowly and carefully.

Arnold Toynbee is probably always going to be a gatherer of lore on file cards, so being a world traveler is all right for him, though it is a shame that most public officials will learn about cities in Toynbee's way. More can be expected of Mosche Safdie, however, and so he must be urged to settle for Montreal, or Jerusalem, or some one place, where his intelligence and sensitivity can lead to places for people to live in that are, like the Arab music, the soul of the land. If and when he does this he will be able rightly to use the architecture machines Nicholas Negroponte is going to build. For the wonderful thing about Negroponte's machines is that they acknowledge their ignorance, they learn their patterns only by seeing and hearing and discovering gradually what is relevant for a particular situation. This acknowledging, this learning, this discovering, is what makes them problem worriers rather than problem solvers, and that makes all the difference.

MUMFORD & FULLER

The servile specialist, eloquently ignorant of any department of thought but his own, and therefore fundamentally ignorant of essential relationships in his own field, was undoubtedly a product of the Brown Decades: but it is our

own fault, not that of the earlier period, that he has become
a chronic malady of our intellectual life, instead of a passing
maladjustment.

Lewis Mumford wrote that forty-two years ago, and we have little
to show for the years since except the knowledge that the chronic
malady has been nurtured into a cancer. Knowledge becomes
special knowledge, expertise, as though that were the only kind
there is, or the only kind that could be trusted.

Mumford and Buckminster Fuller are extraordinarily active
men now in their late seventies. Mumford has just published *Interpretations and Forecasts: 1922–1972*, "the one-volume Mumford: the essential thought," except it isn't, because his writing on
cities is being reserved for a second volume. Something with
Fuller's name on it is appearing all the time. At hand are *Earth,
Inc.*, a small collection of short things done over the last
twenty-five years; *The Dymaxion World of Buckminster Fuller*,
which is mostly a collection of drawings and photographs; *Utopia
or Oblivion*, a reissue of a 1969 collection of some of Fuller's
finest performances; perhaps most welcome of all is the best book
on Fuller yet to appear, *Bucky*, by Hugh Kenner.

Both Mumford and Fuller are well known, but because neither is a specialist, they may have cause for wondering how much
their prolonged and learned efforts have ever really been accepted. We have no name for such people. Specialists employ
ugly terms, ranging from the condescending "generalist" to the
curled lip "amateur" to, at least in Fuller's case, "crank" and
"crackpot." Fuller sometimes calls himself a "comprehensivist,"
which won't do, and not only because it isn't accurate. Mumford
would probably just call himself a writer, but when someone calls
himself that, he is often assumed to be out of a job, and being out
of a job tends to mean being out of a university job, a specialist's
job.

The specialist, looking at Mumford or Fuller, is free to ask:
What do *they* know? What definitive work did they do? The
Library of Congress has trouble classifying their work, bookstores
don't know in what section they belong. We can invite Mumford
and Fuller to give keynote speeches, we can give them impressive sounding awards, but what we really want is the person who

wrote the best biography of Zachary Taylor, the best study of the effects of northern urbanization on first-generation immigrant blacks, the best account of the influence of Milton on Wordsworth. In the sciences we don't even want books at all, just articles that report the findings.

The first thing to say about *Interpretations and Forecasts* is that Mumford's early work is a pleasure to read, or reread. Here is a sample:

> In the bareness of the Protestant cathedral of Geneva one has the beginnings of the hard barracks architecture which formed the stone tenements of seventeenth-century Edinburgh, set a pattern for the austere meeting-houses of New England, and finally deteriorated into the miserable shanties that line Main Street. The meagerness of the Protestant ritual began that general starvation of the spirit which finally breaks out, after long repression, in the absurd jamborees of Odd Fellows, Elks, Woodmen, and kindred fraternities. In short, all that was once made manifest in a Chartres, a Strasbourg, or a Durham minster, and in the mass, the pageant, the art gallery, the theater—all this the Protestant bleached out into the bare abstraction of the printed word. Did he suffer any hardship in moving to the New World? None at all. All that he wanted of the Old World he carried within the covers of a book. Fortunately for the original Protestants, that book was a whole literature; in this, at least, it differed from the later Protestant canons, perpetrated by Joseph Smith or Mary Baker Eddy. Unfortunately, however, the practices of a civilized society cannot be put between two black covers. So, in some respects, Protestant society ceased to be civilized.

Mumford is blessed precisely because he has no subject, only a train of thought he is following; on another occasion he might remind us of the virtues of Mary Baker Eddy or the shortcomings of medieval Christianity. He is free because he is appealing not to our ignorance but to our knowledge, to rearrange what we al-

ready know—Main Street, Odd Fellow jamborees, Chartres—
into a new configuration:

> Once the European, indeed, had abandoned the dream of
> medieval theology, he could not live very long on the mem-
> ory of a classic culture: that, too, lost its meaning; that, too,
> failed to make connections with his new experiences in time
> and space. Leaving both behind him, he turned to what
> seemed to him a hard and patent reality: the external
> world.

It seems almost effortless as Mumford does it. We were
taught that the Renaissance had to do with humanism and that
humanism had to do with the "rediscovery" of ancient literature,
but we were never convincingly told why that should make such
a difference. The reason, Mumford assures us, is that it didn't,
and, furthermore, what we can see as important, like the voyages
to the New World, or Galileo, was indeed what is important. No
need to ask whether Mumford has his facts exactly right, or all
the facts he should have; no need, thus, to argue with him, to
suggest that the Protestant achievements of Spenser, Rembrandt,
and Milton were as impressive as anything in medieval culture.
Fact-mongering, scholastic argumentation are irrelevant, because
Mumford is not driven by a need to be original or definitive; he
appeals, instead, to our sense of the humanly reasonable and possible.

It is what I, however fumblingly, went to college to hear,
and heard all too little, but enough to convince me of the enduring importance of this way of thinking and writing about the past.
Later, of course, would come the stern admonitions. "Historians," even "history majors," and especially "graduate students"
had to be suspicious of such ease, freedom, and generality, such
unscientific and unverifiable assertions. I don't think I ever really
believed such admonitions, work though I did to find out who
wrote the standard biography of Charles II. But what I did do
was to turn to writers like Mumford less often than I once had
done. I remember a splendid review of his of the last four volumes of Toynbee's *Study*, which is regrettably missing from this

collection, but Mumford's new books in those years were called *In the Name of Sanity* and *The Transformations of Man,* and so we drifted apart, and I think now we were both right and both wrong.

My experience did allow me a great sense of freshness in rereading what Mumford has chosen from *The Golden Day, The Brown Decades, Herman Melville,* and the somewhat later *The Condition of Man.* Confident of the greatness of human variousness, Mumford approaches each figure without method or bias: Emerson, Thoreau, Melville, Jesus, Augustine, Aquinas—the portraits are usually small, but lithe, alive, telling. Of course some figures remain obdurately beyond Mumford's temperament, but, one notes, because they are narrow and powerful, like the apostle Paul, Rousseau, and Hume, and Mumford responds best to those who are, like himself, flexible and capacious. But these flaws are just that, the necessary shortcomings of one man just because he is only one man.

To say all this is to imply misgivings about some of Mumford's later work. It is not that his interests have changed, but urgency and gloom have infected him. Look at Mumford, in 1948, linking the overuse of the printing press with the evils of specialization; look at how a fine paragraph is, to my mind, marred in its final sentence:

> . . . the mere multiplication of our mechanical facilities has so swollen the output of printed matter, that if any human being attempted to keep up with it in the most cursory way he would have no time left for any other activity. . . . Each specialist, by agreement, pays attention to the narrow column of water that works his particular turbine, and automatically rejects contributions that flow in any other channels: even as he turns aside, perhaps more decisively, from the broad silt-laden river of human experience from which all these activities derive. . . . Either to explore the past or keep up with the present becomes increasingly impossible: so that our capacity for assimilation may be said to vary inversely with our capacity for production; and eventually this will have an unfortunate effect upon our creativity, indeed on our very rationality. When our frustra-

tions finally become acute, we may be tempted, like Hitler's followers, to seek in mere charlatanism and quackery
some short cut to order.

What, in the next-to-last sentence, is an "unfortunate effect" is
expanded, in a frustrated and unthinking way, into the followers
of Hitler and the rest. Mumford has gained from the war a
bludgeon; faced with an enemy, and in need of a weapon, invoke
the Nazi experience.

   Near the end of the same essay, the sourness becomes more
acute:

   About any and every machine, above all about the technical
   process itself, the critical question is: How much does this
   instrument further life? If it does not promote human welfare, in the fullest sense, an atomic pile is as disreputable as
   a pinball game or a juke box.

Pinballs and juke boxes—disreputable? The cheap horror show
of the fifties is upon us, the endless baiting of popular culture for
its vulgarity, the equally endless denunciations about the stan-
dardization of life and the dehumanization of men in cities. Mumford plunges in, as if unaware that Philip Wylie, or Vance Pack-
ard, or a reasonably literate and would-be cynical sophomore,
sounds just that way:

   If the goal of human history is a uniform type of man, repro-
   ducing at a uniform rate, in a uniform environment, kept at
   a constant temperature, pressure, and humidity, like a uni-
   formly lifeless existence, with his uniform physical needs
   satisfied by uniform goods, all inner waywardness brought
   into conformity by hypnotics and sedatives, or by urgent ex-
   tirpation, a creature under constant mechanical pressure
   from incubator to incinerator, most of the problems of
   human development would disappear. Only one problem
   would remain: Why should anyone, even a computer,
   bother to keep this kind of creature alive?

Much of Mumford's writing of the fifties and sixties is like this.
One need do no more than to compare this passage with the first

passage from Mumford quoted above, which is also about the un-
civilizing of civilization.

The fear of the religion of the machine and the corresponding fear of the religion of centralized power take over, and,
as fear will, it strikes Mumford dumb: "By a total inversion of
human values, the favored leaders and mentors of our age prefer
disease to health, destruction to creativity, pornography to potent
sexual experience, debasement to development"; "In this shift to
a world directed solely by intelligence for the exploitation of
power, all of post-historic man's efforts tend toward uniformity";
"By our overvaluation of physical power and scientific truth, aloof
from other human needs, we have paid the same price Faust had
to pay when he made his compact with Mephistopheles: we have
lost our souls." On and on it goes, essay after essay bloated and
yet empty, the voice urgent, but losing its authenticity in clichés.

Yet, yet. If, in *The Culture of Cities* of the late fifties, we
find this same heavy, effortful, repetitive fear in the later chapters, we also find one grand evocation after another of the culture
of older cities in the earlier ones. Even more striking, more rem-
iniscent of the best in Mumford's earlier work, is the series of
reviews done in the last decade—in the present collection are
reviews of a biography of Audubon, a book on Eakins's photographs, and the notorious and nefarious Belknap Press edition of
Emerson. The piece on Audubon, especially, is splendidly loving, praising, fully critical, detailed, morally and emotionally
flexible. So let it be clearly said that there has been no slowing
down or atrophying of powers; there has, rather, been a tendency
to lapse, to let some familiar and often justified fears of modern
life become absolutes.

This is hardly the occasion for a full assessment of Mumford's
achievement; we need, as I have said, the companion volume on
cities. But I know few in the next generations who combined the
grace, the breadth of inquiry, the urgent yet urbane disinter-
estedness that one finds in Mumford, in Wilson, in Lippmann, in
Parrington, although none of these figures, I think, conveys either the rich sense of individual personality or the enduring wisdom that one finds in the greatest English prose writers of the
late-eighteenth and mid-nineteenth centuries. It may be too soon

to judge what Mumford and the others have left us. They have no heirs of anything like that stature, and few even want to celebrate their virtues.

Of course Mumford and Buckminster Fuller are similar in many ways: the same sort of inquisitiveness, the same distrust of specialization, the same kind of civilized puritanism, the same distaste for the short-sighted and the shoddy. Mumford, however, came of age in what we think of as the usual way; he published his first book in his late twenties, he secured his audience and his insights roughly simultaneously so that we can speak of him as belonging to a particular generation. Fuller spent many years struggling in obscurity, never totally failing but never succeeding either, and so never losing the sense that he was by himself, driven back onto his own native resources.

During the years Mumford wrote *The Golden Day* and *The Brown Decades* Fuller worked for the Armour meat people, tried unsuccessfully to market a substitute for the common brick invented by his father-in-law, developed something he called 4-D, which is still obscure, appeared at the Chicago World's Fair with his Dymaxion car, which impressed many, but never went into production. Then there came the Dymaxion house or dwelling place, the Dymaxion map, and still later the World Game and the famous geodesic domes, of which there are many examples, but which never went into production either; and how-to books about domes, which were not endorsed by Fuller himself, led to more failures than successes. Fuller's career itself is something that never quite worked or went into successful production. He is an interesting man, but neither his admirers nor his denouncers have ever known how to assess him.

Which is why it is good to have Hugh Kenner's *Bucky*. It offers much too favorable a view to satisfy many, but it is often steady or cautious precisely where Fuller himself is most fuzzy, enthusiastic, and heedless; it can be recommended as the work of a sober admirer, and, because Hugh Kenner wrote it, as an exercise of mind. The opening chapter offers a small autobiography that ends:

Such was my own route to what everyone sooner or later confronts: the generic twentieth-century problem, discontinuity. Have we still lines of communication open with Jefferson, Socrates, Christ? Or have we spot-welded about ourselves a world we can't think about? Must you just let it hit you?

Kenner has always discussed literature and history in ways that seem bizarre to a specialist; he doesn't like to take things one at a time, this poem and that writer. In *The Counterfeiters* he discusses Pope and Swift by way of *The Stuffed Owl* anthology, a mechanical duck made by an eighteenth-century Frenchman, Charles Babbage, Buster Keaton, and Andy Warhol. He wants a Whole, what Buckminster Fuller calls a coordinate system, a means whereby history can intelligibly end with the present, and the present can make sense:

A guide, not an outline. His dynamisms don't submit to outline. "People expect one-picture answers," he says, implying that they should think of cinema sequences. There's no more a definitive arrangement than there was for the parts of the Dymaxion Map I bought at Mac's. That map, like his lectures, was meant to correct a misleading view of the world. Yet one of its arrangements can look like Mercator's—which was true enough to sail by, after all—and one of the ways I could arrange this book would make Fuller's talk seem systematic. I could also make it look like a string of platitudes, or like a set of notions never entertained before, or like a delirium. I won't do any of those things. It's a poet's job he does, clarifying the world. That's the emphasis I understand best.

Fuller is a poet, after all, so many can let themselves relax, feeling they no longer have to take Fuller seriously, because poets, they know, clarify no worlds larger than their own private ones. But Kenner's poets have always had a way of doing more than that:

Should we muff our part of the world's work irretrievably—a possibility he does not ignore, though his optimism

is famous—then it will have been Fuller's achievement any-
how to show a vision of what might have been. Pythagoras,
long ago, glimpsed what might have been, a harmonious
civic and intellectual sanity. That vision, what survives of it,
no one thinks mistaken, though Greece itself perished.

The claims are both modest and huge. Fuller can be system-
atized, made platitudinous, or totally original, or delirious, so it is
only a conjuring trick, it seems, that makes him not any of these,
but a poet. Yet the poet does much, clarifies the world, shows
what might be.

Since Kenner's sentences are totally linked to one another, I
cannot possibly reveal the charm and intensity of his proceed-
ings, only indicate emphases and offer an example or two. The
major emphasis is on Fuller as a performer, a tireless world
traveler who gives marathon "lectures," lasting between four and
six hours, many times a year. Those who try to "get" Fuller by
reading him are at a disadvantage and may well be inclined to
think him simple-minded, or a pop scientist, or a fraud, which
must count as a limit both to his capacities and to his ultimate
influence. Those who have heard him, however, know that the
point about him is not the particular "points" he makes, most of
which in isolation are easy to grasp and to discard, but rather the
leaps, the line he casts out between one knot that he ties and the
next. Furthermore, in the cold light of print—and Fuller's most
recent books are transcribed performances—one notices that
things are often not quite right, as Kenner remarks:

> Yet barely a detail is invulnerable to someone's carping.
> Names are wrong, or dates. Paraphrases are hasty. When
> Bucky commences a sentence "Einstein said . . . ," you
> can be sure that an Einstein specialist would take half an
> hour persuading you that what Einstein had in mind was a
> good deal more intricate. As for his irrefutable assertions, a
> committee would tell you that they were fervent platitudes,
> scraps from some specialist's alphabet. His science is "su-
> perficial." His mathematics is "trivial."

One sees how Kenner loads dice; all objections are called carping, and done not by physicists or mathematicians but "Einstein

specialists" and committees. Yet Kenner is right. In performance what is wrong seems to matter little, because Fuller when performing makes the particular points minor, and the star-spinning from one to the next entrancing.

This may indicate why Fuller is so beloved, and scorned, and even feared. He seems to cast a spell that makes interested listeners into something like followers, and those who seek to dismiss him know that spell-binders have been suspect for a number of centuries. Those who claim to chart the universe are often known for having too easy answers; in response to such people, specialists, who could be trusted, came into being, and they soon demonstrated that the universe could not be charted. They piled up such huge storehouses of specialized knowledge that any one person's knowledge of more than a little bit of it would have to be inaccurate, or superficial, or trivial. So let us accept this. As a knower, as someone speaking about history or chemistry or physics or architecture, Fuller is seldom going to be as accurate, as subtle, as comprehensive as at least some and maybe many specialists in each of these "subjects" might be. But is there nothing left? What is left is Fuller's faith, and we should try to say what that faith consists of, for it has often been misunderstood.

Fuller's faith rests on a denial of original sin. "He believes," says Kenner, calling the belief Emersonian, "that Character is by definition disinterested, and that conflict does not arise unless through selfishness, a corruption of character." He also believes that men have been selfish and corrupt because there simply was not enough to go around. The act of making one man rich is the act of making another man poor, said Ruskin, and, replies Fuller, that was much more true a thousand or five thousand years before Ruskin than it was in 1862, and much more true then than now.

The reason is, simply, the human mind, the great anti-entropic force. Men have for centuries been becoming aware of and learning nature's processes, and, since nature always does things in the most efficient way possible, men have learned how to get more from less, how to reduce the amount of slave labor or man hours it takes to build a house, get a boat from Tyre to

Athens, grow grain in a field. Any politics based on a principle of exploitation must, then, someday and perhaps soon, become obsolete; if we continue to believe in the capacity of the mind to understand the processes of nature, we can make men more productive, more at home in the world, less menial, less exploitative, less polluting.

The unborn, says Fuller, are uncorrupted. "Nevertheless," Kenner quickly adds:

> if they are born into our environment they will turn out like us. That is how the sins of the fathers are transmitted; surroundings which model a deficient imagination impress its deficiencies upon the impressionable. The jailor's son believes in jails. The slum child grows up coping with slums. Squares live in cubes, cubes shape the next generation of squares. The *house* is the most immediate environment, and hovering in Bucky's mind between metaphor and reality, the house became his prime theme when he talked of regenerating man.

Fuller no longer makes such an emphasis, but that isn't really important. Let's pick up Fuller at a point where almost anyone would scream:

> Children are born naturally to truth or reason. Protect them in it mechanically and they need never lose it. The new industrially produced home will accomplish this.

The most generous one can be with such a statement taken by itself is that it smacks of pitchmen of the thirties and the 1939 New York World's Fair. But it isn't, again, the example that is crucial; here is Kenner on the principle in question:

> Were houses mass-produced, where would architects' commissions go? But we hardly think to impute to them self-interest, so strongly are we conditioned against the phrase "mass-produced." Yet books are mass-produced. Milton was not offended by the sameness of any two copies of *Paradise Lost*. Sheet music is mass-produced. Prints are mass-produced. The writer, the composer, the designer, each

brings his prototype to the best perfection he can manage, and then entrusts it to a factory. Indeed by the 1960s a constructivist in steel could instruct the factory by telephone. Such things shape our intellectual environment, and our bodies too are produced by automation. The refined prototype, mass-produced: that is nature's way with trees and cats and human frames, and the poet's way and the shipbuilder's.

The house is the example, mass production is the principle, nature is the designer. Does that make the unborn uncorrupted? Yes, say Fuller and Kenner, because only human selfishness and folly corrupt, as they interfere and blunder with nature's processes, of which the unborn are an example. The mind learns to leap, from the apparently abhorrent "new industrially produced home" to Milton's mass-produced poem, to nature's mass-produced trees and people.

But have we done in all this anything more than engineer the term "mass-produced" into a splendid and slick metaphor? At a later point in *Bucky*, Kenner conducts a dialogue with a skeptic who has a go at Fuller's scheme of linked tetrahedra in chemical bonding: "Bucky's is a pretty intuitive model, but it is not chemistry." Kenner answers,

> I will concede a large problem area, in which three different things tend to get mixed up: a coordinate system, a set of quick analogies, and the actual modeling of natural structures. All a coordinate system needs to claim is that it is close enough to actuality to give an economical accounting.

Kenner is right in the sense that Newton's laws of motion are right, and not right. But to make such a claim for coordinate systems is not to make that claim for any one system, including Fuller's, and when Kenner moves off the point here, I feel, as I do more than once in *Bucky*, that I don't know what Fuller's systems teach beyond his articles of faith that nature always works in the most economical way possible and that the mind can understand these workings so as to make man a success in the universe.

To accept "mass-produced" things and not to fear them in a Luddite or even in a Mumfordian way is not of course to guarantee that mass-produced houses will keep the young uncorrupted.

When Kenner's skeptic says, "If there has been no possibility of evidence for human sweetness, then what Fuller must ask is blind faith," Kenner himself is reduced to answering, "True, and it is an endearing faith." It is surely only Kenner's own imperturbability that makes the word that follows "True" not a "but" but an "and." Yet he may well be right:

> Bucky's work, seen part by part, is a story of crisis and failure, buildings that don't get built, industries that don't get financed, theories that don't get heard. Seen whole, it is an effort to develop a vast new paradigm, the synergetic vision. Scientists have evinced no special eagerness for it, because their response is to scientific crises, in between which they feel no need at all for new models of the Universe. No, the crisis to which synergetics is pertinent is a crisis of popular enlightenment, popular faith.

It is almost a political idea, stated that way, much as Fuller and Kenner abhor the mention of politics. One suspects that Fuller has so many followers among the young because they have not yet decided what the world is like and so have no need to reject him. Not yet having become specialists, their curiosity is more easily challenged by Fuller's way of leaping than by his exploring. Yet I myself see nothing naïve in this, however fuzzy or incomplete it may be.

On the last page of *The Dymaxion World of Buckminster Fuller* is a picture of bare mountain crags, Colorado or the moon, over which float two huge spheres. Fuller then describes how, as one increases the diameter of a sphere, one increases the proportion of the weight of the enclosed air to the weight of the sphere. At 100-feet diameter, 3 tons of sphere enclose 7 tons of air; at 400-feet diameter, 15 tons of sphere enclose 500 tons of air; at half-mile diameter the ratio is 1000:1. Next:

When the sun shines on an open frame aluminum geodesic sphere of one-half-mile diameter the sun, penetrating through the frame and reflected from the concave far side, bounces back into the sphere and gradually heats the interior atmosphere to a mild degree. When the interior temperature of the sphere rises only one degree Fahrenheit, the weight of the air pushed out of the sphere is greater than the weight of the spherical geodesic structure. This means that the total weight of the interior air plus the weight of the structure is much less than the surrounding atmosphere. This means that the total assemblage will have to float outwardly, into the sky, being displaced by the heavy atmosphere surrounding it. . . . Many thousands of passengers could be housed aboard one-mile diameter and larger cloud structures. The passengers could come and go from cloud to cloud, or cloud to ground, as the clouds float around the earth or are anchored to mountain tops.

First, such an idea can hardly be original with Fuller—and he makes no such claim. Second, the physicist and the engineer can, I am sure, think up ten problems in five minutes with such a scheme—I wondered how hot it would be inside one of these clouds if it were anchored, say, at Palm Springs, or Cairo. Third, anyone might ask: Who would want to be one of thousands floating in a sphere over the earth? It may be a totally harebrained idea, but such spheres sure as hell save on gas and oil, fuels we seem to know how to use but not how to replace or do without.

I offer the example in part because it is striking, but mostly to show how Fuller has never been simply "for more technology," as is so often assumed. He seldom speaks well of automobiles, and he insists we would not be so stupid about them if we could learn to be afraid of falling out of them and thereby insist they be as economical and safe as ships, planes, and rockets are. Nor does Fuller have much interest in speed for its own sake, except as our best means for becoming conscious of the world as a single space ship; one imagines those floating spheres would not move very fast. His point is not more technology, but better technology, better understanding of nature's processes, so that eventually, and soon, all may share in the energies and fruits of the earth. As Kenner says, Fuller's optimism is famous, though he never has claimed that we will do what he is sure we can do.

It seems to me possible to be attracted to Fuller and yet not to share his faith, or Kenner's in him. I enjoyed *Bucky* very much, and was grateful for the ways it showed me to read Fuller. But when Kenner says of Fuller's axioms, "Who doesn't want to believe them while the taxman cometh," I am not so sure. Part of me isn't even sure how much I care, and a larger part of me knows that although I feel that better technology is essential and possible, neither Fuller nor Kenner has made me care. Always reach for a higher level of generalization, Fuller says, the principles whereby something works. In *Gravity's Rainbow* Pynchon answers, talking about the effects of a drug, "Like other forms of paranoia, it is nothing less than the onset, the leading edge, of the discovery that *everything is connected.*"

To believe that everything is connected seems to me as much grounds for hope as for paranoia and despair, yet what passes through the giant fingers of both Fuller and Pynchon as mere instances of a generalization is for me where I do my living, rooted as I am in particulars, in my cityscape and landscape, in the challenge to understand my own energies, sins, failures, and possibilities, and those of my friends, students, and enemies. Fuller, Kenner, Pynchon too, are rich in intelligence, yet the part of me that is skeptical of them is a part of me I treasure. One way of praising the early work of Lewis Mumford is to say that as he leaps across the apparent boundaries offered by countries and centuries and subjects, he also confronts each person, book, and event as something fresh, by itself, not fodder for generalization, though perhaps an occasion to celebrate the possibilities of generalizing.

Fuller doesn't do that, though in the one performance of his I saw he came close to offering himself not as a principle in action but simply as himself, tired and yet tireless. Sitting on bleachers, watching him at a distance of at least a hundred yards, one could nonetheless feel his presence as something more than charismatic or soothing. He asked, and so received and deserved, only for time and patience, not for belief, or if he asked for that, it was only as a way of asking us to believe more in ourselves. That was memorable, and listening to Fuller as he spins his stars is an experience one should have, and probably more than once.

But, having said that, I feel inclined to let it go at that, and none of the persuasions of Kenner's *Bucky* make me think otherwise. Having long ago decided that life is not simply a matter of despairing and gloomy occasions, I do not feel moved to decide to live in a world of instances of hope and synergetic pattern either. Fuller, like the later Mumford, seeks not just generalization but masterful generalization. Both are decent, on the side of life, but both are imperial, commanding. One can admire them, and live at the heart of empire too, and yet not necessarily want to join in the chorus.